THE FRENCH REVOLUTION AND NAPOLEON

The upheavals, terror and drama of the French Revolutionary and Napoleonic period restructured politics and society on a grand scale, making this the defining moment for modern European history.

This volume collects together a wide selection of primary texts that explain the processes behind the enormous changes undergone by France and Europe between 1787 and 1815, from the Terror to the counter-revolution and from Marie-Antoinette to Bonaparte. While bringing the impact of historical events to life, Philip Dwyer and Peter McPhee provide a clear outline of the period through the selection of key documents, lucid introductory passages and commentary. They illustrate the meaning of the Revolution for peasants, *sans-culottes*, women and slaves, as well as placing events within a wider European context.

Students will find this an invaluable source of information on the Revolution as a whole as well as its international significance.

D1355519

THE FRENCH REVOLUTION AND NAPOLEON

A sourcebook

Edited by
Philip G. Dwyer and Peter McPhee

London and New York

PERM
RES
944·04
P21,5

First published 2002
by Routledge
11 New Fetter Lane, London EC4P 4EE

Simultaneously published in the USA and Canada
by Routledge
29 West 35th Street, New York, NY 10001

Routledge is an imprint of the Taylor & Francis Group

Typeset in Garamond by M Rules, London
Printed and bound in Great Britain by
Biddles Ltd, Guildford and King's Lynn

British Library Cataloguing-in-Publication Data
A catalogue record for this book is available from the British Library

Library of Congress Cataloging-in-Publication Data
A catalog record for this book has been requested

ISBN 0–415–19907–7 (hbk)
ISBN 0–415–19908–5 (pbk)

CONTENTS

CONTENTS

CONTENTS

CONTENTS

ILLUSTRATIONS

ABOUT THE EDITORS

Philip G. Dwyer is Lecturer in Modern European History at the University of Newcastle, Australia. He is the editor of *Napoleon and Europe* (London, 2001), and the author of *Talleyrand* (London, 2002). He is currently working on a study of Napoleon's youth and rise to power.

Peter McPhee is Professor of History at the University of Melbourne, Australia. His books include *A Social History of France, 1780–1880* (London and New York, 1992); *The Politics of Rural Life: Political Mobilization in the French Countryside 1846–1852* (Oxford, 1992); and *Revolution and Environment in Southern France: Peasant, Lords, and Murder in the Corbières, 1780–1830* (Oxford, 1999). He is currently working on a book on daily life during the French Revolution.

PREFACE

This collection offers students a wide selection of primary texts that help illustrate and explain the processes behind the enormous social and political changes undergone by France during the revolutionary and Napoleonic eras. The documents are organized thematically into chapters, and generally follow a chronological progression. Each document is prefaced with a short explanatory note that places it within its precise historical context and links it to the wider course of the French Revolution and Empire.

Some of the documents are here published in English for the first time, such as the *cahiers* from the Berry (p. 5–13), the remarkable statement by a group of children from La Rochelle (p. 91) and some of the reflections French people made on the significance for their lives of the extraordinary period through which they had just lived (pp. 202–8). Others are already well known but nevertheless indispensable for any collection covering this period: the Declaration of the Rights of Man and of the Citizen of 1789 and extracts from the various constitutions drawn up by parliaments seeking to codify the Revolution's achievements and to achieve stability.

The collection is necessarily selective in its choice, but the guiding principle throughout has been to detail the course and impact of the French Revolutionary and Napoleonic era on the people of France and, to a lesser extent, on the peoples of Europe. To this end we have sought to illustrate the gradual development of revolution in France, the rise of the Republican movement, the origins of the revolutionary wars and the continuation of those wars into the Napoleonic era with all the social and political consequences they entailed. In an attempt to go beyond traditional documentary formats students might often find dry, and in an effort to imbue the collection with the vigour and excitement that characterised the era, preference has been given to extracts that let individuals speak for themselves.

We have sought to offer as broad a range of documents as possible. The questions that students of revolutionary and Napoleonic France ask of the period have inevitably changed across time, and some of the documents in this collection offer the opportunity to investigate dimensions of the period which reflect current debates about the meaning and significance of these years. This is particularly so of those documents illustrative of the ways in which revolutionary governments excluded categories of individuals from full citizenship despite the demands of those people (Chapter 4) and of the impact of the

Revolution on the rural environment (Chapter 9). The people who lived through these years experienced privation and horror as well as elation and hope; in particular, the documents on pp. 18, 19, 55, 66, and 99 illustrate moments of collective violence and the reactions to it of eye-witnesses. The Empire, of course, was about much more than Napoleon's rise and fall (Chapters 16, 18, 21 and 22, pp. 195, 200). It brought with it a certain degree of administrative stability to France and Europe (Chapters 17 and 19), but at the same time imposed conscription, war and economic deprivation (Chapters 20 and 21) on many of those who fell under within its orb.

We are grateful to Victoria Peters of Routledge for her patience in dealing with the inevitable delays in this project, and to the anonymous reviewers who provided valuable advice during its early stages. In addition, Peter McPhee wishes to acknowledge the invaluable and skilled assistance provided by Juliet Flesch in the location of original documents and by Julie Kalman in their translation. Judy Anderson found the intriguing document 'A provincial response' (p. 78) in the Archives Départementales de la Gironde in Bordeaux; Jason Taliodoros assisted with the translation of 'Papal Bull *Charitas*, 13 April 1791' (p. 49). Philip Dwyer would like to thank Hélène Jaccomard for her help on a few tricky points of translation, Alan Forrest for kindly providing the documents on banditry and conscription in the Archives Nationales ('Report by the sub-prefect of Nyons (Drôme), 23 January 1802' (p. 146) and 'Conscription frauds in the Ariège, 5 October 1806' (p. 169), and Malcolm Crook for the material on the Napoleonic plebiscites ('The Consulate for Life, 1802' (p. 153), 'Founding the Empire, 1804', (p. 154) and 'The plebiscite of 1815' (p. 200)).

A NOTE ON THE REVOLUTIONARY CALENDAR

On 14 Vendémiaire II (5 October 1793) a new calendar was established by a 'Decree establishing the French Era', in order to mark the significance of the new age opened by the proclamation of the Republic on 22 September 1792 (retrospectively the first day of Year I of the new era). The calendar represented a repudiation of the Gregorian calendar and its saints' names; instead, there would be twelve 'rational' months of thirty days, each with three *décades*, and each day would have a name drawn from nature: in Frimaire, for example, honey, juniper tree and cork. The *décadi* or tenth days were named after farm implements such as pickaxe and shovel. The calendar lasted until New Year's Day 1806; its termination was part of Napoleon's accommodation with the Church.

Autumn:	Vendémiaire (month of grape harvest)	22 September–21 October
	Brumaire (month of fog)	22 October–20 November
	Frimaire (month of frost)	21 November–20 December
Winter:	Nivôse (month of snow)	21 December–19 January
	Pluviôse (month of rain)	20 January–18 February
	Ventôse (month of wind)	19 February–20 March
Spring:	Germinal (month of budding)	21 March–19 April
	Floréal (month of flowers)	20 April–19 May
	Prairial (month of meadows)	20 May–18 June
Summer:	Messidor (month of harvest)	19 June–18 July
	Thermidor (month of heat)	19 June–17 August
	Fructidor (month of fruit)	18 August–16 September

Sans-culottides: 'complementary' days from 17 to 21 September, plus an extra day in leap years. The four-year cycle was known as the *franciade*, 'in memory of the Revolution which, after four years of effort, has guided France to republican government'.

CHRONOLOGY

22 February 1787	Meeting of the Assembly of Notables.
June–August 1787	Refusal of Parlement of Paris to register royal reforms; exile of members of Parlements.
8 May 1788	Lamoignon's reforms seeking to reduce powers of Parlements.
7 June 1788	'Day of the tiles' at Grenoble.
8 August 1788	Estates-General convened for 1 May 1789.
27 December 1788	Royal Council decrees doubling of the number of Third Estate's representatives.
January 1789	Sieyès publishes *Qu'est-ce que le Tiers État?*
March–April 1789	Elections to the Estates-General.
5 May 1789	Opening of the Estates-General at Versailles.
17 June 1789	Declaration by Third Estate of the 'National Assembly'.
20 June 1789	Tennis Court Oath.
23 June 1789	King's Declaration concerning the Estates-General.
27 June 1789	King orders all orders to join the National Assembly.
11 July 1789	Dismissal of Necker.
14 July 1789	Insurrection captures the Bastille.
Late July–early August 1789	Provincial revolutions, peasant revolts, Great Fear.
4–11 August 1789	The August Decrees on feudalism.
10 August 1789	Decree establishing National Guards.
27 August 1789	Declaration of the Rights of Man and Citizen.
11 September 1789	National Assembly grants suspensive, rather than absolute, veto to king.
5–6 October 1789	March of the Parisian women on Versailles; royal family brought back to Paris.
2 November 1789	Church property placed at the disposal of the nation.

14 December 1789	Decree establishing municipalities (*communes*).
19 December 1789	First issue of *assignats* (revolutionary currency).
24 December 1789	Grant of religious liberty to Protestants.
28 January 1790	Sephardim Jews of south-west France granted equal rights.
13 February 1790	Decree prohibiting monastic vows in France.
26 February 1790	Decree dividing France into departments.
22 May 1790	National Assembly renounces wars of conquest.
19 June 1790	Decree abolishing hereditary nobility and titles.
12 July 1790	Voting of the Civil Constitution of the Clergy.
14 July 1790	Fête de la Fédération.
18 August 1790	First counter-revolutionary assembly, at Jalès in southern France.
October 1790	Revolt of slaves and black freemen in Saint-Domingue.
27 November 1790	Decree requiring the clerical oath.
2 March 1791	D'Allarde law abolishing guilds.
13 April 1791	The Papal Bull *Charitas*.
15 May 1791	Descendants of free Blacks in colonies granted equal rights.
14 June 1791	Le Chapelier law on 'associations'.
20–21 June 1791	The king's declaration and flight from Paris.
5 July 1791	The Padua Circular.
16–17 July 1791	Petition and 'massacre' of the Champ de Mars.
27 August 1791	The Declaration of Pillnitz.
3 September 1791	The Constitution of 1791.
14 September 1791	Louis XVI accepts the new Constitution.
14 September 1791	Annexation of Avignon and the Comtat-Venaissin from Papacy.
28 September 1791	Ashkenazim Jews of eastern France granted equal rights.
1 October 1791	First meeting of Legislative Assembly.
9 November 1791	Decree against *émigrés* (vetoed by king 12 November).
29 November 1791	Priests refusing to take an oath to the Constitution suspended from their functions.
9 February 1792	Decree nationalising *émigré* property.
20 April 1792	Declaration of war on Austria.
27 May 1792	Decree on deportation of non-juring priests (vetoed 19 June).
12 June 1792	Dismissal of Girondin ministers.
20 June 1792	Invasion of the Tuileries by the Paris crowd.
11 July 1792	Declaration of the 'Patrie en danger'.

25 July 1792	Publication of the Brunswick Manifesto.
10 August 1792	Storming of the Tuileries and suspension of the king.
19 August 1792	Defection of Lafayette to the Austrian army.
2 September 1792	Fall of Verdun to the Prussian army.
2–6 September 1792	'September massacres' in the prisons of Paris.
20 September 1792	First session of the National Convention.
20 September 1792	Victory of French army at Valmy.
6 November 1792	French victory at Jemappes.
27 November 1792	French annexation of Savoy.
11 December 1792	Appearance of Louis to face charges before the Convention.
14–17 January 1793	King's trial.
21 January 1793	Execution of Louis XVI.
1 February 1793	French declaration of war on England and Holland.
24 February 1793	Decree for a levy of 300,000 men.
7 March 1793	Declaration of war on Spain.
10 March 1793	Creation of special Revolutionary Tribunal.
10 March 1793	Creation of surveillance committees.
10–11 March 1793	Massacres at Machecoul and start of Vendéan insurrection.
19 March 1793	Decree on Public Relief.
28 March 1793	Decree against *émigrés*.
4 April 1793	Defection of Dumouriez to the Austrians.
6 April 1793	Decree on the formation of a Committee of Public Safety.
9 April 1793	Decree establishing 'deputies on mission'.
4 May 1793	The first law of the Maximum.
31 May–2 June 1793	Invasion of Convention by Paris sections; fall of Girondins.
1 June 1793	Proclamation of the Convention concerning the Events of 31 May and 1 June.
June 1793	'Federalist' revolts centred on Bordeaux, Caen and Lyons.
24 June 1793	The Constitution of 1793.
13 July 1793	Assassination of Marat.
17 July 1793	Execution of Chalier in Lyons.
27 July 1793	Robespierre elected to Committee of Public Safety.
1 August 1793	Decree establishing a uniform system of weights and measures.
23 August 1793	Decree establishing the *levée en masse*.
27 August 1793	Toulon surrendered to the British navy.

5–6 September 1793	Popular *journée* pressures the Convention into radical measures.
17 September 1793	The Law of Suspects.
29 September 1793	The Law of the General Maximum.
5 October 1793	Decree establishing the French Era (14 Vendémiaire II) and new calendar.
9 October 1793	Suppression of 'Federalist' insurrection in Lyons.
10 October 1793	Declaration of Revolutionary Government (19 Vendémiaire II).
16 October 1793	Execution of Marie-Antoinette.
31 October 1793	Execution of the Girondin leaders.
4 December 1793	The Constitution of the Terror (Law of 14 Frimaire Year II).
8 December 1793	Decree concerning Religious Liberty (18 Frimaire II).
19 December 1793	Decree concerning Public Education (29 Frimaire II).
4 February 1794	Abolition of slavery in French colonies.
3 March 1794	The decrees of 13 Ventôse II.
13–24 March 1794	Arrest and execution of Hébertistes.
30 March–6 April 1794	Arrest and execution of Dantonists.
8 June 1794	Festival of the Supreme Being in Paris.
10 June 1794	The Law of 22 Prairial II.
26 June 1794	French victory at Fleurus.
23 July 1794	Introduction of wage regulation in Paris.
27 July 1794	9 Thermidor: overthrow of Robespierre.
28 July 1794	Execution of Robespierre, Saint-Just and associates.
12 November 1794	Closure of Jacobin Club.
17 November 1794	Decree on Primary Schools (27 Brumaire III).
24 December 1794	Abolition of General Maximum.
28 December 1794	Decree reorganising the Revolutionary Tribunal (8 Nivôse III).
1 April 1795	Germinal: popular *journée* in Paris.
5 April 1795	The Treaty of Basle with Prussia (16 Germinal III).
April–May 1795	'White Terror' in southern France.
16 May 1795	The Treaty of The Hague (27 Floréal III).
20 May 1795	*Journée* of Prairial: invasion of Convention by Parisian crowd.
8 June 1795	Death of Louis XVII; comte de Provence becomes pretender to French throne (Louis XVIII).
22 July 1795	Peace signed with Spain.

22 August 1795	The Constitution of Year III (5 Fructidor III).
5 October 1795	Vendémiaire IV: royalist rising in Paris.
25 October 1795	Decree concerning the Organisation of Public Education (3 Brumaire IV).
26 October 1795	Dissolution of the Convention.
3 November 1795	Installation of the Directory.
19 February 1796	Withdrawal of the *assignats*.
2 March 1796	Bonaparte appointed general-in-chief of the army in Italy.
10 May 1796	Conspiracy of the Equals; Babeuf arrested.
December 1796	Failure of Hoche's Irish expedition.
March–April 1797	Royalist successes in legislative elections.
27 May 1797	Execution of Babeuf.
4 September 1797	18 Fructidor V: *coup d'état* against royalist deputies.
17 October 1797	Treaty of Campo Formio (27 Vendémiaire VI).
11 May 1798	22 Floréal VI: removal from office of extreme Republican deputies.
19 May 1798	Bonaparte leaves on Egyptian campaign.
1 August 1798	Battle of the Nile: French fleet defeated.
August 1798	Failure of French invasion of Ireland.
5 September 1798	The Jourdan or General Conscription Law (19 Fructidor VI).
March 1799	War of the Second Coalition.
April 1799	Legislative elections favour neo-Jacobins.
9 October 1799	Bonaparte's return to France.
18 October 1799	Decree on Francs and Livres (26 Vendémiaire VIII).
9–10 November 1799	Napoleon's *coup d'état* (18–19 Brumaire VIII).
13 December 1799	The Constitution of Year VIII (22 Frimaire VIII).
15 December 1799	Proclamation of the Consulate.
28 December 1799	Churches reopened for worship on Sundays.
17 January 1800	Suppression of sixty out of the seventy-three existing Parisian newspapers.
13 February 1800	Creation of the Bank of France.
17 February 1800	Law on the administrative organisation of France.
2 March 1800	*Émigrés* are granted an amnesty.
14 June 1800	Battle of Marengo.
5 November 1800	Start of the negotiations for the Concordat.
24 December 1800	Plot to kill Napoleon.
9 February 1801	Treaty of Lunéville.
16 July 1801	Concordat concluded with Pius VII.

23 July 1801	Start of discussions on the Code civil.
26 January 1802	Napoleon president of the Republic of Italy.
25 March 1802	Treaty of Amiens.
2 August 1802	Proclamation of the Consulate for life.
4 August 1802	The Constitution of Year X.
28 March 1803	Rupture of the Treaty of Amiens and renewal of war with Britain.
9 March 1804	Arrest of Cadoudal.
21 March 1804	Execution of the duc d'Enghier.
18 May 1804	Proclamation of the Empire.
28 June 1804	Execution of Cadoudal.
2 December 1804	Napoleon is crowned emperor.
March 1805	Creation of the Kingdom of Italy.
18 May 1805	Napoleon is crowned king of Italy in Milan.
August 1805	Third Coalition formed against France.
20 October 1805	Battle of Trafalgar.
2 December 1805	Battle of Austerlitz.
26 December 1805	Treaty of Pressburg with Austria.
July–August 1806	Creation of the Confederation of the Rhine.
July 1806	Fourth Coalition against France.
14 October 1806	Battles of Jena-Auerstädt.
7 February 1807	Battle of Eylau.
14 June 1807	Battle of Friedland.
July 1807	Tilsit. Creation of the Kingdom of Westphalia, and the Duchy of Warsaw.
November–December 1807	Occupation of Portugal by the French.
23 November and 17 December 1807	Milan decrees extending the terms of the Continental Blockade.
1 March 1808	Senatus Consultum organising the imperial nobility.
April–May 1808	The meeting at Bayonne.
2 May 1808	The 'Dos de Mayo'; Madrid rises in revolt.
May–June 1808	Spain rises in revolt.
10 September 1808	Married and widowed men are exempt from military service.
September–October 1808	Meeting between Napoleon and Alexander at Erfurt.
April 1809	Fifth Coalition formed against France.
21–22 May 1809	Battle of Aspern-Essling.
5–6 July 1809	Battle of Wagram.
14 October 1809	Treaty of Schönbrunn with Austria.
30 November 1809	Napoleon decides to divorce Josephine.
15 December 1809	Divorce is officially pronounced.
1–2 April 1810	Marriage of Marie-Louise and Napoleon.

20 March 1811	Birth of the king of Rome.
June 1812	Start of Russian campaign.
7 September 1812	Battle of Borodino.
14 September 1812	Napoleon enters Moscow.
23 October 1812	The Malet affair.
29 October 1812	Malet and his accomplices are shot.
October 1812	Start of retreat from Moscow.
16–19 October 1813	Battle of Leipzig.
1 March 1814	Treaty of Chaumont.
31 March 1814	Paris surrenders to the Allies; Alexander moves into Talleyrand's hotel.
1 April 1814	Talleyrand elected president of the provisional government.
2 April 1814	Napoleon deposed by the Senate.
6 April 1814	Napoleon abdicates at Fontainebleau. The Senate offers the throne to Louis XVIII.
3 May 1814	Louis XVIII enters Paris.
30 May 1814	First Treaty of Paris.
November 1814	Opening of the Congress of Vienna.
February 1815	Napoleon escapes from Elba.
20 March 1815	Start of the Hundred Days (to 22 June).
18 June 1815	Battle of Waterloo.

1

THE *ANCIEN RÉGIME* CHALLENGED

Lamoignon on the principles of the French monarchy, 19 November 1787

This extract is from a speech delivered by Chrétien-François de Lamoignon (1735–89), Garde des sceaux, at a royal sitting of the Parlement of Paris, on 19 November 1787. The Garde des sceaux, literally 'keeper of the seals', was the Minister of Justice. Earlier in 1787 an Assembly of Notables and the Parlement of Paris had rebuffed ministerial appeals for reform and financial assistance to the State. Lamoignon, a leading Notable and former president of the Parlement, here reminds his peers of Louis XVI's pre-eminence by dismissing their call for a meeting of the Estates-General in return for approval of a loan. The following May Lamoignon issued six edicts aimed at undermining the judicial and political power of the Parlements, provoking rioting in Paris and provincial centres. In July Louis decided that he would, after all, convoke an Estates-General in May 1789, and Lamoignon was dismissed.

These principles, universally accepted by the nation, prove:

> that *sovereign power in his kingdom belongs to the king alone;*
> that he is accountable only to God for the exercise of supreme power; that the link that unites the king and the nation is by nature indissoluble; that the reciprocal interests and duties of the king and his subjects ensure the perpetuity of this union; that the nation has a vested interest that the rights of its ruler remain unchanged; that the king is the sovereign ruler of the nation, and is one with it; finally that legislative power resides in the person of the sovereign, depending upon and sharing with no-one.

These, sirs, are the invariable principles of the French monarchy. . . .

It results from these ancient maxims of the nation, testified to on each page of our history:

> that the right to convene the Estates-General belongs to the king alone;
> that he alone must judge whether such a convocation is useful or necessary;
> that he needs no special powers to administer his kingdom; that a king of France, in the representatives of the three orders of the State, would find only a more wide-ranging advisory council, made up of members chosen from a family of which he is the head, and that he would always be the supreme arbiter of their representations or of their grievances. . . .

When our kings established the Parlements, sirs, they wished to appoint officers whose duty it was to administer justice and to maintain the edicts of the kingdom, and not to build up a power to rival royal authority.

Source: *Archives parlementaires,* 19 November 1787, Series 1, vol. 1, pp. 265–9.

'Memoir of the Princes of the Blood', 1788

The 'Memoir of the Princes of the Blood' was sent to Louis XVI on 12 December 1788, at the close of the second Assembly of Notables, which had expressed its anxiety at mounting pressure for the doubling of the size of the Third Estate representation at the approaching Estates-General. Five of the seven princes signed the document. While Louis' youngest brother, the comte d'Artois, signed, a notable absence was the next youngest brother, the comte de Provence, by now building a reputation for the relative moderation of his views.

Your Majesty has stated to the princes of the blood that, when they wish to tell him what might be useful in his service and to the State, they may address themselves to him.

The comte d'Artois, Prince de Condé, the duc de Bourbon, the duc d'Enghien and Prince Conti believe it to be their duty to respond to this invitation from Your Majesty.

It is in effect the princes of the blood who by their rank are the first of your subjects, who by their position are your born counsellors, who by their rights are concerned to defend yours; above all, it is their duty to tell you the truth, and they believe it to be equally their duty to make known to you their feelings and thoughts.

Sire, the State is in danger; your person is respected, the virtues of the

2

monarch ensure the homage of the nation; but Sire, a revolution is brewing in the principles of government; it is being brought on by the ferment of opinion. Reputedly sacred institutions, which this monarchy has made to prosper for so many centuries, have become matters for debate, or are even described as injustices.

The writings which appeared during the Assembly of Notables, the reports which have been delivered to the undersigned princes, the demands put forward by various provinces, towns or corporations; the objectives and the style of these demands and these reports: everything proclaims, everything reveals a system of deliberate insubordination and contempt for the laws of the State. Each author sets himself up as a legislator; eloquence or the ability to write, even when devoid of study, knowledge and experience, seems to be sufficient to determine the constitution of empires: whoever puts forward a daring proposition, whoever proposes to change the law, is sure of having readers and an audience.

Such is the unhappy progress of this agitation that opinions which a short time ago might have seemed reprehensible, today appear to be reasonable and fair; and that which good people are indignant about today will in a short time perhaps pass as regular and legitimate. Who can say where the recklessness of opinions will stop? The rights of the throne have been called into question; the rights of the two orders of the State divide opinions; soon property rights will be attacked; the inequality of fortunes will be presented as an object for reform; the suppression of feudal rights has already been proposed, as the abolition of a system of oppression, the remains of barbarism. . . .

May the Third Estate therefore cease to attack the rights of the first two orders; rights which, no less ancient than the monarchy, must be as unchanging as its constitution; that it limit itself to seeking the reduction in taxes with which it might be burdened; the first two orders, recognising in the third citizens who are dear to them, will, by the generosity of their sentiments, be able to renounce those prerogatives which have a financial dimension, and consent to bear public charges in the most perfect equality.

Source: *Archives parlementaires*, 12 December 1788, Series 1, vol. 1, pp. 487–9.

━━━━━━━━━━━━

Sieyès, *What is the Third Estate?*, January 1789

During the debate over the composition of the Estates-General, a 40-year-old priest of bourgeois background, Emmanuel-Joseph Sieyès, contributed the most remarkable of his several pamphlets, titled *What is the Third Estate?*. Sieyès attacked the nobility's obsession with its 'odious privileges', and issued a stirring declaration of commoner capacity. Significantly, Sieyès wrote of just one privileged order, assuming that the clergy, too, were irrevocably divided between noble élite and commoner parish priests. However, Sieyès was no democrat: women and the poor could not hope to vote or represent their fellow citizens; nor could wage earners, whom he saw as too dependent on their masters. Despite his profession, Sieyès was elected a deputy for the Third Estate of Paris in 1789.

This document is set out quite simply. We have three questions to ask ourselves.

1. What is the Third Estate?—everything.
2   What has it been until now in the political order?—nothing.
3   What is it asking?—to be something.

We shall see if these answers are correct. . . .

Who would thus dare to say that the Third Estate does not contain everything that is needed to make up a complete nation? It is like a strong and robust man who still has one arm in chains. If the privileged orders were removed, the nation would not be worse off for it, but better. So, what is the Third? Everything, but a fettered and oppressed everything. What would it be without the privileged order? Everything, but a free and flourishing everything. Nothing can happen without it; everything would be infinitely better without the others. . . .

It would be useless for the Third Estate to expect the restitution of its political rights and the plenitude of its civil rights with the support of all the orders; the fear of seeing abuses reformed inspires fear in the aristocrats more than the desire they feel for liberty. Between it and a few odious privileges, they have chosen the latter. The soul of the privileged has identified with the favours of servitude. Today, they dread the Estates-General that they once called for with such fervour. All is well for them; they complain only about the spirit of innovation; they no longer want for anything; fear has given them a constitution.

The Third Estate must realise, from the movement of minds and of events, that it can rely only on its knowledge and its courage. Reason and justice are on its side; it must at the very least ensure their full strength. No, it is no longer the moment to work for the reconciliation of all parties. What agreement can be hoped for between the energy of the oppressed and the rage of the oppressors? They have dared to pronounce the word *scission*. They have threatened the king and the people with it. Oh! Dear God! It would be a happy day for the nation for this so desirable scission to be made forever! How much easier it would be to do without the privileged! How difficult it will be to induce them to be citizens! . . .

There cannot be in any form liberty or rights without limits. In all countries the law has settled on certain characteristics without which one can be neither a voter nor eligible. Thus, for example, the law must decide on an age below which one is incapable of representing one's fellow citizens. Thus women everywhere, for better or worse, are precluded from this form of authority. It is a fact that a vagabond or a beggar cannot be given the responsibility of the political trust of the people. Would a domestic servant and anyone who depends on a master, or a foreigner who is not naturalised, be allowed to be counted among the representatives of the nation? Thus political freedom has its limits, as does civil freedom.

Source: Emmanuel Sieyès, *Qu'est-ce que le Tiers État?* (Paris, 1789).

===≫○○○≪===

Cahiers de doléances, province of Berry, spring 1789

The First Estate of Bourges

Members of the First Estate envisaged a rejuvenated feudal order under the auspices of a Catholic monopoly of worship and morality. However, as commoners by birth, many parish priests showed a lively concern to reform the system of justice and taxation in the interests of their parishioners. Here the Dean of the cathedral of Bourges in central France and thirty-one clergy in the cathedral chapter outline their advice to the king. Such men were not as critical of the élite of the clergy as were parish priests; even here, however, they condemned those who held important positions *in absentia*.

Respectful grievances from the metropolitan church of Bourges.
  Article 1. The chapter of the metropolitan church of Bourges will ceaselessly wish for the prosperity and long reign of His Majesty. It blesses the Lord for having inspired him with the generous resolution to assemble the Estates-General of this kingdom. A father who looks after the interests of a family that is dear to him acquires new rights to the love of his children. . . .
  Article 2. . . . May it please His Majesty to order that all those who, through their writings, seek to spread the poison of incredulity and attack religion and its mysteries, discipline and dogmas, be seen as enemies of the Church and the State and severely punished; that printers be once again forbidden to print books contrary to religion; to forbid also bookshops and pedlars to spread such books. To order that judges, accompanied by educated and enlightened clergymen, designated by the bishop, will from time to time visit printers and

bookshops, and that all the books contrary to religion and good morals be seized and confiscated, and that the said offending printers and bookshops will be prosecuted according to the severity of the law.

Article 3. The apostolic and Roman Catholic religion is the only true religion. More ancient than the monarchy, she ascended to the throne of our kings with Clovis and has never descended from it.

May she reign alone in the kingdom, the only friend of kings! . . .

Article 6. The spirit of religion and of piety is being extinguished in all social orders, the divine and human laws that order the sanctity of Sundays and holidays are violated publicly and with impunity, both in the city and in the countryside. The roads are full of carriages; workshops, shops, cabarets and gaming houses are open on these holy days, even during the hours devoted to the divine service and the education of the faithful. Abuses continue despite the severity of the laws. . . .

RESIDENCE

Article 9. For a long time the public has been upset by and complains about this innumerable crowd of ecclesiastics and benefice holders, who from all parts of the kingdom flood towards the capital; it is much to be desired that His Majesty forbid a scandal which is no less contrary to canon law than to the temporal and spiritual well-being of the provinces.

Cathedral churches are especially devoted to public worship; the majesty of religion, the pomp of the ceremonies requires that there are always in these churches a certain number of canons to conduct divine offices and to help the bishops with their functions; but the cathedrals will soon be deserted if this multitude of useless commissions and positions is not abolished in the households of the king and the princes of the blood. . . .

JUSTICE

Article 14. . . . May it please His Majesty to reduce the overly widespread jurisdiction of the Parlements; to reduce also the number of courts of law; to simplify further the conventions of justice, and have the code—both civil and criminal—reformed. . . .

SALT TAX

Article 16. All France sees the salt tax as the most disastrous of taxes, even though it weighs most unequally on different parts of this kingdom. Berry, which is in the region of greatest salt tax (*grande gabelle*), is one of the provinces which has the most reason to complain; besides the enormous sum that the salt it consumes costs it, and which is nearly equivalent to that of the direct tax (*taille*), poll tax (*capitation*) and others, its inhabitants are regularly troubled by all the fiscal searches and the surveillance that its proximity to a retithed [lighter taxed] region necessitates, where salt is reasonably priced; . . . fraud, whose cunning cannot be calculated, always finds ways to bring salt from the retithed region into those that are not. . . . What a happy change Berry would undergo if the price of salt were sufficiently modified so that its inhabitants could give it to their animals! This would protect them from many sicknesses. . . .

CONCLUSIONS
These are the respectful grievances of the metropolitan church of Bourges, those that love for religion and zeal for the public good have dictated.

May the assembly of Estates-General re-establish the empire of morals, make religion reign, reform abuses, find a remedy for the evils of the State, be the era of prosperity in France and profound and durable glory for His Majesty.
Signed: Beugy, Dean, and thirty-one other clergy

Source: *Archives parlementaires, États Généraux 1789. Cahiers, Province du Berry,* pp. 509–12.

The Second Estate of Berry

Eleven noble representatives gathered in Bourges on 28 March to draw up this *cahier*. The Second Estate of Berry here demonstrated both its goodwill towards its fellow citizens and its intransigence on critical issues relating to the status and privileges of nobles and the survival of the seigneurial regime. A stirring statement of preparedness to join with the Third Estate in the programme of reform was coupled with qualifying clauses that effectively negated this initial gesture. Like the other orders, the Second Estate looked forward to a permanent sharing of power with the king, but insisted on the special role for nobles. The nobles commonly used the term *subsides* or grants instead of taxes.

GENERAL GATHERING
Of the order of the nobility of the Province of Berry for the Estates-General

FOREWORD
. . . The spirit of unity and agreement, which had always reigned between the three orders, is equally manifest in their *cahiers*. The question of voting by head in the assembly of the Estates-General was the only one to divide the Third Estate from the other two orders, whose constant wish has been to deliberate there by order . . . it is with the greatest satisfaction that the orders have seen that their *cahiers*, although separate, could be seen as effectively comprising only one, motivated by the same spirit.

TITLE 1

Constitution
Article 1 . . . The deputies will seek to discuss any other matter . . . only when they will have stated in the most positive manner and in the form of fixed and unalterable law:

1. The recognition of administrative power belonging fully to the king;
2. the rights of the nation to consent to laws as well as to grants [taxes], their sharing out and collection;
3. public and individual freedom, from which derives that of the press, guaranteed according to the law;
4. the sacred and inviolable right of property, the stability of the courts, the irremovability of their officers. . . .
7. the periodic return of the Estates-General.
8. the establishment of provincial Estates in each province . . .

TITLE 3

Grants {taxes}
Article 1. The deputies will present to the Estates-General a picture of abuses resulting from the arbitrariness employed in assessments of the *taille*, *capitation*, one-twentieth levies [*vingtièmes*], contributions to roads, and will demand the abolition, modification, combination or conversion of these taxes.

Article 2. They will demand the abolition of the salt tax and the replacement of this imposition by another that is less onerous. . . .

TITLE 4

Finances . . .
Article 9. The deputies, having fulfilled all the obligations that the preceding articles have imposed on them, will concern themselves with regulating the grants that the nobility, through their generous, patriotic, fraternal and unanimous support, have decided to bear equally with the two other orders of the State. . . .

TITLE 5

Demands unique to the province
The deputies will ask: . . .

Article 8. That all bourgeois who are privileged inhabitants of towns give up all exemptions, immunities, privileges, under whatever designation they are presented, even under the title of public teaching or whatever else it may be. . . .

Article 14. That the current rate of poll tax for nobles and privileged men in this province not serve as a basis for the new distribution of taxes, given that it has been recognised as being excessive and disproportionate. . . .

TITLE 6

Demands relating to the order of the nobility
The deputies of the order of the nobility of Berry at the Estates-General will ask:

Article 1. That all venal nobility be abolished.

Article 2. That the provincial Estates be able to present to the king those of their fellow citizens whose services rendered put them in the position of obtaining nobility.

Article 3. That in each province a nobiliary be formed by a court made up of nobles.

Article 4. That seigneurial justice be preserved (while taking the necessary measures to improve its administration), as well as all honorific and useful rights, inherent in lands or people, excepting all the same those of pure and personal servitude, which will always be repugnant to the generous heart of the nobility.

Article 5. The deputies will especially occupy themselves with all that concerns the interests and glory of the nobility of the provinces, having the least access to the favours of the court.

. . .

Done and settled in the special hall for the order of the nobility assembled to this effect in Bourges, this Saturday, 28 March 1789. Signed by all the members of the order of the nobility, and particularly by the eleven representatives named for the drawing up of this register.

Source: *Archives parlementaires, États Généraux 1789. Cahiers, Province du Berry,* pp. 319–22.

The Third Estate of Berry

Parish *cahiers* (see the extracts below from the Levet and Marcilly parish *cahiers*) were collated into a general *cahier* for the Third Estate at a district (*bailliage* or *sénéchaussée*) level. In a parallel manner, parish delegates were sent to district capitals where they elected the Third Estate deputies for Versailles. This meant that district *cahiers* tended to reflect urban middle-class grievances and aspirations, just as the deputies were almost exclusively urban men from the professions, public service or commerce. Nevertheless, the sharp contrast in the outlook of prominent members of the Third Estate of Bourges and that of the nobility (see the extract above) is readily apparent, as are some startlingly radical attitudes to individual freedoms.

Cahier of grievances, petitions and remonstrations of the Third Estate of the *bailliage* of Berry, 23 March 1789

May it please the king and the assembled nation to order:

Article 1. That the Third Estate will have in perpetuity at the Estates-General a number of voters at least equal to that of the two other orders united; that the three orders will deliberate in common. . . .

Article 3. That a law can be made only with the participation of the king and the Estates-General.

Article 4. That no tax be legal or be collectable unless it has been consented to by the nation in the assembly of the Estates-General; and the said Estates can consent to it only for a limited rate, and until their following meeting, so that if this subsequent meeting is not held, all taxes will cease. . . .

Article 10. That the press will be free, on the condition that the author will remain responsible for what is produced. Printers will equally be responsible for anonymous writings. . . .

Article 13. That internal customs and duties collected on entering and leaving [the provinces] be abolished, and replaced by the duties collected on entering the kingdom. . . .

Article 17. That taxes remaining or to be established will be borne equally and on the same roll by all orders of the State, at the rate of individual properties or capacity to pay; and the Third Estate, sensitive to the justice and the disinterest of the first two orders of the province, cannot record their wish here without offering them testimony of their gratitude. . . .

Article 19. That provincial Estates will be established in Berry, organised in the same manner as those newly re-established in the province of Dauphiné. . . .

Article 23. That positions and offices without function be abolished, or at least that the salaries that accompany them be greatly reduced.

Article 24. That all non-Catholic subjects will enjoy all the rights of the citizen, with the exercise of public worship reserved only for the Catholic religion.

Article 25. That purely personal constraints, and other supposed duties resulting from the said personal constraints, as well as toll duties, will be abolished without compensation, and that the Estates-General will advise on ways to destroy the slave trade, and to prepare for the abolition of the slavery of Negroes.

Article 26. That landed and seigneurial dues, in wheat, cash and poultry, territory, *banalités* [monopolies], and all other real existing servitudes, as much over holdings in the country as in the towns, will be refundable to lords and ecclesiastic and secular property owners, without prejudice to the *seigneurie* and the rights of *directe* [justice]; the said refund will be made at the

10

rate of twenty-five times the annual worth, according to the product of the last ten years. . . .

Article 30. That the laws excluding the Third Estate from civil and military ranks be abolished.

Article 31. That the ballot for the militia be abolished; and that the Estates-General advise on ways to replace it.

Article 32. That municipal officers be elected, as in the past. . . .

Article 37. That the reformation of civil and criminal justice will be undertaken. . . .

Article 44. That there be, in the future, only one sole weight and one sole measure in all of France.

Decided in the assembly of the Third Estate of the *bailliage* of Berry, 23 March 1789.

Source: *Archives parlementaires, États Généraux 1789. Cahiers, Province du Berry*, pp. 323–5.

The parish of Levet

Levet, 18 km south of Bourges, was a village of about 500 people and seventy-seven households in 1789. Four *laboureurs* (farmers) and thirty *manoeuvres* (labourers) gathered on 1 March to draw up this *cahier*; only four of them were able to sign it. A *laboureur* and a *manoeuvre* were elected as deputies to attend the Third Estate meeting in Bourges on the 16th. Levet was remarkable for the number of privileged persons— seventeen ecclesiastics or orders and nine lay persons—who extracted revenue from its territory: among the former were the parish priest and several religious orders from Bourges: the Benedictines, Ursulines, Carmelites and Visitandines.

His Majesty is entreated by the inhabitants of the parish of Levet to order:

Article 1. That the Third Estate vote by head at the assembly of the Estates-General. . . .

Article 3. That the *aides* [indirect taxes] and the salt tax, and also customs duties, having become arbitrary after the abuse of an infinity of decisions surprising to the opinion of the Council, be and remain abolished, the province of Berry giving the king in some other way the same net funds. . . .

Article 4. That all types of exemptions be abolished, such as those concerning the *taille*, *capitation*, lodging of soldiers, etc., entirely borne by the most unfortunate class of the Third Estate. . . .

Article 5. That the abuses be dealt with which are committed by soldiers in the parishes where they are sent and where they pass their days in the most vexatious manner, usually in debauchery and at the cabaret.

Article 6. That a regulation will be created for farm workers requiring them to continue their service instead of abandoning it at the moment they are most needed.

Article 7. That the ballot for militia in the countryside be conducted by the closest official, who will go there to that end in order to avoid the expense and travel of farm workers who take advantage of the occasion to spend entire weeks in debauchery.

Article 8. That priests be forbidden to absent themselves from their parishes for more than twenty-four hours without a replacement priest, in order to avoid the abuses which are committed daily in the parishes.

Article 9. That seigneurial justice be abolished and those called to justice instead plead before the closest royal judge.

Source: Alfred Gandilhon, *Cahiers de doléances du bailliage de Bourges et des bailliages secondaires de Vierzon et d'Henrichement pour les États-Généraux de 1789* (Bourges, 1910), pp. 170–84.

The parish of Marcilly

Fewer than 300 people and forty-three households lived in the tiny village of Marcilly, to the east of Bourges, in 1789. Among the forty men at the assembly on 1 March were three tenant-farmers, three farmers, thirteen labourers, a blacksmith and a longsawyer; only eight of them could sign their names. Two of the farmers were elected deputies. Three nobles and a priest had seigneurial rights or privilege land in Marcilly. Like the preceding extract, this *cahier* reveals the targets of peasant dissatisfaction.

Article 1. His Majesty will be entreated by the deputies of the Third Estate of the province of Berry to order that the Third Estate vote by head in the general assembly of the Estates-General.

Article 2. That the province of Berry be made a part of the provincial Estates [a *pays d'État*].

Article 3. That there be only one custom, one law, and one system of weights and measures. . . .

Article 6. That all financial privileges be abolished; consequently, that the three orders no longer be exempt from any of the public responsibilities and taxes that the most unfortunate class of the Third Estate alone endures and pays, such as statute labour (*corvée*), lodging of soldiers, and all incidental costs for the *taille*, etc.

Article 7. [repeats Article 3 on p. 11 above] . . .

Article 10. That each of the poor beg only in their parish, enabling us thus to provide for the needs of our own.

Article 11. That for some years huts have been constructed, as much in our parish as in other parishes that border the main road from Bourges to La Charité and that unfortunate incidents provoked by those who inhabit them could be feared; that a great number are idle and send their children to get them bread; request the demolition of the huts. . . .

Article 14. That all [salaries of] priests be reduced, that is: for those without a curate to 1,200 livres and for those with a curate to 1,800 livres, with the use of their house and garden only. . . .

Article 17. That the Chartreuse communities be abolished, the monks secularised and each given 800 livres; the surplus of their income to belong to His Majesty.

Article 18. That the Ambrosian and Genovefain canons and other pensioned orders be each reduced to the sum of 800 livres and that the surplus of their income will belong to His Majesty.

Article 19. [repeats Article 5 on p. 12 above]

Source: Alfred Gandilhon, *Cahiers de doléances du bailliage de Bourges et des bailliages secondaires de Vierzon et d'Henrichement pour les États-Généraux de 1789* (Bourges, 1910), pp. 187–91.

Cahier de doléances, Parisian flower sellers, spring 1789

The *cahiers* of urban *menu peuple* (working people) were compiled at meetings of master craftsmen, parish assemblies and, very occasionally, groups of tradeswomen such as the flower sellers of Paris. Most urban working people were too poor to meet the minimal property requirements necessary to participate: in Paris only about one in five men over 25 years was eligible. This *cahier* reveals the antipathy of small shopkeepers and traders to free trade and competition, but at the same time their confidence in the Third Estate deputies, most of whom, nevertheless, were committed to economic liberalism.

The freedom given to all citizens to denounce abuses that press on them from all sides to the representatives of the nation is doubtless a certain omen of an impending reform. Confident of this, the flower sellers formerly forming the community of the female sellers of flowers and bonnets of flowers of the city and suburbs of Paris dare to address themselves to you our lords [the Estates-General]. It is not simple abuses that they request be put right. It is their profession, the entire existence of which the doubtless involuntary error of one of the former ministers of His Majesty has deprived them, that they ask for at this time. . . .

In 1735, through the kindness of Louis XV the flower sellers obtained confirmation of their community and new rulings, whose fulfilment was ordered in the letters of patent of 26 November 1736, registered in the Parlement on 18 December 1737.

The flower sellers who had undergone an apprenticeship of three years and who had paid considerable fees for the right enjoyed their profession in peace, when they suddenly found themselves deprived of it by the abolition of their community. . . .

Moreover, the complaints of the supplicants stem from an important question whose resolution is submitted to the Estates: that of knowing whether it would be useful or not to grant to all individuals the undefined freedom to practise any sort of business.

May the supplicants be permitted to venture a few reflections at this point that may perhaps pave the way to deciding on this major question.

In policing business and the arts [trades], two things must be considered. Professional bodies should be organised in such a way that individuals who devote themselves to a profession may support themselves and their children from their work. However, access to the professions, and particularly to those that are especially comprised of the less fortunate class, must not be made so difficult as to exclude the poor from business and stifle competition.

This combination, on which rest the common happiness and the prosperity of business, would necessarily be destroyed by unlimited freedom.

The excessive liberty resulting from the edicts of 1776 and 1777 has made all professions only too conscious of the inconveniences of this freedom. The multitude of sellers is far from producing the salutary effect that we apparently should expect from competition. As the number of consumers does not increase proportionately with the number of producers, they necessarily do each other damage, as buyers will give them preference only if they decrease the price of their merchandise. Distress and the necessity to sell at a low price lead them to make poor merchandise or to be misleading about the quality of what they sell; if, in doing that, they delay their ruin, they inflict mortal blows on commerce.

The more restricted is a profession, and the less it offers in resources, the more important it is to reduce the number of competitors. . . . Today, when everyone can sell flowers and make bouquets, their modest profits are divided up to the point of no longer giving the means to subsist.

The lure of these earnings, however, limited as they are, and even more a strong propensity to idleness, encourages a crowd of young people of the fair sex to practise the profession of the supplicants; and, since their profession cannot feed them, they seek the resources they lack in licentiousness and the most shameful debauchery. The supplicants' cause is also that of morality. . . .

The supplicants particularly lodge their just claims in the hands of the deputies of the Third Estate. They, even more especially than others among their representatives, are their friends and their brothers, and it is to them that it falls to plead the cause of the destitute. . . .

The supplicants will not cease to send wishes to heaven for the preservation and prosperity of the representatives of the nation.

> Signed: The said merchants, represented by Madame Marl,
> syndic of the community.

Source: 'Doléances particulières des marchandes bouquetières fleuristes chapelières en fleurs de la ville et faubourgs de Paris', in Charles-Louis Chassin, *Les Élections et les cahiers de Paris en 1789*, 4 vols (Paris, 1888–9), vol. 2, pp. 534–7.

2

REVOLUTIONARY ACTION

The Tennis Court Oath, 20 June 1789

The immediate issue at Versailles was that of voting procedures: should the Estates-General meet in three separate chambers or in a common assembly? The Third Estate deputies refused to vote separately, but the nobility were clearly in favour of this, as, very narrowly, were the clergy. The resolve of the bourgeois deputies was strengthened by defections from the privileged orders, particularly by parish priests. On 17 May the deputies of the Third Estate declared that 'the interpretation and presentation of the general will belong to it. . . . The name National Assembly is the only one which is suitable'. Three days later, finding themselves locked out of their meeting hall (apparently by accident), the deputies moved to a nearby indoor royal tennis court and, under the presidency of the astronomer Jean-Sylvain Bailly, insisted by oath on their 'unshakeable resolution' to continue to act as the national representation. Only one deputy voted against the motion.

M. Mounier presents an opinion that is supported by MM. Target, Chapelier and Barnave; he points out how strange it is that the hall of the Estates-General is occupied by armed men; that other premises have not been offered to the National Assembly; that its president was only informed by letters from the Marquis de Brezé, and the national representatives by notices; that they have finally been obliged to meet at the Jeu de Paume, rue de Vieux-Versailles, so as not to interrupt their work; that, their rights and their dignity wounded, aware of the great intensity of the intrigue and of the relentlessness of the efforts to push the king to take disastrous measures, the representatives of the nation must bind themselves to the public good and the interests of the nation though a solemn oath.

This proposition is approved through universal applause.

The Assembly immediately decides the following:

Figure 1 The Tennis Court Oath (detail). Jacques-Louis David became an increasingly enthusiastic supporter of the Revolution. Here he has immortalised the signing of the Tennis Court Oath in June 1789 by the new 'National Assembly' presided over by Bailly. In the foreground, the abbé Grégoire embraces the Catholic monk Dom Gerle and the Protestant pastor Rabant St-Etienne. Source: Bibliothèque nationale de France.

The National Assembly, whereas it is called on to lay down the Constitution of the kingdom, implement the regeneration of public order, and maintain the true principles of the monarchy, can be stopped by nothing from continuing its deliberations in whatever place it may be obliged to establish itself, and that finally, anywhere its members are gathered together, that is the National Assembly.

It is decided that all the members of this Assembly will now swear a solemn oath never to separate, and to gather together anywhere

17

that circumstances demand, until the Constitution of the kingdom is established and consolidated on solid foundations, and that the said oath being sworn, each and every one of the members will confirm this unshakeable resolution with their signature.

Source: *Gazette nationale ou le Moniteur universel*, no. 10, 20–24 June 1789, vol. 1, p. 89.

The storming of the Bastille, 14 July 1789

In a context of political stand-off and economic crisis (the price of the standard 4-pound loaf of bread had risen from 8 to 14 sous), the dismissal of Louis' one non-noble minister, Jacques Necker, convinced Parisians that they and the Third Estate were under attack. On the 14th, up to 8,000 armed Parisians, chiefly artisans, wage-earners and shopkeepers, laid siege to the fortress; the governor, the marquis de Launay (or de Launai), refused to surrender and, as crowds forced their way into the courtyard, ordered his soldiers to fire upon the crowd, killing perhaps one hundred. Only when two detachments of Gardes Françaises sided with the crowd and trained their cannon on the main gate, did he surrender. In the first issue of one of the new newspapers which rushed to report on the unprecedented events, *Les Révolutions de Paris*, a young journalist from Bordeaux named Elysée Loustallot sought for the words to describe de Launay's killing.

DETAILS OF TUESDAY, 14 JULY . . .

Already the great drawbridge is lowering; the governor is sought; each tries to find him: good Arné, that intrepid grenadier, notices him; he rushes to him and arrests him; de Launai tries to pierce his chest, Arné disarms him and hands him over to M. Hullin and M. Elie, to die in another place where danger calls him. Meanwhile the traitorous governor is already in the hands of his conquerors, his badges of honour are torn from him, he is treated like one who is loathsome; he will be dragged into the midst of an enormous crowd; he urges the young man who accompanies him, who still wishes to protect him from the insults of the populace: 'Ah!' he says to him, torn by remorse, 'I have betrayed my fatherland!' and his voice is choked with sobs. Meanwhile the vice-governor, the major, the captain of the gunners and all the prisoners of war have already been taken; the dungeons are opened; liberty is given to innocent men, and to venerable old men surprised to see the light. For the first time,

18

august and sacred liberty finally entered this abode of horrors, this dreadful asylum for despotism, monsters and crimes.

Meanwhile we fall into step, we exit into an enormous crowd, applause, excesses of joy, insults, curses thrown at the perfidious prisoners of war, all of them mingled; cries of vengeance and of pleasure come from all hearts; the glorious victors covered in honour carrying the weapons and the spoils of the vanquished, the flags of victory, the militia among the soldiers of the fatherland, the praise offered them from all sides, all make a fearsome and superb spectacle. On arriving, these people who were so impatient to avenge themselves allowed neither de Launai nor the other officers to go into the city court; they tore them from the hands of their conquerors and trampled them underfoot one after the other; de Launai was pierced by countless blows, his head was cut off and carried on the end of a spear, and his blood ran everywhere. And there were already two bodies being shown there before the disarmed guards from the Bastille appeared. They arrived, and the people demanded their execution, but the generous French Guards asked for their pardon, and on their request votes were taken, and the pardon was unanimous.

This glorious day must surprise our enemies, and portends finally the triumph of justice and freedom.

This evening, the city will be illuminated.

Source: *Les Révolutions de Paris*, no. 1, 12–18 July 1789, pp. 17–19.

The killing of Bertier and Foulon, 22 July 1789

The seizure of the Bastille saved the National Assembly and legitimised a sharp shift in power. The control of Paris by the Third Estate was institutionalised by a new city government under Bailly and a bourgeois civil guard commanded by the French hero of the American War of Independence, Lafayette. Later in the month Lafayette would join the white of the Bourbon flag to the red and blue colours of the city of Paris: the revolutionary tricolour cockade was born. On 17 July, Louis formally accepted what had occurred by entering Paris to announce the withdrawal of troops and the recalling of Necker. However, the retribution meted out to de Launay after the storming of the Bastille was to be repeated. On the 22nd, the royal governor (Intendant) of Paris since 1776, Louis Bertier de Sauvigny, and his father-in-law Joseph Foulon, who had replaced Necker in the ministry, were captured as they fled the capital. Foulon had allegedly stated that if the poor were hungry they should eat straw. This time Loustallot was less tolerant of popular vengeance.

DETAILS OF WEDNESDAY, 22 JULY

This day was frightening and dreadful; it was a sign of the people's vengeance against their oppressors. As early as five o'clock in the morning it was announced that Foulon, full of ambition, who, so many times, incited public hatred through his odious speculations and the incredible growth of a fortune that was surprising, even incredible: Foulon had just been arrested 5 leagues from Paris, on the Fontainebleau road. . . . Vainly did the Electors come down from the city, and seek to harangue the people; words of peace had no effect on a people in a state of fury, who desired only blood. M. Bailly got up before them; his eloquence, which was always persuasive, was lacking for the first time; he was not heard. What else could one hope for from a people who were no longer moved by expressions of feeling?

. . . the rope was waiting for him, he was already under the fatal street-lamp whose post has served as a gallows to so many traitors, he was already suspended, the cord broke, and suddenly it was mended, one thousand hands, one thousand arms were busy with his execution: in brief, he was no more, and his severed head separated far from his body presenting the horrific spectacle of the bloody proscriptions. This head was carried at the end of a pike through all the streets of Paris; a handful of hay was in its mouth, a striking allusion to the inhumane sentiments of this barbarous man; his body that was dragged through the mud and carried all over the place announced the terrible vengeance of a people rightly angry towards the tyrants! . . .

The Intendant of Paris, M. Bertier, having been recognised in Compiègne by a man of the people, was immediately arrested. . . . The cruel joy of the people is painted on every face; doors, balconies, windows, along his path they are all full, everything is occupied, their desirous expectation increases their interest. Finally he appears, this iniquitous Intendant; his face is still tranquil! Thus a habit of infamy, as well as innocence, also inspires tranquillity! No, Bertier did not imagine he was walking to his execution: but what horrible scene has just begun! Who would believe it? The bloody head of that loathed outlaw, his father-in-law, is presented to him. O what a dreadful spectacle! Bertier is trembling! . . .

Already, Bertier is no more; his head is already nothing more than a mutilated mass, separated from his body; already a man—a man! Oh the gods! The barbarian!—tears out his heart from his palpitating entrails. What do I say? He is avenging himself on a monster! This monster had [allegedly] killed his father. . . .

I feel it, oh my fellow citizens, I feel to what extent these revolting scenes grieve your souls; like you, they have penetrated me; but consider how ignominious it is to live and to be a slave! Consider with what torture the crimes of lèse-humanity should be punished; consider, finally, what fortunes, what satisfactions, what happiness await you, you and your children and your descendants, once august and holy liberty has placed its temple among you! Nonetheless, do not forget that these proscriptions offend humanity and make nature tremble.

Source: *Les Révolutions de Paris*, no. 2, 18–25 July 1789, pp. 18–25.

Arthur Young in France, July 1789

The English agronomist Arthur Young (1741–1820) used his farm near Bradfield, Suffolk, to carry out scientific agricultural experiments. In the summer of 1789 he was making his third visit to France; his observations on his travels are an invaluable source for social conditions and political opinion in these years. In July he was in the eastern province of Lorraine at the same time as revolution was occurring in Paris.

The 9th

This spirit of reading political tracts, they say, spreads into the provinces, so that all the presses of France are equally employed. Nineteen-twentieths of these productions are in favour of liberty, and commonly violent against the clergy and nobility; I have today bespoke many of this description, that have reputation; but enquiring for such as had appeared on the other side of the question, to my astonishment I find there are but two or three that have merit enough to be known. Is it not wonderful, that while the press teems with the most levelling and even the seditious principles, that if put in execution would overturn the monarchy, nothing in reply appears, and not the least step is taken by the court to restrain this extreme licentiousness of publication. It is easy to conceive the spirit that must thus be raised among the people. But the coffee-houses in the Palais Royal present yet more singular and astonishing spectacles; they are not only crowded within, but other expectant crowds are at the doors and windows.

The 10th

Everything conspires to render the present period in France critical: the want of bread is terrible: accounts arrive every moment from the provinces of riots and disturbances, and calling in the military, to preserve the peace of the markets. The prices reported are the same as I found at Abbeville and Amiens—5 sous a pound for white bread, and $3\frac{1}{2}$ to 4 for the common sort, eaten by the poor: these rates are beyond their faculties, and occasion great misery.

It appears plain to me, that the violent friends of the commons are not displeased at the high price of corn, which seconds their views greatly, and makes any appeal to the common feeling of the people more easy, and much more to their purpose than if the price was low.

The 12th

Walking up a long hill, to ease my mare, I was joined by a poor woman, who complained of the times, and that it was a sad country; demanding her reasons, she said her husband had but a morsel of land, one cow, and a poor little horse, yet they had a *franchar* [42lb] of wheat, and three chickens, to pay as a quit-rent to one Seigneur; and four *franchar* of oats, one chicken and 1F to pay to another, besides very heavy *tailles* and other taxes. She had seven children, and the cow's milk helped to make the soup. But why, instead of a horse, do you not keep another cow? Oh, her husband could not carry his produce so well without a horse; and asses are little used in the country. It was said, at present, *that something was to be done by some great folks for such poor ones, but she did not know who nor how,* but God send us better, *car les tailles & les droits nous écrasent.* This woman, at no great distance, might have been taken for sixty or seventy, her figure was so bent, and her face so furrowed and hardened by labour,—but she said she was only twenty-eight.

An Englishman who has not travelled, cannot imagine the figure made by infinitely the greater part of the countrywomen in France; it speaks, at the first sight, hard and severe labour: I am inclined to think, that they work harder than the men, and this, united with the more miserable labour of bringing a new race of slaves into the world, destroys absolutely all symmetry of person and every feminine appearance. To what are we to attribute this difference in the manners of the lower people in the two kingdoms? To GOVERNMENT.

Source: Arthur Young, *Travels in France during the years 1787–1788–1789 undertaken more particularly with a view of ascertaining the cultivation, wealth, resources and national prosperity of the Kingdom of France* (London, 1792), pp. 196–8.

The Great Fear: letter from the steward of the Duke of Montmorency, 2 August 1789

Rural people had placed great hopes in the meeting of the Estates-General. Now news of the storming of the Bastille tempered such hopes with fears that the nobility would take revenge on the Third Estate. Villages formed popular militias. The bands of destitute roaming country roads were the focus of suspicion as anxious peasants waited for crops to ripen. In such a situation rumour spread like wildfire from five separate epicentres, engulfing every region but Brittany and the east. When noble revenge failed to eventuate, village militias instead turned their weapons on the seigneurial system itself, compelling *seigneurs* or their agents to hand over feudal registers to be burned on the village square. This extraordinary revolt came to be known as the 'Great Fear'. This example comes from the parish of Montmartin, to the north-east of Paris.

Sir, so as not to disturb your peace, I have not revealed to you the justifiable concerns that have been perturbing me for some time, but now I would believe it unwise to leave you unaware of them. Brigandage and pillage are practised everywhere. The populace, attributing to the lords of the kingdom the high price of grain, is fiercely hostile to all that belongs to them. All reasoning fails: this unrestrained populace listens only to its own fury and, in all our province, the vassals are so outraged that they are prepared to commit the greatest excesses; moreover, in this very parish, persuaded that the Baron of Breteuil and his family are in the castle, it is said aloud that it will be set on fire. You must believe, Sir, that in such circumstances, I take all possible care. Each night, I and my own keep watch in great secrecy so as not to show concern that could be detrimental to us. Even though I know very well the people who have such feelings, I feign ignorance of it and I redouble my friendliness towards everyone. Another concern that tears at my heart is not knowing whether our lords are protected from the popular fury. If it is within your power, please be so good, I beg of you, as to write something of it to me.

Just as I was going to finish my letter, I learnt . . . that approximately 300 brigands from all the lands associated with the vassals of Mme the marquise de Longaunay have stolen the titles of rents and allowances of the *seigneurie*, and demolished her dovecotes: they then gave her a receipt for the theft signed *The Nation*. The same men, 4 days ago, entered a castle of the Prince of Monaco located 4 leagues from Thorigny to steal the titles from there also; not finding them, they unleashed their fury on the furniture in the castle and reduced it to dust. The tax collector and his family were lucky enough to escape.

Thorigny castle is under threat, and there is no doubt that it will be pillaged. What, therefore, must we do and become?

The paupers of this parish are dying of hunger: I will help them a little in this dreadful destitution and, to try to stop it, distribute 50 crowns or so. . . .

Source: *Annales historiques de la Révolution française*, 1955, pp. 161–2.

3

CREATING A REGENERATED FRANCE

The August 1789 decrees on feudalism

The response of the National Assembly to the news of the 'Great Fear' was initially one of panic. On 4 August a series of prominent nobles made sweeping gestures to renounce their privileges. Over the succeeding days, however, the Assembly made a crucial distinction between instances of 'personal servitude', which were abolished outright, and 'property rights' (seigneurial dues payable on harvests) for which peasants had to pay compensation before ceasing payment. The distinction was to create years of litigation and unrest in the countryside. State taxes and church tithes were also to continue for the time being. Nevertheless, the decrees were of great importance in legislating that henceforth all French people were to be citizens equal before the law and that careers were 'open to talents'. The age of privileged corporations and provinces was over.

Article 1. The National Assembly destroys the feudal regime completely. It decrees that both feudal and *censuel* [that is, levied on crops] rights and dues which stem from real or personal servitude or *mortmain* [a lord's inalienable hold over some land], and those who represent them, are abolished without compensation; all the others are declared redeemable, and the price and the manner of the redemption will be set by the National Assembly. Those of the said rights that are not abolished by this decree will continue nonetheless to be collected until redemption has been made.

Article 2. The exclusive right to bird shelters and dovecotes is abolished. Pigeons will be confined for periods determined by communities; during this time, they will be regarded as game, and each man will have the right to kill them on his land.

Article 3. The exclusive right to hunting and open rabbit warrens is equally abolished, and any property owner has the right to destroy and have destroyed, on his own property alone, any type of game, except in conformity with police regulations that may be made in relation to public safety.

All *capitaineries* [hunting jurisdictions], even royal ones, and all hunting preserves, under whatever denomination, are equally abolished; and the preservation of the personal pleasures of the king will be provided for in a manner compatible with the respect due to property and liberty.

The President will be given the responsibility of requesting from the king the freeing of galley slaves and those banished for the simple fact of hunting, the release of prisoners currently detained, and the abolition of the existing procedures in this respect.

Article 4. All seigneurial courts are abolished without compensation, but nonetheless the officers of these laws will continue their duties until the National Assembly has provided for the establishment of a new judicial order.

Article 5. Tithes of any nature, and taxes that take their place, under whatever denomination that they be known and collected, even by subscription, and *possessed by secular and regular bodies*, by beneficed clergymen, vestries and all people in *mortmain*, even by the Order of Malta, and other religious and military orders . . . are abolished, subject to advice on the means to meet in another manner the costs of divine worship, the maintenance of ministers of religion, the relief of the poor, the repairs and reconstruction of churches and presbyteries, and all the establishments, seminaries, schools, colleges, hospitals, communities and others to whose maintenance they are currently assigned. And meanwhile, until provision has been made, and the former possessors are furnished with their equivalent, the National Assembly orders that the said tithes will continue to be collected according to the law and in the accustomed manner. . . .

Article 6. All perpetual ground rents, be they in kind or in money, whatever be their type, whatever be their origin, and to whomever they be due, owners of *mortmain*, owners of domains, privileged persons, those of the Order of Malta, will be redeemable; seigneurial rights to a part of the tenant's harvest, of all types and all denominations, will be so also, at a rate to be set by the Assembly. It will be forbidden in the future ever to create a non-redeemable due.

Article 7. The venality of judicial and municipal positions is abolished henceforth. Justice will be rendered freely. Nonetheless the incumbents of these positions will continue to fulfil their functions and to receive their emoluments until the Assembly has provided for means of securing their reimbursement.

Article 8. The occasional charges levied by country priests are abolished, and will cease to be paid as soon as the increase of the *portion congruë* and vicars' stipends has been provided for, and a ruling will be given to ascertain the lot of town priests.

Article 9. Pecuniary, personal or real privileges, in matters of taxation, are abolished for ever. Levies will be made on all citizens and on all possessions, in the same manner and the same form; and the ways of effecting proportional payments of all contributions will be advised, even for the last six months of the current year of taxation.

Article 10. A national constitution and public freedom being more beneficial to the provinces than the privileges that some of them enjoyed, and the sacrifice of which is necessary for the unity of all parts of the kingdom, it is declared that all special privileges of provinces, principalities, counties, cantons, towns and communities of inhabitants, be they financial or of any other nature, are abolished without compensation, and will be absorbed into the common rights of all French people.

Article 11. All citizens, without distinction of birth, may be admitted to all ecclesiastical, civil and military employments and positions. . . .

Article 14. Plurality of benefices will no longer exist, once the income from the profit to which one is entitled exceeds the sum of 3,000 livres. . . .

Article 16. The National Assembly decrees that, in memory of the great and important deliberations that have just been undertaken for the happiness of France, a medal will be struck, and that in thanksgiving a 'Te deum' will be sung in all the parishes and churches of the kingdom.

Article 17. The National Assembly solemnly proclaims King Louis XVI to be *Restorer of French liberty*.

Article 18. The National Assembly will appear as a body before the king, in order to present to His Majesty the decree that it has just adopted, to bring him the homage of its most respectful gratitude, and to beg him to allow the *Te Deum* to be sung in his chapel, and that he himself be present. . . .

Source: *Gazette nationale ou le Moniteur universel*, no. 40, 11–14 August 1789, vol. 1, pp. 332–3.

———❧———

The Declaration of the Rights of Man and of the Citizen, August 1789

With the August decrees on feudalism, the Declaration of the Rights of Man and of the Citizen represents the foundation document of the regenerated society and polity which it was believed would emerge from the Revolution of 1789. The Declaration may be read as a critique of the *Ancien Régime*, as the previous system was now called, for each article targeted a specific feature of pre-1789 France. However, it was also one of the great statements of the fundamental, universal principles of liberalism. It was nonetheless ambiguous in its silences about providing the means for the poor to enjoy these rights and in the distinction it made between 'man' and 'citizen'.

The representatives of the French people, constituted as a National Assembly, considering that ignorance, forgetfulness or disregard for the rights of man are the sole causes of public misfortunes and of the corruption of governments, have resolved to set out, in a solemn declaration, the natural, inalienable and sacred rights of man, so that this declaration, constantly present for all the members of the social body, may ceaselessly remind them of their rights and their duties; so that the acts of the legislative body and those of the executive body, being comparable with the goal of all political institutions, be the more respected for it; and so that the demands of citizens, based henceforth on simple and incontestable principles, may be always directed towards the main-tenance of the Constitution and the happiness of all men.

Consequently, the National Assembly, in the presence and under the aus-pices of the Supreme Being, recognises and declares the following rights of man and of the citizen:

Article 1. Men are born and remain free and equal in rights. Social distinc-tions may only be based on common usefulness.

Article 2. The goal of every political association is the preservation of man's natural and imprescriptible rights. These rights are liberty, property, security, and resistance to oppression.

Article 3. The principle of all sovereignty resides essentially in the nation. No body or individual may exercise authority that does not expressly emanate from it.

Article 4. Liberty consists in being able to do anything that is not harmful to others. Thus, the only limits to the exercise of the natural rights of each man are those that ensure the enjoyment of the same rights for other members of society. Only the law may determine these limits.

Article 5. The law has the right only to forbid acts that are harmful to soci-ety. Anything that is not forbidden by the law may not be prevented, and no one may be constrained to do what it does not command.

Article 6. The law is the expression of the general will. All citizens, or their representatives, have the right to work solemnly towards its formulation. It must be the same for all, whether it protects or punishes. All citizens, being equal in its eyes, are equally admissible to all public dignities, posts and employment, according to their abilities, and without any distinction other than that of their virtues and their talents.

Article 7. No man may be accused, arrested or detained, other than in those cases determined by the law, and according to the conventions it has pre-scribed. Those who solicit, expedite or execute arbitrary orders, or have arbitrary orders executed, must be punished; but any citizen who is sum-moned or apprehended by virtue of the law, must obey immediately; he makes himself guilty through resistance.

Article 8. The law may only establish punishments that are strictly and clearly necessary, and a man may be punished only by virtue of a law that is established and promulgated prior to the crime, and legally enforced.

Article 9. All men being presumed innocent until they have been declared guilty, if it is deemed indispensable to arrest a man, any severity that is not necessary in the apprehension of his person must be severely repressed by the law.

Article 10. No man may be harassed for his opinions, even religious ones, as long as their manifestation does not trouble the public order established by the law.

Article 11. The free communication of thoughts and opinions is one of the most precious rights of man; thus any citizen may speak, write and print freely, on condition that he will have to answer for the abuse of this freedom in those cases set down by the law.

Article 12. Guaranteeing the rights of man and the citizen necessitates a public force: thus this force is instituted for the benefit of all, and not for the individual use of those to whom it is entrusted.

Article 13. To maintain the public force, and for administrative costs, a common tax is indispensable; it must be equally divided among all citizens, on the basis of their property.

Article 14. All citizens have the right to observe for themselves, or through their representatives, the need for public taxation, to consent to it freely, to scrutinise its use, and to determine the quota, the basis on which it is assessed, its payment and duration.

Article 15. Society has the right to request an account of his administration from any public agent.

Article 16. Any society in which the guarantee of rights is not ensured, nor the separation of powers established, has no constitution.

Article 17. Property being an inviolable and sacred right, no man may be deprived of it, unless in cases where public necessity, legally recorded, clearly demands it, and on condition of just and prior compensation. The National Assembly, wishing to establish the French Constitution on the principles it has just recognised and declared, irrevocably abolishes those institutions that wounded the liberty and equality of rights.

Source: *Gazette nationale ou le Moniteur universel*, no. 44, 20 August 1789, vol. 2, pp. 362–3.

The march of Parisian market-women on Versailles, October 1789

Louis refused to sanction both the August decrees and the Declaration of the Rights of Man. For the second time, the *menu peuple* of Paris intervened to safeguard a revolution that they assumed was theirs. This time, however, it was particularly the women of the markets. On 5 October, up

Avant-Garde des femmes Allant à Versailles

Figure 2 The Parisian market-women en route to Versailles on 5 October to make their protest to the king and the Assembly. Contemporaries disagreed as to whether some of the market-women who marched to Versailles were men in disguise, and about who led them. There is no doubt, however, that their intervention in the political stand-off was crucial in securing the king's acceptance of the Declaration of the Rights of Man and of the Citizen and the August decrees on feudalism, and in forcing the royal family and Assembly to move to Paris. Source: Bibliothèque nationale de France.

to 7,000 women marched to Versailles, belatedly followed by the National Guard. At Versailles the women invaded the Assembly. A deputation was then presented to the king, who agreed to sanction the decrees. It soon became apparent, however, that the women would be satisfied only if the royal family returned to Paris; on the 6th it did so, and the Assembly followed soon after. The Assembly again owed its success to the people of Paris. However, it was now determined to put an end to such popular intervention, and ordered an enquiry into the 'crimes' of 5–6 October. Among the hundreds of people interviewed was Madelaine Glain, a 42-year-old cleaner, who made a link between the imperatives of securing cheap and plentiful bread and the fate of the key revolutionary decrees.

LXXXIII

Madelaine Glain, aged 42, cleaner, wife of François Gaillard, office assistant in the Oratoire district, with whom she lives, no. 40 rue Froidmanteau, states that having been forced, like many other women, to follow the crowd that went to

Versailles on Monday, 5 October last, and having arrived at Sèvres near the porcelain factory, a man with a black sash having asked them where they were going, they told them that they were going to ask for bread at Versailles; that this man urged them to be well behaved; but a woman whom she knows to be a prostitute, and who has since lived with Lagrement, café owner, rue Bailleul, having said that she went to Versailles to bring back the head of the queen, this woman was strongly reprimanded by the others; that arriving at the avenue of Versailles, this same woman stopped a king's guard who was on horseback, and she roundly abused him, threatening him with a rusty old sword that she was carrying; that this king's guard told her she was poor wretch, and to make her let go of his horse's bridle that she was holding, struck her and wounded her in the arm; that then going to the castle, with the intention of informing His Majesty of the motives of their actions, the witness found herself caught, that is to say, her skirts were caught in two uprights of the railings, from which a Swiss man helped her out; after which she went with the other women to the hall of the National Assembly, where they entered in great numbers; that some of these women having demanded 4 pounds of bread at 8 sous, and meat at the same price, the witness begged for silence, and then she said that they asked that they no longer want for bread, though not at the price that the said women wished to have it; that she did not go in a delegation to the castle, but came back with M. Maillard and two other women to the Paris town hall, bringing the decrees that were given to them in the National Assembly; that the mayor and the representatives of the commune were highly satisfied, and they were received with joy, and that then the witness was taken by the National Guard to the Oratoire district to make known the good news; that she can give us no information on what happened at Versailles on Tuesday the 6th, but learned, without being able to say from whom, that the man called Nicholas, a model at the academy, who was living with Poujet, rue Champfleuri, had, on the said Tuesday, cut off the heads of two of the king's guards who had been massacred by the people, and that since, the said Nicholas has not reappeared in the district.

Source: *Réimpression de l'Ancien Moniteur, seule histoire authentique et inaltérée de la Révolution française, depuis la réunion des États-Généraux jusqu'au Consulat*, 32 vols. (Paris, 1847), vol. 2, 1789, p. 544.

Law on inheritance, March 1790

This measure introducing equal inheritance of both sons and daughters was taken more with a view to breaking the power of great noble patriarchs than to strengthening the economic position of women. Henceforth, however, no child could be disinherited as a result of parental decisions. If a farm was to be left intact to one child, other children would have to be compensated. The legislation was to have a dramatic impact in those regions (for example, most of the south and Normandy) where testamentary freedom had favoured first-born sons; in western regions such as Maine and Anjou, on the other hand, partible inheritance was already the norm.

Article 11. All privileges, all feudalism and nobility of property being destroyed, birthright and rights of masculinity with regard to noble fiefs, domains and ancestors, and unequal distribution by reason of someone's quality are abolished.

Consequently, the Assembly orders that all inheritances . . . will be, without regard for the ancient noble quality of possessions and persons, shared between heirs according to the laws, statutes and customs that regulate distributions between all citizens, and repeals and destroys all the laws and customs contrary to this.

Excepted from the present decree are those who are currently married or widowed with children, who in the distributions to be made between them and their fellow heirs, for all inheritances of personal goods and real estate, direct and collateral, that may fall to their share, will enjoy all the advantages that the former laws grant them.

Furthermore it is declared that younger children and girls, in the customs where they have up to now had more benefits from possessions held in fiefs than from non-feudal possessions, will continue in the above fiefs to take the parts assigned to them by the said customs, until the National Assembly decides on a definitive and uniform form of inheritance for all the kingdom.

Source: *Archives parlementaires*, 15 March 1790, p. 173.

The Festival of the Federation, 14 July 1790

The popular alliance of the Third Estate and its allies among the clergy and 'patriotic' nobility continued to draw on a powerful sense of national unity and regeneration well into 1790. This unity was enacted in Paris by the great 'Fête de la Fédération', on the first anniversary of the storming of the Bastille. On the Champ de Mars, which had been levelled by voluntary labour, Louis, Talleyrand (the former Bishop of Autun) and Lafayette proclaimed the new order in front of an estimated 300,000 Parisians. This ceremony occurred in different forms in towns and villages all over France.

Meanwhile, an army of workers finished preparations in haste on the Champ de Mars, in spite of the abundant rain; and in several districts tickets were being distributed for entry to it the next day. . . .

Forty-two departments, in alphabetical order, the deputation of the ground and sea troops, [then] the forty-one remaining departments made up the federal army; a detachment of grenadiers and guards on horseback closed the parade.

From the boulevard, the procession passed through the rues Saint-Denis, Ferronerie and Saint-Honoré, rue Royal, Louis XV Square, the Queen's Walk and Chaillot Wharf, and made for the Champ de Mars via the bridge of boats that had been laid across the Seine, opposite the Filles Sainte-Marie convent.

A great spectacle greeted the eyes of the federates as they arrived; 300,000 spectators, men and women, all of them decorated with ribbons *à la nation*, were seated on benches which, extending from a triple triumphal arch, form a sloping boundary whose top blends with the branches stretching from the trees like wings, and whose bottom dominates an immense platform, in the middle of which an altar had been raised. . . .

A moment later, the National Assembly swore an oath; there was a cry of 'Long live the king!', a few voices attempted 'Long live the National Assembly!'; either by error, or deliberately, [but] these cries were stifled. Finally, the king stood up; immediately a double row of people was formed from the throne to the altar, but he did not judge it timely to go to it, and from his place, he said out loud, and with a highly satisfied look, the oath decreed by the National Assembly. The cries of 'vive le roi' began again. A moment later, the queen held up her son to the people, and the covered gallery, where entrance had been by ticket, shouted 'vive la reine', which was echoed with cries of 'vive le dauphin'. A few salvoes announced the end of the celebration at about six o'clock in the evening.

Source: *Révolutions de Paris*, no. 53, 10–17 July 1790, pp. 3–5, 8.

Le Chapelier law, 14 June 1791

The Declaration of the Rights of Man had been silent on economic matters, but in 1789–91 the Assembly passed a series of measures revealing its commitment to economic liberalism. Impediments to freedom of occupation were removed with the abolition of guilds (the d'Allarde law, March 1791) and, most importantly, a free market in labour was imposed by the Le Chapelier law of 14 June 1791 outlawing associations of employers and employees. Le Chapelier, an ennobled lawyer, had presided over the session of 4 August 1789 in the National Assembly, and was one of the radical Breton deputies who had founded the Jacobin Club. While these laws were decisive in the creation of a *laissez-faire* economy, they were also aimed at the 'counter-revolutionary' practices and privileges of the *Ancien Régime*. No longer were there specific orders of clergy or nobility, or guilds, provinces and towns which could claim particular monopolies, privileges and rights. The old world of corporations was dead.

Article 1. The destruction of all types of corporations of citizens of the same trade and profession being one of the fundamental bases of the French Constitution, it is forbidden to re-establish them in fact, under any pretext or in any form whatsoever.

Article 2. Citizens of the same trade or profession, entrepreneurs, those who have shops, workers and craftsmen of whatever art, may not, when they find themselves together, name a president, secretary or syndic, keep registers, make decrees or decisions, or form regulations on their supposed common interests.

Article 3. It is forbidden to all administrative or municipal bodies to receive any address or petition under the denomination of a trade or profession, [and] to answer it; and they are charged to declare null the decisions that could be made in this manner, and to ensure that no result or implementation comes from them.

Article 4. If, against the principles of liberty and the Constitution, citizens attached to the same professions, arts and trades make decisions or created agreements between themselves which would lead them to refuse, or only make available at a set price, their industry or their work, the said decisions, accompanied by an oath or not, are declared unconstitutional and detrimental to liberty and to the Declaration of Human Rights, and null and void; administrative and municipal bodies are obliged to declare them as such; the authors, leaders and instigators who have incited them, drawn them up or presided over them will be summoned before the police court, at the request of the prosecutor of the commune, and given a 500-livre fine, and suspended for a year from exercising all the rights of active citizens, and from entry into the assemblies. . . .

Article 6. If the said decisions or agreements, posted or distributed by circular, were to contain any threat to foreign entrepreneurs, tradesmen, workers or day labourers who may come to work in the area, or to those who are content with a lower wage, all authors, instigators and signatories of the deeds or writings will be punished through a fine of 1,000 livres each, and three months in prison.

Article 7. If the individual freedom of entrepreneurs and workers were to be attacked through threats of violence on the part of these coalitions, the authors of the violence would be pursued as disturbers of the public peace.

Article 8. Coalitions of workers having as their goal to hamper the freedom that the Constitution grants to industry, and to oppose police rulings or the execution of judgements to that effect, will be seen as insurgents, and consequently punished.

Source: *Gazette nationale ou le Moniteur universel*, no. 166, 15 June 1791, p. 662.

4

EXCLUSIONS AND INCLUSIONS

Petition from Jewish Communities, 28 January 1790

The Declaration of the Rights of Man had already held out the promise that henceforth all citizens would share equal rights to freedom of conscience and the external practice of their faith. By the end of 1789 full citizenship had been granted to Protestants and, the following January, to the Sephardic Jews of Bordeaux and Avignon (by only 374 votes to 280). The Assembly hesitated to grant equality to Ashkenazim Jews of eastern France in the face of the anti-Semitism of deputies from Alsace, such as Jean-François Reubell from Colmar, who opposed citizenship for eastern Jews at the same time as he campaigned for the rights of slaves. This prompted this spirited reminder from eastern Jews in January 1790. Only during the final sessions of the National Assembly in September 1791 were the eastern Jews granted full equality and the right to stand for election.

We remember that the National Assembly, in granting to non-Catholics who fulfil the conditions of eligibility the right to be chosen for all grades of administration, and to possess civil and military positions like other citizens, declared in the same decree that it did not mean to make any premature judgement on the Jews, on whom it would decide later. It is on this indefinite adjournment, which left the fate of 50,000 Jews established in France in suspense, that their deputies come, in their name, to present this petition to the National Assembly. The Jews of Bordeaux have asked, at the same time, to enjoy the active rights of citizens, for which they possess the statement declared in the letters patent. Their petition was presented to the Assembly by a prelate as distinguished for his wisdom as for his patriotism, and who, thanks to his good principles and good example, has the good fortune to be honoured in the same degree, both in the esteem of good citizens, and the hatred of the enemies of the public good. Despite the prejudicial cries and tumultuous movements of one section of the hall, which for several hours violated the sanctuary of its deliberations, the National Assembly proclaimed the great act of justice that was asked of it, by admitting to the enjoyment of the rights of active citizenship all the *Portuguese, Spanish and Avignonnais* Jews. The other part of the Jews established in France is thus in the same state as it was on 24 December. Their rights are in the same state of uncertainty. The time when these rights are to be discussed is not even set, in spite of the request for adjournment to a set day, made on 28 January by the Abbé Grégoire, one of the first and most eloquent defenders of the Jews. Whatever may be the time for a discussion that the imperious law of justice does not allow to be much delayed, its success can hardly be seen as doubtful. It could be believed, as it is by the authors of this petition, *that it is not the intention of the National Assembly that men whose religion and principles are the same have a different existence in France, because they do not live in the same province.* . . .

Thus the Jews prove that France must, from justice and interest, grant them the rights of citizenship, in that their home is in this empire, that they live there as subjects, that they serve their fatherland through all the means that are in their power, that they contribute to the maintenance of the public force like all the other citizens of the kingdom, independently of the onerous, degrading, arbitrary taxes that ancient injustices, ancient prejudices, supported by the old regime, accumulated on their head: that is, they say, there can only be two classes of men in a State: citizens and foreigners; to prove that we are not foreigners is to prove that we are citizens.

. . . The same objections that are made at the moment against the Jews were made, two years ago, against the Protestants, and it can be remembered with what success. Then, like today, it was said, printed, pronounced, with most imposing gravity, that any innovation of this type would be a sign of general subversion. Catholic blood and Protestant blood were already seen to be flowing from the daggers of fanaticism in all parts of France. Tender and timid souls, stirred up by vigorous souls, moaned in advance about so many horrible calamities, and beseeched heaven not to punish with such a vengeance the crimes of *modern philosophy*. Meanwhile the *tolerance* law (as it was then called) was proclaimed: it was peacefully enacted from one end of France to the other; the terrors were in vain, the manoeuvres remained powerless; and these same men, for whom the right of *tolerance* was disputed in 1787, in 1789 received all civil rights with no type of contradiction.

In this paper, the Jews respond to all the objections that are made to them regarding their religion. They prove that the vices of some among them, far from being inspired by their religious principles, are the work of the people who gave them sanctuary, and that the degrading of the others is the fruit of the institutions that surrounded them; that the usury for which all the Jews are reproached is practised only by a few among them, and that it is so because all means of living are refused them; that even, for a great number of years, the courts have resounded only rarely with complaints of usury against Jews; that

their religion authorises neither deception nor dishonesty; that far from ordering that foreigners be hated, it stipulates that they love them, that they be
offered consolation and help; that the law of Moses is full of these principles of
love and charity, etc. They respond again in a very decisive manner to other less
specious objections, raised against them in the National Assembly and in
public, and end their petition by stating the right and the interest they have
to be admitted, without restriction and without delay, to the enjoyment of the
station of citizen.

Source: *Gazette nationale ou le Moniteur universel*, no. 46, 15 February 1790, vol.
2, pp. 368–9.

Civil rights for free Blacks, 15 May 1791

The Revolution threatened the livelihoods of those whose wealth was
drawn from the slave system as slave traders or colonial planters if the
principles underpinning the Declaration of the Rights of Man were
extended to the Caribbean colonies. An angry debate opposed the
colonial lobby (the Club Massiac) to the Société des Amis des Noirs,
which included Brissot, Robespierre and Grégoire. The Assembly
changed nothing in its first decree, on 8 March 1790. Its next response,
in May 1791, granted 'active' citizen status to free Blacks ('men of
colour') with free parents and the necessary property, but avoided the
issue of slavery.

M. ROBESPIERRE: All that M. Barnave has just said has been sufficiently
  answered during the course of the discussion. . . . He claims that, having
  already sanctioned slavery through a decree, we must not, or, to put it
  better, you must not be so difficult about the rest. But did you speak the
  word *slavery* completely freely? . . . If you have adopted a decree, the idea
  of which the colonisers would not have dared suggest to you six months
  ago, as the price of such a sacrifice, one finds it strange that you would
  seek to establish the principles of liberty with regard to those whom you
  found free. For myself, I feel that I am here to defend the rights of men; I
  cannot consent to any amendment, and I demand that the principle be
  adopted in its entirety. *(M. Robespierre steps down from the platform to the
  repeated applause of the left and of all the galleries.)* . . .
M. L'ABBÉ MAURY: The precautions that the legislator must take in order to ensure
  justice and good morals lead me to suggest a minor amendment to you: it is

to say: 'The National Assembly decrees that it will never deliberate on the station of people of colour who are not *born of a free father and mother, and proving the legitimacy of their birth.'* . . . No one wished to deprive men of colour of the exercise of political rights indefinitely; but it was wished that they be brought to that point calmly; it was wished that the white colonisers indicate to you the precautions to be taken. It was not said to you that free Negroes are more worthy of interest than men of colour; they have earned emancipation through their services, while men of colour often owe their existence to nothing other than the most shameful prostitution. . . .

The article proposed by M. Reubell is put to the vote.—It is decreed in the following terms:

> The National Assembly decrees that it will never deliberate on the station of people of colour who are not born of a free father and mother, without the prior, free and spontaneous wish of the colonies; that the colonial assemblies currently in existence will stay on; but that people of colour born of a free father and mother will be admitted to all future parish and colonial assemblies, if they moreover have the required qualities.

(The chamber echoes with applause.)

Source: *Gazette nationale ou le Moniteur universel*, no. 136, 16 May 1791, vol. 8, p. 404.

An attack on the slave trade by Frossard, 12 December 1793

The rebellion of hundreds of thousands of mulattos and slaves in Saint-Domingue, beginning in August 1791, pressured the Legislative Assembly in April 1792 into extending civil equality to all 'free persons of colour'. The extension of the revolutionary wars against England and Spain into the Caribbean early in 1793 intensified support inside France for abolition for slavery, as in this pamphlet. In Saint-Domingue, the offer in June 1793 of freedom for slaves who would fight for the Republic was followed by a general emancipation in July–August, extended to all French colonies by the law of 4 February 1794.

Black slave trading is the greatest crime that a government can allow and that man can commit; for it allows and encourages all infamies. Its successes create curses, its intervals the blessings of Providence. Through it, human beings have become merchandise; and the greatest affront to our nature is that in this business, only physical strength is valued, without intellectual capacity being held in any regard, without even allowing that one may have a soul. . . .

From this political axiom, the following consequences can be deduced, and they will form the basis of the arguments, whose analysis I take the liberty of presenting to you, in favour of the abolition of the trading of black slaves.

No man has the right to reduce his fellow man to servitude; nor even to sell his own person. Liberty is an inalienable property. It cannot be represented by any value; and the pact that would bind it is null as a result of this, all the more so as it is unjust and unequal.

For all the more reason, no man can be seen as a slave, if he has not consented to the transaction, if he has not received the price at which his liberty was estimated.

It is no more permitted to go and take slaves in Guinea, than in Spain, England or Italy. All nations are united by a common law, whose exclusive covenants are infractions, rather than exceptions.

In vain will be put forward the pretext that we require labour for our agricultural work. This necessity, however pressing it may be, fades before that of natural rights, whose laws are even more pressing; and man becomes a criminal the moment he bases his individual interests on the misery of his fellow men.

Source: B. S. Frossard, *Observations sur l'abolition de la traite des nègres, présentées à la Convention nationale* (Paris, 1793), pp. 1–3.

Olympe de Gouges on women's rights, 1791

The contradiction between the inclusive, universal promises of the Declaration of the Rights of Man and of the Citizen and the exclusions enshrined in subsequent legislation was not lost on politically active women. In Paris, the Fraternal Society of Citizens of Both Sexes, gathering up to 800 men and women at its sessions, deliberately sought to integrate women into institutional politics. The rights of women were also advocated by individual activists such as Olympe de Gouges, the marquis de Condorcet, Etta Palm and Théroigne de Méricourt, and the Cercle

39

Social urged the vote for women, the availability of divorce, and the abolition of inheritance laws which favoured the first-born son. In 1791 de Gouges published a draft social contract for marriage arrangements concerning children and property and a Declaration of the Rights of Woman and of the Citizeness.

DECLARATION OF THE RIGHTS OF WOMAN AND OF THE CITIZENESS
To be decreed by the National Assembly in its last meetings or in that of the next legislature.

PREAMBLE
Mothers, daughters, sisters, female representatives of the nation, ask to be formed into a National Assembly. Considering that ignorance, forgetfulness or disdain for the rights of women are the only causes of public unhappiness and government corruption, [they] have resolved to set out in a solemn declaration the natural, inalienable and sacred rights of women, so that this declaration, constantly before all members of the social body, will remind them ceaselessly of their rights and duties, so that the power of women, and the power of men being at any moment comparable with the goal of any political institution, be better respected, so that the complaints of female citizens, founded henceforth on simple and incontestable principles, always focus on the maintenance of the Constitution, of good morals, and the happiness of all people.

Consequently, the sex that is superior in beauty as it is in courage in maternal suffering, recognises and declares in the presence and under the auspices of the Supreme Being, the following rights of woman and of the citizeness.

Article 1. Woman is born free and remains equal to man in rights. Social distinctions can only be founded on common utility.

Article 2. The goal of any political association is the preservation of the natural and imprescriptible rights of Woman and Man: these rights are liberty, property, safety and most especially resistance to oppression.

Article 3. The principle of all sovereignty resides essentially in the nation, which is merely the bringing together of woman and man: no body, no individual, can exercise authority that does not expressly emanate from it.

Article 4. Freedom and justice consist in recognising all that belongs to others; thus the practice of woman's natural rights has no limits other than the perpetual tyranny which man opposes to her; these limits must be reformed by the laws of nature and reason.

Article 5. The laws of nature and reason forbid all actions harmful to society: all that is not forbidden by these wise and divine laws cannot be prevented, and no-one can be compelled to do what they do not order.

Article 6. The law must be the expression of the general will; all female and male citizens must assist personally, or through their representatives, in its formation; it must be the same for all: all female and all male citizens, being equal in its eyes, must also be eligible for all public dignities, positions and employments according to their abilities, and without any distinction other than that of their virtues and their talents.

Article 7. No woman is excepted; she is accused, arrested and detained in cases determined by the law. Women obey this strict law as do men.

Article 8. The law must only establish strictly obvious and necessary punishments, and no-one may be punished unless it is by virtue of a law established and promulgated before the crime and legally applied to women.

Article 9. Any woman being declared guilty will be judged according to the letter of the law.

Article 10. No-one may be troubled for their own personal opinions; woman has the right to climb the scaffold, she must equally have that to come forward and speak, as long as her protestations do not affect the public order established by the law.

Article 11. Free communication of thought and opinions is one of the most precious rights of woman, since this freedom ensures the legitimacy of fathers towards their children. Any citizeness can thus say freely, *I am the mother of a child that belongs to you*, without a barbaric prejudice forcing her to hide the truth, except to respond to the abuse of this freedom in cases determined by the law.

Article 12. The guarantee of the rights of woman and of the citizeness requires a public force; this guarantee must be introduced for the benefit of all and not for the special use of those women to whom it is entrusted.

Article 13. For the maintenance of the public force, and the expenses of administration, the contributions of woman and man are equal; she has a part in all the drudgery, in all the painful tasks; she must therefore have an equal part in the distribution of positions, employment, offices, dignities and industry.

Article 14. Female and male citizens have the right to judge for themselves, or through their representatives, the need for public contributions. Citizenesses can only adhere to it through the admission of equal shares, not only in fortune, but also in public administration, and to determine the quota, the basis, the levying and the duration of them.

Article 15. The mass of women, united with men as tax payers, has the right to demand an account of their administration from any public agent.

Article 16. Any society in which the guarantee of rights is not assured, nor the separation of powers determined, has no Constitution; the Constitution is null if the majority of individuals who make up the nation have not cooperated in its drafting.

Article 17. Properties belong to both sexes, united or separate; they are for both an inviolable and sacred right; no-one can be deprived of them as a true inheritance of nature, unless it is when public necessity, legally recorded, clearly requires it, and under condition of a just and prerequisite compensation.

FORM OF THE SOCIAL CONTRACT OF MAN AND WOMAN

We, X and X, separate through our own will, unite together for the term of our life, and for the duration of our mutual tendencies, under the following conditions: We intend and desire to hold our fortunes in common, reserving nonetheless the right to separate them in favour of our children, and of those for whom we may have a special liking, recognising mutually that our goods belong directly to our children, from whatever bed they come, and that all have the right without distinction to carry the name of the fathers and mothers who acknowledge them, and we fully subscribe to the law that punishes the denial of one's own blood. We equally commit ourselves, in the case of our separation, to share out our fortune, and to deduct our children's portion as indicated by the law, and, in the case of a perfect union, whoever died could withdraw half of their goods in favour of their children; and if one died without children, the survivor would inherit by right, unless the one dying disposed of half of the common possessions in favour of whomsoever they might judge suitable.

Source: Olympe de Gouges, *Écrits politiques* (Paris, 1993), pp. 206–11.

5

THE CHURCH AND THE REVOLUTIONARY STATE

The debate on Church reform, May 1790

There was widespread agreement in the *cahiers* on the need for extensive reform to the Church, resulting in the Civil Constitution of the Clergy voted on 12 July 1790. There was no question of separating Church and State: the public functions of the Church were assumed to be integral to daily life, and the Assembly accepted that public revenues would support the Church financially after the abolition of the tithe. Most contentious, however, was the issue of how the clergy were to be appointed in future. To the trenchant objections from clerical deputies in the Assembly that the hierarchy of the Church was based on the principle of divine authority and on inspired appointment by superiors, other deputies retorted that this had resulted in nepotism.

THE ARCHBISHOP OF AIX: Does the ecclesiastical committee know how useful is the influence of religion on citizens? It is the brake that stops the wicked, it is encouragement for virtuous men. Religion is the seal on this declaration that provides man with his rights and his freedom; it is steadfast in its dogmas; its morals cannot change, and its doctrine will always be the same. The committee wishes to remind the clergy of the purity of the original Church. It is not bishops, successors to the apostles, it is not pastors, responsible for preaching the gospel, who can reject this method; but since the committee reminds us of our duties, it will allow us to remind it of our rights and of the sacred principles of ecclesiastical power. It must therefore be reminded of the essential authority of the Church; it is a question of the truths of religion. I will speak of them with all the confidence that befits ministers of the Lord. Jesus Christ passed on his mission to the apostles and to their successors for the salvation of the faithful; he entrusted it neither to the magistrates nor to the king; we are speaking of an order which magistrates and kings must obey. The mission that we

43

have received through ordination and consecration goes right back to the apostles. . . .

Doubtless, abuses must be righted, and a new order of things be brought about. We believe that the ecclesiastical powers must do all they can to reconcile your wishes with the interests of religion; but it is with much sorrow that we witness these culpable designs to make episcopal powers disappear. . . .

Therefore we propose that you consult the Gallican Church by means of a national council. There resides the power that should watch over the centre of faith; it is there that, informed of our duties and our wishes, we will reconcile the interests of the people with those of religion. Thus we come to place the declaration of our sentiments in your hands. We most respectfully beg the king and the National Assembly to allow the convening of a national council. Should this proposition fail to be adopted, we declare ourselves unable to participate in the deliberations. . . .

M. TREILHARD: The principles of the French government had corrupted all classes of citizens; and the clergy, despite the virtues of some of its members, could not resist the influence of a bad constitution. Institutions with no purpose, useless men highly paid, useful men without reward, such are the evils that the current organisation of the clergy presents. Discussion is open as to the decree that the ecclesiastical committee has presented to you. Are the proposed changes useful? Do you have the right to prescribe them? These are the only objects of this discussion. . . .

But is it not clear that the way of elections will ensure the Church the pastor most suitable for such important responsibilities? . . . The first to be appointed after Jesus Christ, Saint Matthew, was elected by all the disciples, who numbered seventy-two. Two people had been chosen, and fate chose between them. The honourable member who said yesterday that pastors were elected solely by fate was thus telling only half the truth. . . . How can we re-establish an ancient order that gave the Church its splendour? Through elections entrusted to the people. It is said that these elections will give rise to cabals; but how many profane motives determined the old choices? . . . Let us throw a veil over the past: my aim, in this discussion, is neither to flatter malice nor to criticise the old régime. Yesterday it was said that non-Catholics would compete in the elections. I say, firstly, that in the current state of things many non-Catholics are appointed for benefices, even to the responsibility of souls; and secondly, it could be required of all electors that they declare that they profess Catholicism. I believe I have shown that the proposed changes are useful, and that they are established on foundations that should lead to good reforms.

It is time to examine whether you have the right to order these changes. Yes, you have the right to do it. Far from undermining religion, in ensuring that the faithful have the most honest and virtuous ministers, you are paying it the most worthy homage. He who believes that this would be to wound religion is forming a truly false idea of religion.

Source: *Gazette nationale ou le Moniteur universel*, no. 150, 30 May 1790; no. 151, 30 May 1790, pp. 491–2, 498–9.

———————<>o<>o<>=————————

Decree on the Civil Constitution of the Clergy, 12 July 1790

The deputies believed that the Civil Constitution concerned itself only with the temporal organisation of the Church (hence the term 'civil'); there was therefore no need to consult the Church. Most parish priests were to be materially advantaged by the new salary scales. However, the Assembly reallocated diocesan and parish boundaries, eliciting a chorus of complaints from small communities and urban parishes whose churches had been closed and who were now required to worship in a neighbouring church. Most important, in applying popular sovereignty to the choice of priests and bishops, the Assembly crossed the narrow line separating temporal and spiritual life. In the end, it proved impossible to reconcile a Church based on divinely ordained hierarchy and dogma and a certainty of one true faith with a Revolution based on popular sovereignty, tolerance and the certainty of earthly fulfilment through the application of secular reason.

The National Assembly, having heard the report from its ecclesiastical committee, has decreed and decrees that which follows, as constitutional articles:

TITLE 1
On ecclesiastical duties
Article 1. Each department will be comprised of one diocese only, and each diocese will have the same area and the same boundaries as the department. . . .
Article 5. All churches and parishes in France, and all French citizens, are forbidden from recognising, in any case and under any pretext whatever, the authority of a . . . bishop whose see is established under the domination of a foreign power . . . all of this without prejudice to the unity of faith and the communion that will be maintained with the visible head of the universal Church. . . .
Article 7. On the advice of the bishop and the district administration a new formation and territory for all the parishes of the kingdom will be established

shortly. Their number and the area will be determined according to the rules that are to be established. . . .

Article 16. In all the towns and villages that do not contain more than 6,000 souls, there will be only one parish; the other parishes will be abolished and joined with the main church.

Article 17. In towns where there are more than 6,000 souls, each parish can be made up of a greater number of parishioners, and it will be retained as long as the needs of the people and the towns demand it. . . .

TITLE 2

Nomination to ecclesiastical positions

Article 1. Counting from the day of publication of the present decree, only one manner of filling bishoprics and cures will be known, that is through elections.

Article 2. All elections will be conducted by ballot and absolute plurality of votes.

Article 3. The election of bishops will be done in the prescribed form and by the electoral body indicated in the decree of 22 December 1789 on the nomination of members of the departmental assembly. . . .

Article 7. To be eligible for a bishopric, it will be necessary to have fulfilled, for at least fifteen years, the duties of an ecclesiastical minister in the diocese in the capacity of priest, priest in charge, or vicar, or as a vicar superior, or as vicar-director of the seminary.

Article 8. The bishops whose seats are abolished by the present decree may be elected to bishoprics that are currently vacant, as well as those that will become vacant, or that are established in some departments, even if they have not had fifteen years of exercise. . . .

Article 10. Also eligible to be elected will be those who are presently priests who have ten years of exercise in a parish of the diocese, even if they have not in the past fulfilled the duties of a curate.

Article 11. It will be the same for priests whose parish has been abolished by virtue of the present decree; and their time of exercise will be counted from the period passed since the abolition of their parish. . . .

Article 19. The new bishop may not apply to the pope in order to obtain any confirmation from him; but he will write to him [only] as the visible head of the universal Church, as an expression of the unity of faith, and of the communion that he must maintain with him. . . .

Article 21. Before the consecration ceremony begins, the elected bishop will, in the presence of the municipal officers, the people and the clergy, make the solemn promise to watch with care over the faithful of the diocese that is entrusted to him, to be faithful to the nation, to the law and to the king, and to maintain to the best of his power the Constitution decreed by the National Assembly, and accepted by the king. . . .

Article 25. The election of priests will be carried out in the prescribed manner, and by the electors indicated in the decree of 22 December 1789 for the nomination of members of the local administrative assembly. . . .

Article 29. Each elector, before putting his ballot paper in the ballot box, will swear to name only the candidate he has chosen in all honesty, as the most worthy, without having been induced by gifts, promises, enticements or threats. This promise will be made for the election of bishops, as for that of priests.

Article 30. The election of priests may only be conducted or begun on a Sunday in the main church of the main town of the district, at the conclusion of the parish Mass, which all electors will be obliged to attend.

Article 31. The proclamation of the elected will be made by the president of the electoral body in the main church before the solemn Mass, which will be celebrated to that effect, in the presence of the people and the clergy.

Article 32. To be eligible for a parish, it will be necessary to have fulfilled the duties of curate in a parish, or in a hospital and other house of charity of the diocese, for at least five years.

Source: *Archives parlementaires*, 12 July 1790, pp. 55–60.

The clerical oath

The decree of 27 November 1790

Most clerical deputies opposed the Civil Constitution, but the Assembly was resolute and was determined not to accede to pressure from the bishops. It sought to force the issue by requiring elections to be held early in 1791, with those elected to swear an oath of loyalty to the law, the nation and the king.

The National Assembly, having heard the report given to it in the name of its ecclesiastical committee . . . decrees the following:

Article 1. Bishops, former archbishops and priests whose see or parish has been preserved, and who are absent from it, for whatever reason and under whatever pretext there may be, excepting, however, those who are members of the National Assembly, will go to their respective dioceses and parishes within a fortnight for those who are in France, and within six weeks for those who are among foreigners; all of the above dating from the publication of the present decree.

Article 2. Within a week of this decree, all bishops and priests currently present in their dioceses and cures will solemnly swear, if they have not already done so, to carefully watch over the faithful of the dioceses and parishes that are entrusted to them, to be faithful to the nation, to the law and to the king, to maintain the Constitution decreed by the National Assembly and accepted by the king, to the best of their ability; and those among the absent who have not taken the above oath will swear it in the same manner and in the same form in the fortnight following their arrival in their diocese or parish. . . .

Article 7. In the case where bishops, former archbishops and priests fail to take the oath, be it by refusing to obey the decrees of the National Assembly, accepted or sanctioned by the king, or by forming or exciting opposition to the carrying out of the said decrees of the National Assembly, accepted or sanctioned by the king, they will not only be deprived of their salary or pension, but also their rights as French citizens will be declared forfeit, and they will be incapable of any public office. . . .

Article 9. In the same way, all ecclesiastical or secular persons who ally themselves to form or to excite opposition to the decrees of the National Assembly sanctioned by the king will be pursued and punished for having disrupted the public peace.

Source: *Gazette nationale ou le Moniteur universel*, no. 332, 28 November 1790, vol. 6, p. 484.

The declaration of a parish priest, January 1791

All over France the oath faced parish priests with an agonising choice of conscience. The Civil Constitution had been sanctioned by the king, but did that quieten their anxiety that the oath contradicted loyalty to the pope and long-established practice? Many priests sought to resolve the dilemma by taking a qualified oath, such as the priest of Quesques et Lottinghem in the north of the north-eastern department of Pas-de-Calais. Ultimately, only a handful of bishops and perhaps half the parish clergy took an unqualified oath. By mid-1791 two Frances had emerged, contrasting the pro-reform areas of the south-east, the Paris basin, Champagne and the centre with the 'refractory' west and south-west, the east, the north, and the southern Massif Central.

TO THE MUNICIPALITY OF THE PARISH OF QUESQUES

DECLARATION OF THE PARISH PRIEST REGARDING THE OATH REQUIRED BY THE ASSEMBLY

I declare that my religion does not allow me to take an oath such as the National Assembly requires; I am happy and I even promise to watch over as well as one possibly can the faithful of this parish who are entrusted to me, to be true to the nation and the king and to observe the Constitution decreed by the National Assembly and sanctioned by the king in all that is within the competence of his power, in all that belongs to him in the order of purely civil and political matters, but where the government and the laws of the Church are concerned, I recognise no superior and other legislators than the pope and the bishops; you Christians would certainly not wish to be led by apostates and schismatics and I would be such a one if I had had the cowardice to take an oath such as the National Assembly requires, for according to our faith the sovereign pontiff is not only at the centre of Catholic unity and has primacy of honour in all the Church, but also primacy of jurisdiction. Is it not refusing him this primacy of jurisdiction in France to forbid the entire Church and all French citizens to recognise his authority and his jurisdiction in any case and under any pretext that may arise and to reject any other communication with him than that of faith? It is still said in the Scriptures that Jesus Christ established his bishops to govern over the Church, *posuit episcopos regere ecclesiam dei*. Nonetheless, by taking this oath I would have sworn no longer to recognise our holy father the pope and head of the Church, or the bishops as its governors, since the National Assembly wishes to attribute this right to itself alone; my confidence in refusing the oath that the National Assembly requires will teach you, Christians, that neither the fear of being pursued nor this interest that we are often reproached for having at the wrong moment can make me betray my conscience. This will be an example for any of you who may lose your possessions, your fortune, even your life if necessary, rather than abandon your faith, your religion and offend your God. These are the sentiments of he who has the honour of being your most humble servant.

Sirs, with much fraternal feeling

J. A. Baude, parish priest of Quesques et Lottinghem

Source: *Annales historiques de la Révolution française*, 46 (1974), p. 289.

━━━━━━◦◦◦◦◦━━━━━━

Papal bull *Charitas*, 13 April 1791

A large proportion of priests who had taken the requisite oath subsequently retracted when, in April 1791, the pope, already antagonised by the absorption of his lands in and around Avignon into the new nation and by revolutionary decrees granting religious freedom to Jews and Protestants, now condemned the Civil Constitution and the Declaration of the Rights of Man as inimical to a Christian life. The pope specifically singled out as schismatics and heretics Talleyrand and other bishops who had taken the oath.

Our beloved sons, venerable brothers, most beloved sons, greetings and apostolic benediction. Love, which, in the teaching of the apostle Paul, is patient and kind, supports and sustains all things for as long as some hope remains, and, through gentleness, counters those errors that have now begun to encroach upon us. But if these errors increase daily, and extend as far as they do now, so that matters slide towards schism, then the laws of love itself, with the laws of apostolic function in which we unworthy ones engage, the laws which are joined with the offices, demand and entreat that a certain paternal, yet prompt and efficacious, remedy ought to be applied to the growing sickness, to which those in error are exposed by the horror of their guilt and by the seriousness of canonical punishment to which they are subject. For in this way it may be that those who have retreated from the way of truth will recover their senses, and turn back to the Church with errors renounced, and, as they turn back, will be embraced as by a kind mother, with open arms; and as the rest of the faithful opportunely avoid the frauds of the pseudo-pastors, who, coming from elsewhere than through the gate to the fold of Christ, seek nothing else but to steal, afflict and destroy. . . .

We call upon you to witness, however, in the name of the Lord, beloved sons, Catholics who in the kingdom of the Gauls are united, being mindful of your religion and the faith of your fathers, we counsel you from the innermost feelings of our heart lest you secede from it, inasmuch as it is the one and the true religion, which bestows eternal life and protects citizens, even societies, and makes them prosperous. Take special care lest you proffer ears to the insidious voices of this secular sect, whose voices furnish death, and avoid in this way all usurpers whether they are called archbishops, bishops or parish priests, so that there is nothing in common between you and them, especially in divine matters . . . in one word, cling to us: for no-one can be in the Church of Christ unless he is unified with the visible head of the Church itself and is strengthened in the cathedral of Peter. . . .

Given at St Peter of Rome, on this day 13 April 1791, in the seventeenth year of our papacy.

PIUS WHO IS ABOVE

Source: Augustin Theiner, *Documents inédits relatifs aux affaires religieuses de la France* (Paris, 1857), pp. 75, 85, 88.

6

MONARCHY AND REVOLUTION

The King's proclamation on his flight from Paris, 21 June 1791

Louis had sanctioned the Civil Constitution of the Clergy, but was increasingly distressed by the divisions it had brought to the surface. The Estates-General he had convened to offer him advice in May 1789 had developed into a sovereign parliament that had sharply limited his powers. Louis fled Paris on 21 June, presumably for the safety of Bouille's garrison at Nancy, leaving behind a lengthy document which publicly repudiated the direction the Revolution had taken. Louis made an appeal to his subjects to return to the certainties they had once known.

As long as the king was able to hope to see the order and happiness of the kingdom revived through the methods employed by the National Assembly, and through his residence close to this Assembly in the capital of the kingdom, no personal sacrifice has aggrieved him; he would not even put forward the complete lack of freedom, which has made void all the steps he has undertaken since the month of October 1789, as an excuse, if this wish had been fulfilled: but today, when the only recompense for so many sacrifices is to witness the destruction of the kingdom, to see all authority ignored, personal property violated, people's safety everywhere in danger, crimes remaining unpunished, and a complete anarchy established above the law, without the appearance of authority that the new Constitution grants him being sufficient to repair even one of the evils that afflict the kingdom: the king, having solemnly protested against all the decrees that were issued by him during his captivity, believes it to be his duty to put a picture of his behaviour and that of the government that has been established in the kingdom under the eyes of the French and of all the universe. . . .

From the spirit that reigns in the clubs, and the way in which they seize control of the new primary assemblies, what can be expected from them is apparent; and if they show any sign of some tendency to go back over something, it is in order to destroy what is left of royalty, and to establish some metaphysical and philosophical government which can never be achieved in reality.

People of France, is that what you intended when you sent your representatives to the National Assembly? Did you wish for the anarchy and despotism of the clubs to replace the monarchical government under which the nation prospered for 1,400 years? Did you wish to see your king showered with insults, and deprived of his liberty, while his only goal was to establish yours? . . .

People of France, and especially you Parisians, inhabitants of a city that the ancestors of His Majesty delighted in calling 'the good city of Paris', be wary of the suggestions and lies of your false friends; come back to your king; he will always be your father, your best friend. What pleasure will he not have in forgetting all his personal wrongs, and to see himself once again in your midst, when a Constitution that he has freely accepted ensures that our holy religion will be respected, that the government will be established on a stable footing, and will be useful through its actions, that each man's goods and position will no longer be disturbed, that laws will no longer be infringed with impunity, and that, finally, liberty will be placed on a firm and unshakeable base.

Source: *Archives parlementaires*, 21 June 1791, pp. 378–83.

———————

Reactions to the king's flight

The Abbé Grégoire

The royal family's desperate flight to safety was a series of blunders from the outset. On the evening of 21 June Louis was recognised by Drouet, the postmaster at Sainte-Menehould, who dashed to the next town, Varennes, to arrest him. The Assembly was stunned: Louis was suspended from his position as king. Louis' return was humiliating, the roads lined with his resentful subjects, reportedly refusing to remove their hats in his presence. During his suspension by the Assembly, Jacobins such as the Abbé Grégoire argued that he should be forced to abdicate.

Whatever my opinion may be, I will speak according to my conscience (*From the right:* Ah! ah!) . . . and, instead of comparing my opinion with my station, I ask that I be refuted; where the rest is concerned, gentlemen, once the

Assembly has pronounced I will be submissive to its decrees . . . *(From the right:* Just as well!) and I will never allow myself to protest against it . . . *(Applause from the left.)* . . .

The premier public servant abandons his post; he arms himself with a false passport; after having said, in writing to the foreign powers, that his most dangerous enemies are those who spread alleged doubts about the monarch's intentions, he breaks his word, he leaves the French a declaration which, if not criminal, is at the least –however it is envisaged—contrary to the principles of our liberty. He could not be unaware that his flight exposed the nation to the dangers of civil war; and finally, in the hypothesis that he wished only to go to Montmédy, I say: either he wanted to content himself with making peaceful observations to the National Assembly regarding its decrees, and in that case it was useless to flee; or he wanted to support his claims with arms, and in that case it was a conspiracy against liberty. . . .

But if, unfortunately, the committees' project were to be adopted by the Assembly, if it was decided that inviolability is total, that the king can never be called into question, then, gentlemen, so as to be consistent, you must judge the National Guard of Varennes, and those who worked for the king's arrest, as though they were guilty of a serious crime. *(Loud applause from the left and in the galleries.)*

Source: *Archives parlementaires*, 15 July 1791, pp. 378–83.

A monarchist petition from the provinces

The king's flight and the Assembly's response had divided the country. Despite Louis' humiliating capture and return, the Assembly reinstated him and on 15 July decreed that he had been 'kidnapped' and that the monarchist provisions of the Constitution of 1791 would stand. On 19 July, a delegation from Chartres representing the governing body of the department of Eure-et-Loir was warmly received into the Assembly. The delegates expressed their delight that the Assembly had decided that Louis would retain his throne and that the Constitution would be presented to him.

To love the Constitution, to defend it and die for it, this is the sacred motto of the Directory of the department of Eure-et-Loir; it is also the motto of the administrative bodies that assist and share in its work.

The great principles that dictated the wise provisions of the decree that you have just pronounced had already been engraved in our hearts. We even dare to go further, gentlemen; they were engraved in the hearts of all the inhabitants of the beautiful land that we administer.

Gentlemen, we have not come to flatter you with vain adulation unworthy both of you and of us; we come to declare to you in the name of a department, in the name of a district, in the name of a town, all passionate friends of the Revolution, that they see true unshakeable liberty and happiness for the French nation only in the constitutional articles that served as a basis for your decree of the 15th of this month. We have come to assure you, with the most exact truthfulness, that this decree that decides the empire's destiny, was received with joy and gratitude by all the citizens of the department; that it has only added to the confidence, the admiration that is due to you on so many grounds. Finally, we have come to repeat at your hands the solemn oath to shed the last drop of our blood for the fulfilment of the law and the upholding of the Constitution. (*There is applause.*)

Source: *Gazette nationale ou le Moniteur universel*, no. 201, 20 July 1791, vol. 10, p. 170.

Barnave on ending the Revolution, 15 July 1791

The decree of 15 July met with varying responses, particularly in Paris. The Cordeliers Club took the initiative to call on all citizens to assemble at the Champ de Mars on 17 July to sign a petition calling for Louis' abdication. This occurred in the context of a wave of strikes and demonstrations by wage earners and the unemployed in the capital, and continuing unrest in the countryside. To leading conservatives in the Assembly, such as Barnave, Louis had become a symbol of stability against the increasingly radical demands of 'passive' citizens and their supporters.

(Barnave stands up to speak; he is greeted by applause from a large majority of the Assembly.)

Gentlemen, the French nation has just suffered a violent shock; however, if we are to believe all the omens that are manifesting themselves, this latest event, like all those that preceded it, will only serve to hasten the date, to ensure the stability of the Revolution that we have created. Already the nation, in showing its unanimity, in noting the immensity of its strength in a time of concern and peril, has proved to our enemies what they would have to fear from the result of their attacks. Today, by attentively examining the Constitution she has given herself, she is developing a profound knowledge of it, something that she would perhaps not have acquired for a long time if the principles of morality, seemingly contradictory to those of politics, if a deep sentiment, contrary at this time to the national interest, had not obliged the Assembly to look closely into these great and important questions, and to demonstrate to all of France what those who had examined it already knew in principle, but what the masses perhaps did not yet know; I am speaking of the nature of the monarchical government, its bases, its true usefulness for the nation to which you have given it. . . .

I say: any change today is fatal: any prolonging of the Revolution is disastrous; this is the question that I put here, and it is indeed here that it is marked by the national interest: are we going to finish the Revolution, are we going to recommence it? (*Repeated applause.*) If you defy the Constitution once, at what point will you stop, and more importantly, where will our successors stop? . . .

A great evil is done us in the perpetuation of this revolutionary movement that has destroyed all there was to destroy, that has taken us to the point where we had to stop, and that will cease only with peaceful determination, common determination, a reconciliation, if I may so put it, of all that in the future could make up the French nation. Consider, gentlemen, consider what will happen after you: you have done what was good for liberty, for equality; no arbitrary power was spared, no usurpation of pride or property escaped: you have made all men equal before the civil law and the political law; you have taken back, you have returned to the State all that had been taken from it. From there comes this great truth, that if the Revolution takes one more step, it cannot do so without danger; if it is in the direction of liberty, the first act to follow could be the destruction of royalty; if it is in the direction of equality, the first act to follow could be the violation of property. (*Applause.*) . . . is there still to be destroyed an aristocracy other than that of property?

Source: *Archives parlementaires*, 15 July 1791, pp. 326–34.

The massacre on the Champ de Mars, 17 July 1791

On 17 July an unarmed demonstration gathered on the Champ de Mars to sign a petition demanding Louis' abdication, on the same 'altar of the homeland' on which the Fête de la Fédération had been celebrated a year earlier. Lafayette, the commander of the National Guard, was ordered to disperse the petitioners. He ordered the red flag raised as a signal that troops would fire if the crowd did not disperse, then ordered the National Guard to fire on the petitioners, killing perhaps fifty of them. This was the first large-scale bloodshed within the Parisian

Third Estate which had helped make the Revolution in 1789. The original petition was destroyed by the fire of the Hôtel de Ville in Paris in 1871; we know its substance from this extract from Elysée Loustallot's newspaper.

The unhappy day of 17 July 1791
Blood has flowed on Federation Field; the altar of the fatherland has been stained with it; men's and women's throats have been cut; citizens are dismayed. What will become of freedom? Some say that it has been wiped out, that the counter-revolution is complete; others assert that liberty has been avenged, the Revolution unshakeably consolidated. . . .

Petition to the National Assembly composed on the
altar of the fatherland, 17 July 1791.

Representatives of the nation, you are coming to the end of your work; soon successors, all nominated by the people, will walk over your traces, without meeting the obstacles that the deputies of the two privileged orders, necessary enemies of all the principles of holy equality, placed before you.

A serious crime is being committed; *Louis XVI is escaping;* he is abandoning his post without dignity; the empire is within an inch of anarchy. Citizens arrest him in Varennes, and he is brought back to Paris. The people of this capital earnestly ask you not to make any pronouncement on the fate of the guilty man without having heard the expression of the wishes of the eighty-two other departments.

You defer it; a multitude of addresses arrives at the Assembly; all the sections of the empire demand simultaneously that Louis be judged. You, gentlemen, you had decided that he was innocent and inviolable, in declaring, in your decree of the 16th, that the constitutional charter will be presented to him once the Constitution has been completed. Legislators! That was not the wish of the people, and we thought that your greater glory, that your very duty consisted in being the organs of the public will. Doubtless, gentlemen, you were led to this decision by the crowd of those resisting deputies, who voiced their protests against the entire Constitution in advance. But, gentlemen . . . but, representatives of a generous and trusting people, remind yourselves that those 290 protesters had no voice at all in the National Assembly; that the decree is therefore null in form and in substance; null in substance because it is contrary to the wishes of the sovereign; null in form because it is brought by 290 individuals without quality.

These considerations, all these views of the general good, this imperious desire to avoid anarchy, to which a lack of harmony between the representatives and the represented would expose us, all have made it imperative to ask you, in the name of all of France, to reconsider this decree, to take into consideration the fact that Louis XVI's crime is proven, that the king has abdicated; to receive his abdication, and to call a new constituent body so as to proceed in a truly national fashion with the judgement of the guilty party, and especially with the replacement and organisation of a new executive power.

. . . They return to the altar of the fatherland, and they continue to sign. The young people have fun dancing; they make circles and sing the tune 'Ça ira' ['Things will turn out fine']. A storm comes unexpectedly (were the heavens seeking to portend that which would sweep down on the heads of the citizens?), they are no less eager to sign in spite of it. The rain stops, the heavens become calm and serene once more; in less than two hours there are 50,000 people on the plain . . .

Suddenly the noise of drums is heard, people look at one another; the members of the different patriotic societies assemble, they were about to withdraw . . . one section of the troops enters from the far side where the military school is, another by the passage that is located a little further down, a third through the one that leads into the Grande Rue de Chaillot; that was where the red flag was. Hardly had it been noticed by those who were at the other side, and there were more than 15,000 of them, than a salvo is heard: *let us not move, they are firing blanks, we must come here to publicise the law.* . . .

Alas! They paid dearly for their courage and their blind trust in the law. Men, women, a child were massacred there; massacred on the altar to the fatherland!

Source: *Les Révolutions de Paris*, 16–23 July 1791, pp. 53–4, 60–1, 64–5.

<hr />

The Constitution of 1791

On 14 September Louis promulgated the Constitution which embodied the Assembly's work since 1789. France was henceforth to be a constitutional monarchy in which power would be shared between the king, as head of the executive, and a legislative assembly elected by 'active citizens' meeting a restrictive property franchise. However, the issues of Louis' loyalty and of whether the Revolution was complete were far from being resolved. Within a year, chapter 2, on the person of the king, was to be of acute political importance.

TITLE 1   Fundamental provisions guaranteed by the Constitution
The Constitution guarantees, as natural and civil rights:

that all citizens may be admitted to positions and jobs, without any distinction other than that of their virtues and talents;
that all taxes will be shared between all citizens, equally, in proportion to
their capacity to pay;
that the same crimes will be given the same punishment, without any distinction between individuals.

The Constitution guarantees in the same manner, as natural and civil rights:

the freedom for all men to go, stay, leave, without being arrested, accused or
detained except in cases determined by the law, and in accordance with
the forms it has prescribed;
the freedom for all men to speak, write and print their thoughts and to
practise the rites of the religion to which they are attached;
the freedom for citizens to assemble peacefully and without arms, within the
policing laws;
the freedom to address petitions signed individually to the constituted
authorities.

As liberty consists only in being able to do all that does not harm the rights
of others or the public safety, the law may put in place sentences against those
acts which, attacking either public safety or the rights of others, would be
harmful to society.

The Constitution guarantees the inviolability of ownership, or the just and
prior compensation for that which public necessity, legally recorded, demands
the sacrifice.

Property which, according to the above, is intended to serve the public use
belongs to the nation; that which was allocated for religious expenses is at its
disposal.

A general body for *public aid* will be created and organised, for the relief of
the poor who are infirm, and those able-bodied poor who are without work.

Public education, common to all citizens, free in regard to the parts of instruction that are necessary for all men, will be created and organised, and its
establishment will be distributed gradually, in a report combined with the
divisions of the kingdom. . . .

CHAPTER 1 *On the National Legislative Assembly*
Article 1. The National Assembly, forming the legislative body, is permanent,
and made up of only one chamber.

Article 2. It will be formed every two years through new elections.
Each period of two years will make up a legislature. . . .

Article 3. The legislative body may not be dissolved by the king. . . .

Article 1. When it is necessary to form the National Legislative Assembly, active citizens will meet as primary assemblies in towns and in districts.

In order to be an active citizen, it is necessary to:

be French, or to have become French;
have reached the age of 25;
have lived in the town or district for at least one year;
pay, in some area of the kingdom, a direct contribution at least equal to the price of three days' work, and to show proof of it;
not be in a domestic post, that is a paid servant;
be registered in the locality of residence on the roll of the National Guard;
have sworn the civic oath . . .

CHAPTER 2   ON ROYALTY, REGENCY AND MINISTERS

Article 1. Royalty is indivisible and delegated hereditarily to the reigning race, from male to male, in order of primogeniture, in perpetual exclusion of women and their issue. . . .

The king's person is inviolable and sacred; his sole title is *king of the French.*

There is no authority in France higher than that of the law. The king only reigns through it, and it is only in the name of the law that he can demand obedience. . . .

Article 6. If the king places himself at the head of an army and directs the forces thereof against the nation, or if he does not, by formal statement, oppose any such undertaking carried out in his name, he shall be deemed to have abdicated the throne. . . .

Article 8. After express or legal abdication, the king shall be classed as a citizen, and as such he may be accused and tried for acts subsequent to his abdication.

Source: *Gazette nationale ou le Moniteur universel*, no. 218, 6 August 1791, vol. 9, pp. 312–20.

7

THE REVOLUTION AT WAR

The renunciation of foreign conquests, 22 May 1790

In its decree of 22 May 1790 placing the power to declare war and make peace in the hands of the Assembly rather than the king, the Assembly declared that in its view the era of wars fought by crowned heads over territory was ended. The king, however, remained at the head of the armed forces and responsible for the conduct of foreign policy.

The National Assembly decrees to be constitutional articles:

The right of declaring peace and war belong to the nation. War may only be decided upon through a decree from the National Assembly. . . .

The care of looking after the external safety of the kingdom, of maintaining its rights and its possessions, is delegated, through the Constitution, to the king; only he may maintain foreign political relationships, direct negotiations, choose the agents for the former, undertake preparations for war proportionate to those of neighbouring states, distribute the forces of land and sea, as he will judge proper, and determine their direction in the case of war.

In the case of hostilities that are imminent or that have already commenced, regarding an ally to be supported, or regarding a right to be preserved by force of arms, the king will be obliged to give due notification to the legislative body without any delay, and to make known its causes and its motives; and if the legislative body is not in session, it will meet immediately.

On such notification, if the legislative body judges that the hostilities that have already commenced are culpable aggression on the part of ministers, or of certain other agents of the executive authorities, the author of this aggression will be prosecuted for *lèse-nation*; the National Assembly declaring to this effect that the French nation renounces the undertaking of any war with a view to making conquests, and that it will never use its forces against the freedom of any people.

On the same notification, if the legislative body decides that war must not be waged, the executive authorities will be obliged to take immediate measures to have any hostility halted or prevented, the responsibility for time limits being left to the ministers; any declaration of war will be made on these terms ON BEHALF OF THE KING AND IN THE NAME OF THE NATION.

Over the entire course of the war, the legislative body may require the executive authorities to negotiate for peace, and the executive authorities will be obliged to defer to this requirement.

At the moment when the war ceases, the legislative body will settle on the time within which those troops placed at the ready beyond the commencement of peace will be dismissed, and the army reduced to its standing state; the pay of the said troops will be continued only until the same time, after which, if the special troops remain assembled, the minister will be responsible and will be prosecuted for *lèse-nation*; It will be up to the king to make and sign all agreements with foreign powers necessary for the good of the State; and the treaties for peace, alliance and trade will only be executed inasmuch as they will have been ratified by the legislative body.

Source: *Gazette nationale ou le Moniteur universel*, no. 143, 23 May 1790, vol. 4, p. 432.

The decree against *émigrés*, 9 November 1791

Outside France, monarchs expressed concern at Louis' safety after his unsuccessful attempt to flee the country in June 1791, and their fears that the Revolution might spread to their lands, in threatening declarations from Padua (5 July) and Pillnitz (27 August). The declarations were not supported by troop movements, but served to convince the followers of Brissot in the Assembly that the Revolution was increasingly menaced by hostile foreign powers in league with internal enemies and *émigrés*. On 9 November, the Assembly passed a sweeping law, effectively declaring the *émigrés* outlaws should they not return by the start of the new year. Three days later, the king used his suspensive veto to block the legislation.

Article 1. Those Frenchmen gathered beyond the kingdom's borders are, from this moment, declared to be suspected of conspiracy against the fatherland.

Article 2. If, on 1 January 1792, they are still gathered in the same way, they will be declared guilty of conspiracy; as such they will be prosecuted, and punished with death . . .

Article 4. The income of the accused, condemned *in absentia*, will be, during their lifetime, collected for the nation's profit, without prejudice to the rights of the wives, children and creditors of the condemned.

Article 5. From this moment, the incomes of French princes who are absent from the kingdom are impounded. No payment of any salary, pension or income whatsoever may be made directly or indirectly to the said princes, nor to their proxies or representatives. . . .

Any officer, whatever his rank, who abandons his duties without having given his prior resignation, will be prosecuted as being guilty of desertion, and given the same punishment as that for soldiers. (*There is repeated applause.*)

Article 14. There will be a stay on the export of arms, ammunition and implements of war. Administrative and municipal bodies will pay particular attention to the execution of this article. The regular seizures will be placed in storage by the local municipality, which will send a copy of the report to the district Directory, which will make the legislative body aware of it.

Article 15. The committee for legislation is given the responsibility of shortly presenting measures, which the king will be requested to take in the name of the nation, regarding neighbouring powers that protect the groups of *émigrés* on territories bordering the French empire. (*There is applause.*)

Source: *Gazette nationale ou le Moniteur universel*, no. 313, 9 November 1791, vol. 10, p. 325.

The declaration of war, 20 April 1792

By early 1792, most deputies had convinced themselves that the *émigrés* and the rulers of Austria and Prussia in particular were engaged in aggression towards the Revolution. Within the Assembly the 'Brissotins' argued that the Revolution would not be safe until this foreign threat was destroyed. A military strike at Austria and Prussia, which would supposedly be brief because of the welcome the commoners in those countries would give their liberated French brothers, would also serve to expose internal counter-revolutionaries in an armed conflict between old and new Europe.

The National Assembly, deliberating on the formal proposition of the king, considering that the Court of Vienna, in contempt of treaties, has not ceased to grant open protection to rebel Frenchmen, that it prompted and took concerted action with several European powers against the independence and safety of the French nation;

that François I, king of Hungary and Bohemia, has, by his messages of 18 March and 7 April, refused to renounce this action;

that in spite of the proposition that was put to him in the message of 11 March 1792, to reduce the troops on the borders to a state of peace on both sides, he has continued and increased preparations for hostilities;

that he has formally conspired against the sovereignty of the French nation, by declaring his desire to support the pretensions of the German princes with possessions in France, to whom the French nation has never ceased to offer compensation; . . .

considering finally that this refusal to respond to the latest dispatches of the king of the French no longer leaves it any hope of obtaining, by means of amicable negotiation, the righting of these different grievances, and is equivalent to a declaration of war;

decrees that there is a state of emergency.

the National Assembly declares that the French nation, true to the principles established in the Constitution *not to undertake war with a view to making conquests, and never to use its forces against the freedom of a people*, only takes up arms in order to maintain its liberty and its independence; that the war that it is obliged to support is in no way a war of nation against nation, but the rightful defence of a free people against the unjust aggression of a king;

that the French will never confuse their brothers with their true enemies; that they will neglect nothing to soften the curse of war, to take care of and preserve property, and to make all the miseries inseparable from war fall only on those who are in league against its liberty;

that it adopts in advance all those foreigners who, renouncing the cause of its enemies, come to line up under its flag and dedicate their efforts to the defence of its liberty; that it will even encourage, by all the means that are in its power, their establishment in France;

deliberating on the king's formal proposition, and after having decreed an emergency, decrees war on the king of Hungary and Bohemia.

Source: *Procès-verbal (Assemblée législative)*, vol. 7, p. 355.

———————⟩∘∘∘⟨———————

Decree of 'La Patrie en danger', 11 July 1792

The Brissotins' promise that the war would be brief proved to be illusory. The initial months of the war were disastrous for the revolutionary armies, which were in a state of disarray after the defection of most of the officer corps, of whom about 6,000 emigrated in 1791. On 11 July the Assembly was forced to declare publicly to the nation that 'the homeland is in danger' and appealed for total support in a spirit of self-sacrifice.

Address to the French people

Your Constitution rests on the principles of eternal justice; a league of kings has been formed in order to destroy it, their battalions are advancing, they are numerous, subject to rigorous discipline, and trained long ago in the art of war. Do you not feel a noble ardour arousing your courage? Would you allow foreign hordes to spread like a destroying torrent over your countryside? To ravage our harvest? To devastate our fatherland through fire and murder? In a word, to fetter you with chains dyed in the blood of that which you hold the most dear?

Our armies are yet barely brought to completion, an imprudent sense of security moderated the spirit of patriotism too early; the recruitment which was ordered did not have as much success as your representatives had hoped. Interior agitation increases the difficulty of our position; our enemies indulge in foolish hopes which are an outrage against you.

Make haste, citizens, save liberty and avenge your glory.

The National Assembly declares that the homeland is in danger.

Nonetheless, be wary of believing that this declaration is the result of a terror unworthy of it and of you; you swore the oath to *live freely or to die*. It knows that you will keep it, and it swears to be an example to you in this; but it is not a question of braving death, we must conquer: and you can do it, if you renounce your hatreds; if you forget your political differences; if you all rally to the common cause; if you keep watch with untiring activity over the enemies within; if you avoid all disturbances and the individual violence that begets them; if, maintaining the authority of the law within the kingdom, and answering, through orderly movements, the homeland that calls on you, you fly to the borders and into our camps, with the generous enthusiasm of liberty, and the profound sentiment of the duties of citizen soldiers.

Men of France, who for the last four years have struggled against despotism, we warn you of the dangers assailing you in order to invite you to make the efforts necessary to surmount them. We are showing you the precipice; what glory awaits you when you have crossed over it! Nations contemplate you; surprise them with the majestic display of your forces and of your great traits, unity, respect for the law, unshakeable courage, and soon victory will crown the altar of liberty with its palm, and soon the people who today are being armed against your Constitution will strive to unite with you through the ties of a sweet brotherhood; and soon, consolidating, through a glorious peace, the basis of your government, you will finally gather all the fruits of the revolution, and you will have prepared, through your happiness, that of posterity.

Source: *Gazette nationale ou le Moniteur universel*, no. 194, 12 July 1792, vol. 13, p. 108.

The deportation of non-juring priests, 26 August 1792

The military defeats of the summer of 1792 made the position of the non-juring clergy impossible. Not only were many such clergy now in exile, but the defeats of French armies were by armed forces which believed themselves to be conducting a religious crusade against a godless revolution. On 26 August the Assembly required all non-juring clergy to leave the kingdom within a fortnight.

The National Assembly, considering that the unrest excited in the kingdom by priests who are not under oath is one of the major causes of danger to the fatherland; that at this time, when all Frenchmen have need of unity and of all their strength to drive back the external enemies, must take all measures possible to ensure and guarantee peace within the nation, decrees that there is a state of emergency. . . .

Article 1. All clergy who, being liable to the oath prescribed by the law of 26 December 1790 and that of 17 April 1791, have not sworn it, or who, after having sworn it, have retracted it, and who have persisted in their retraction, will be obliged to leave the borders of their district and department of residence within eight days and the kingdom within a fortnight. These different deadlines will be counted from the day of publication of the present decree.

Consequently, they will each appear before the Directory or the Council of their district of residence, to declare to it the foreign country into which they intend to withdraw, and a passport containing their declaration, their description, the route that they must take, and the time within which they must have left the kingdom, will be delivered to them on the spot.

Article 2. Once the fourteen-day deadline stipulated above has expired, those clergy not under oath who have not obeyed the above provisions will be deported to French Guyana. The district Directories will have them arrested and taken from brigade to brigade to the nearest seaport. . . .

Article 4. Any clergyman who remains within the kingdom after having made his declaration to leave and obtained a passport, or who returns after having left, will be condemned to a punishment of ten years' detention. . . .

Article 7. Excepted from the preceding provisions are the disabled, whose disability has been recorded by an officer of health who will be designated by the general council of the town of their place of residence, and whose certificate will be verified by the same general council; also excepted are sexagenarians whose age will also be duly recorded. . . .

Source: *Gazette nationale ou le Moniteur universel*, no. 241, 26 August 1792, vol. 13, p. 540.

The September massacres, 1792

On 2 September, word reached Paris that the great fortress at Verdun, just 250 km from the capital and the last major obstacle to invading armies, had fallen to the Prussians. The news generated a surge in the number of volunteers leaving Paris for the front, but also a resolve to punish those blamed for the military crisis. Parisians were convinced that 'counter-revolutionaries' (whether nobles, priests or common law criminals) in prisons were waiting to break out and welcome the invaders once the volunteers had left for the front. Hastily convened popular courts sentenced to death about 1,200 of the 2,700 prisoners brought before them. Among those put to death were about 240 priests who had failed to leave France as required. The killings were observed by Restif de la Bretonne, perhaps the most acute and informed observer of revolutionary Paris.

August 10 had renewed the Revolution and brought it to its conclusion: 2, 3, 4 and 5 September cast a sombre horror over it. These atrocious events must be described with impartiality and the writer must be cold when he makes his reader tremble. He must be moved by no passion; otherwise he becomes a declaimer instead of being a historian. . . .

Then the killing began at Le Châtelet: they were going to the Force Prison. But I didn't go there; I believed I was fleeing from these horrors by going home. I went to bed. A sleep troubled by the fury of the carnage allowed me only a difficult rest, often interrupted by the start of a frightened awakening. But that was not all. At about two o'clock, I heard a troop of cannibals pass by my windows, and not one of them seemed to me to have a Parisian accent; all were foreign: they sang, they bellowed, they yelled. In the middle of all that, I heard: 'Let's go to the Bernardines! . . . Let's go to Saint-Firmin!' Saint-Firmin was a priests' prison. . . . Some of these murderers cried out 'Long live the nation!' One of them, whom I would have liked to see so as to read his hideous soul on his atrocious face, cried out maniacally: 'Long live death!' . . . I heard it, as well as the galley convicts, and the priests of Saint-Firmin. Among the latter was the Abbé Gros, ex-Constituent, once my parish priest at Saint-Nicolas-du-Chardonneret, at whose home I had dined with two ladies from Auxerre. That very evening he even reproached me for having lacked integrity in making a comment in my 'Life of my father' on the celibacy of priests. This Abbé Gros saw, among the murderers, a man with whom he had had some dealings. 'Ah! There you are my friend! Hey! What have you come here for at this time of the night?'—'Oh!' the man replied, 'we come here at an evil time (for misery). You were good to me . . . So, why have you retracted your oath?' This man turned his back on him, as the kings and Richelieu used to do to their victims, and signalled to his comrades. The Abbé Gros was not stabbed; he was given a more gentle death, he was thrown from the window. His brains gushed out on impact, he did not suffer. I won't speak of the convicts. . . .

The murderers were at the Conciergerie, at the Force. They killed, in these two prisons, as well as at Le Châtelet, all night. . . .

Finally, I saw a woman appear, pale as her underclothing, held up by a counter clerk. They said to her in a harsh voice: 'Cry out: "Long live the nation!"' 'No! no!' she said. They made her climb onto a heap of corpses. One of the murderers seized the counter clerk and took him away. 'Ah!' cried the unfortunate woman, 'don't hurt him!' They told her again to cry out 'Long live the nation!' She refused disdainfully. Then a killer seized her, tore off her dress and opened her belly. She fell, and was finished off by the others. Never had such horror offered itself to my imagination. I tried to flee; my legs failed. I fainted. When I came to my senses, I saw the bloody head. I was told that it had been washed, its hair curled, and that it had been put on the end of a pike and carried under the windows of the Temple. Pointless cruelty! . . .

What is, therefore, the true motive for this butchery? Several people think that it was actually so that volunteers, departing for the frontiers, would not leave their wives and children to the mercy of brigands whom the courts could discharge with a pardon, whom malevolent people could help escape, etc. I wanted to know the truth and I have finally found it. They only wanted one thing: to get rid of non-juring priests. Some even wanted to get rid of all of them.

Source: Restif de la Bretonne, *Les Nuits de Paris*, part XVI (Paris, 1963), pp. 277–84.

8

THE END OF THE MONARCHY

The Brunswick Manifesto, 25 July 1792

Early in August 1792 Parisians learnt of a manifesto issued by the commander-in-chief of the Prussian armies, the Duke of Brunswick. Its
language provoked both anger and resolve, threatening as it did sum-
mary justice on the people of Paris and the destruction of their city if
Louis and his family were further harmed or threatened. The threat
added to the popular conviction that Louis and Marie-Antoinette were
complicit in the defeats being suffered by the army.

DECLARATION OF THE DUKE OF BRUNSWICK TO THE
INHABITANTS OF FRANCE
. . . His Majesty the King of Prussia with His Imperial Majesty, through the
ties of a close and defensive alliance, and himself a preponderant member of the
Germanic body, could thus not refrain from going to the aid of his ally and of
his co-State; and it is under this double relationship that he takes up the
defence of this monarch and of Germany.

To these major interests is joined yet another equally important goal, and
one which is close to the heart of the two sovereigns, that is, to have the anarchy within France cease, to stop the attacks being made on the throne and the
altar, to re-establish legal power, to return to the king the safety and freedom
of which he is deprived, and to place him in a position to exercise the legitimate authority which is his due.

Convinced that the healthy part of the French nation abhors the excesses of
a faction that subjugates it, and that the majority of the population waits
impatiently for the moment of aid to openly declare themselves against the
odious enterprises of their oppressors, His Majesty the emperor and His Majesty
the king of Prussia call on them and invite them to return without delay to the
voice of reason and justice, of order and peace. It is with this in view, that I the
undersigned, commander general in chief of the two armies, declare: . . .

That the inhabitants of the towns, market towns and villages who dare to defend themselves against the troops of Their Imperial and Royal Majesties, and to shoot at them, either in the open countryside, or through the windows, doorways and openings of their homes, will be punished immediately, according to the severity of the law of war, or their homes demolished or burned down. On the other hand, all the inhabitants of the said towns, market towns and villages who hasten to submit themselves to their king, by opening their doors to the troops of Their Majesties, will forthwith be under their immediate safeguard; their persons, their goods, their effects will be under the protection of the law, and the general safety of all and each of them will be provided for.

The city of Paris and all its inhabitants, without distinction, will be obliged to submit themselves, immediately and without delay, to the king, to give this prince full and complete freedom, and to guarantee for him, as well as for all royal personages, the inviolability and the respect which the right of nature and of men obliges from subjects towards sovereigns; Their Imperial and Royal Majesties make personally responsible for all events, to be punished militarily, without hope of pardon, all members of the National Assembly, of the district, of the municipality, and of the National Guard of Paris, the justices of the peace and all others whose business it is; their said Majesties declare moreover, on their honour and word as emperor and king, that if the Château of the Tuileries is taken by force or insulted, that if the least violence is done to it, the least outrage to Their Majesties the king, the queen and the royal family, if their safety, their preservation and their freedom are not immediately provided for, they will wreak an exemplary and for ever memorable vengeance, by delivering up the city of Paris to a military execution, and total destruction, and the rebels guilty of assassinations to the execution that they have earned. On the contrary, Their Imperial and Royal Majesties promise the inhabitants of the city of Paris to use their good offices with His most Christian Majesty, to obtain a pardon for their wrongs and their errors, and to take the most energetic measures to ensure their person and their goods, if they obey the above injunction promptly and exactly.

Source: *Gazette nationale ou le Moniteur universel*, no. 216, 3 August 1792, vol. 13, p. 305–6.

━━━━━━◦◇◦━━━━━━

Decree concerning the king, 10 August 1792

From the outset of the Revolution Louis' indecision had exacerbated the great difficulties he faced in accommodating himself to working as a constitutional monarch within institutions based on popular sovereignty. The critical military situation made his position impossible. On 10 August a force of *sans-culottes* from the newly democratised National Guard and *fédérés* (volunteers from the provinces on their way to the front) assaulted and took the Tuileries palace. After Louis took refuge in the nearby Assembly, it decided to suspend him pending the election of a National Convention.

The National Assembly, believing that the dangers to the fatherland have reached their peak;

> that for the legislative body it is the most sacred of duties to employ all means to save it;
> that it is impossible to find effective ones, as long as the task of staunching the source of the evils is not undertaken;
> believing that these evils derive principally from the suspicions that the conduct of the head of the executive authority has aroused, in a war undertaken in his name against the Constitution and national independence;
> that these suspicions have inspired, in different parts of the empire, a wish that aims for the revocation of the authority delegated to Louis XVI; . . .

Article 1. The people of France are invited to form a National Convention. The special commission will present a draft indicating the mode and the period of this convention tomorrow.

Article 2. The head of the executive authority is temporarily suspended from his responsibilities, until the National Convention has delivered a verdict regarding the measures that it believes it necessary to adopt so as to ensure the sovereignty of the people and the reign of liberty and equality.

Article 3. The special commission will present a method for organising a new ministry within twenty-four hours. . . .

Article 8. The king and his family will remain within the legislative body until calm has been re-established in Paris. . . .

Article 10. Any government official, soldier, non-commissioned officer, officer, whatever his rank, and army general, who in these dangerous days abandons his post, is declared to be evil (*infâme*) and a traitor to the fatherland.

Article 11. The department and the municipality of Paris will have the present decree proclaimed immediately and with ceremony.

Article 12. It will be sent by special courier to the eighty-three departments, which will be obliged to have it delivered within twenty-four hours to the municipalities of their jurisdiction so it can be proclaimed there with the same ceremony.

Source: *Gazette nationale ou le Moniteur universel*, no. 225, 12 August 1792, vol. 13, pp. 380–1.

Indictment of Louis XVI, 11 December 1792

The indictment read to Louis in the National Convention on 11 December effectively held him responsible for all the vicissitudes of the Revolution. From the outset of the trial the deputies of the Convention agreed on Louis' guilt but were divided over the appropriate punishment for him. Louis himself was dignified and consistent during his trial. Again and again, as his accusers went over the list of crises faced by the Revolution since 1789, Louis simply denied his personal responsibility.

A profound silence reigns in the Assembly.

THE PRESIDENT: Louis, the French nation accuses you. The National Assembly decreed, on 3 December, that you would be judged by it; on 6 December it decreed that you would be brought before its bar. The act stating the crimes that are ascribed to you will be read to you.—You may be seated. (*Louis sits. One of the secretaries reads the entire act aloud. The president, repeating each item of accusation, calls on Louis to respond to each different charge contained in it.*) Louis, the French people accuses you of having committed a multitude of crimes in the establishment of your tyranny, and in destroying its freedom. On 20 June 1789, you violated the sovereignty of the people, by suspending the assemblies of its representatives, and by driving them out from the place of their meetings with violence. The proof of this is in the report drawn up at the Versailles tennis court, by the members of the Constituent Assembly. On 23 June, you tried to dictate laws to the nation; you surrounded its representatives with troops, you presented two royal declarations to them, subversive of all freedom, and you ordered them to disperse. Your declarations and the reports from the Assembly record these violations. What do you have to say in response?

LOUIS: I was the ruler of the troops at that time; but I never intended to spill blood. . . .

THE PRESIDENT: Following your arrest at Varennes, the exercise of executive power was for a moment suspended from your hands, and still you conspired. On 17 July the blood of citizens was spilled at the Champ de Mars. A letter from your hand, written in 1790 to Lafayette, proves that a criminal coalition existed between you and Lafayette, with which Mirabeau was complicit. The recruiting began under these cruel auspices; all types of corruption were used. You paid for lampoons, pamphlets and newspapers destined to pervert public opinion, to discredit *assignats* and to support the cause of the *émigrés*. The

Septeuil registers show the enormous sums that were put to the use of these *liberticide* manoeuvres to kill liberty. What do you have to say in response?

LOUIS: What happened on 17 July can have nothing to do with me; as far as the rest is concerned, I have no knowledge of it. . . .

THE PRESIDENT: Nîmes, Montauban, Mende, Jalès, all had experienced great unrest from the first days of liberty; you did nothing to smother this seed of counter-revolution, until the moment when the Dusaillant conspiracy broke. What do you have to say in response?

LOUIS: For all of those, I gave all the orders the ministers suggested to me.

Source: *Gazette nationale ou le Moniteur universel*, no. 348, 13 December 1792, vol. 14, pp. 720–1.

———————◦◦◦◦◦———————

Extracts from the trial of Louis XVI, January 1793

While the deputies present during the king's trial agreed on his guilt, Girondins such as Condorcet argued variously that his fate should be decided by a referendum, that he should not be sentenced to death or that he should be reprieved. Specific provisions of the Constitution of 1791 seemed to support their legalistic position that abdication was the proper punishment for a monarch's treason. In contrast, the great strength of the Jacobin argument during this dramatic and eloquent debate was that to spare Louis would be to admit his special nature. Was not Louis Capet a citizen guilty of treason? Robespierre, Marat and Saint-Just argued that, as an outlaw, he should simply be summarily executed: 'the people' had already judged him. However, most Jacobins argued for a full trial: the king's flight in 1791 had effectively nullified any constitutional protection and now he should be tried like any other alleged traitor. In this extract Condorcet and Thomas Paine (here spelt Payne) offer different views on Louis' fate.

CONDORCET: I admit that in comparing [the dangers] of execution within twenty-four hours with those of reprieve, I was undecided, and I had trouble making up my mind. Among these dangers, there is one that is more imminent, and I admit that that is the only one that frightened me. This danger is in prompt execution; but at the same time I have looked to see if there were not a remedy. I will speak to you only of these dangers and of the ways of avoiding them. Until now we have had to fight only those kings and armies for whom the habit of obedience meant subjection to their wishes, without examining whether or not they were right. The people are suspending their judgement, but the kings hope perhaps to gain from Louis' punishment ways in which to advance their general revenge. They can hope to attach to their cause those people who reign, and to find some supporters among us. The method they would use is the one so familiar to the courts, that is, that of slander. They will tell the people that the Convention sacrificed Louis only to satisfy its vengeance; they will paint us as men greedy for blood; they will paint our revolution as leading to anarchy and disorder. Citizens, that is the real way to harm us, the one which the despots hold in their hands; I don't know that they have any others. If we are united, if we take wise measures, we have nothing to fear. These are the ways I propose to you to oppose these dangers.

When I saw my colleagues climb on the podium to speak their minds, I noticed several, among the firmest patriots, pronounce the death penalty only in moans. Well! abolish the death penalty for all private offences, while reserving the chance to examine whether it should be kept for offences against the State, because the questions here are different, raising considerations that do not count elsewhere.

Until now you have shown proof of an active wish to maintain liberty; you have been accused of taking it too far. I do not suggest that you decrease it, but I ask that you add a measure of charity.

Make haste to decree laws that will establish adoption; make haste to assure the fate of those children born outside wedlock; see to it that the labels 'abandoned children' and 'bastards' be longer in use in the French language.

The needs of the State oblige that taxes be established; ways exist to do so in order that these taxes do not burden the poor; make haste to see to it.

(Thomas Payne climbs the podium. Bancal, secretary, reads his opinion.)

PAYNE: Citizens, I present you with my reasons for opposing the resolution to inflict the death penalty on Louis. The manuscript containing my motives was placed in the president's hands immediately after the first discussion was commenced; but, as many members had the floor before me, and since the discussion was closed before it came to my turn, I was not able to make the assembly aware of the motives for my opinion. I regret this today, not only because my speech contained particular motives that had bound me to prefer Louis' reclusion for the duration of the war to the death penalty, and his banishment after the war, but in relation to what I have to say on the new question. The question of reprieve will have less effect on those who have not read my words, and may perhaps seem obscure.

MARAT: In my view, Thomas Payne should not be able to vote on this question; he is a Quaker, so his religious principles are opposed to the death penalty. . . . *(There are murmurs; demands are made that the person who interrupted be brought to order.—The secretary continues.)*

PAYNE: Citizens, all that has passed since then has only served to prove to me the rightness of the motives that helped me to decide. I most sincerely regret the vote that was adopted yesterday in the Convention for the death penalty.

I personally have the advantage of some experience: it is about twenty years since I committed myself to the cause of liberty, contributing to the revolution of the United States in America. My language has always been the language of liberty and humanity, and I know from experience that nothing exalts the soul of a nation so much as the union of these two principles in all circumstances. I know that the public spirit of France, and particularly that of Paris, has been fired up and inflamed by the dangers to which people there have been exposed; but if we carry our ideas before us, and towards the end where these dangers and the inflammation they have produced will be forgotten, then we will be able to see that what today seems to us to be an act of justice, will seem then only to be an act of vengeance. *(Murmurs are heard in one of the far corners of the hall.)*

My concern for the cause of France has now become my concern for her honour; and if I had the opportunity, after my return to America, to write the story of the French Revolution, I would prefer to have to remember a thousand errors dictated by humanity than just one inspired by an overly severe justice.

I voted against the 'call to the people' because it seemed to me that the Assembly, where this question was concerned, had exhausted itself for no reason; but I voted in this way in the hope that the Assembly would pronounce against Louis the same punishment that the nation would have voted for, at least in my opinion, that is, reclusion during the war, and banishment after peace had been made: this is in effect the most effective punishment, since it includes the entire family at the same time, which is not possible with any other punishment. I am still against this call to the primary assemblies, because a better method exists. . . .

France now has only one ally, the United States of America, and this ally is the only nation that can supply her with naval provisions, for the kingdoms of northern Europe, who ordinarily obtain them for her, are or will soon be at war with her. Now here, unfortunately, the person who is the subject of the current discussion is seen, in the United States, as their greatest friend, as the one who obtained their freedom for them. I can assure you that his execution will spread a universal affliction there, and it is in your power to spare your closest friends from this affliction. If I could speak French, I would descend to the podium, and in the name of all my American brothers I would present a petition to defer Louis' execution.

Source: *Gazette nationale ou le Moniteur universel*, no. 23, 23 January 1793, vol. 15, pp. 247–8.

Les Tricoteuses Jacobinès, ou de Robespierre.

Elles étoient un grand nombre, à qui l'on donnoit 40 Sols par jour pour aller dans la tribune des Jacobins applaudir les motions Révolutionnaires.

An 2.

Figure 3 The Jacobin *tricoteuses*, lowest class of women radicals, who met to applaud radical motions in the Jacobin Club. Conservatives and many Jacobins were horrified by the participation of women in the clubs which proliferated in Paris and provincial towns after 1789. Few women's clubs were established during the Revolution; instead, working women chose to attend the meetings of men's clubs as observers. Source: RMN-Bulloz.

Louis XVI's execution, 21 January 1793

On 16 and 17 January 361 deputies voted for death; 360 voted instead for other punishments. The Jacobins then successfully defeated the Girondins' final appeal for clemency, by 380 votes to 310. Louis went to the scaffold on 21 January, evidently with courage. His death not only deepened the gulf between republicans and monarchists inside France; it also resulted in the international war against the Revolution expanding to include England and Spain.

From Paris

Monday, 21 January was the day set for the carrying out of the death decree pronounced against Louis Capet. Hardly had the proclamation of the provisional executive council been made known to him, in relation to his execution, than he asked to speak to his family; the guards, having shown him their embarrassment, proposed to have his family brought to his apartment, which he accepted. His wife, his children and his sister came to see him; they conferred together in the room where it was his custom to eat; the interview took two and a half hours; the conversation was very heated. . . . After his family had left, he said to the guard that he had reprimanded his wife well.

His family had begged him to allow them to see him in the morning; he dealt with this question by answering neither yes nor no. Madame did not see him again. Louis cried out in his room: 'The executioners! the executioners!' . . . Speaking to her son, Marie-Antoinette told him: 'Learn from the misfortunes of your father not to avenge his death.' . . .

The day of his death, Louis had asked for scissors to cut his hair; they were refused him. . . . When his knife was taken away from him, he said: 'Do they believe me to be so cowardly as to destroy myself?'

The major general and the commissioners of the commune went at half past eight in the morning into the apartment where Louis Capet was. The major made known to him the order he had just received to take him to his execution: Louis asked for three minutes to speak to his confessor, which was granted him. . . .

Louis crossed the first courtyard on foot; in the second he climbed into a carriage where were his confessor and two policemen. (The executioner was waiting for him at the place de la Révolution.) The procession followed the boulevards to the place of execution; a great silence held sway along the entire way. Louis read the prayers of the dying; he arrived at the place de la Révolution at ten past ten. He undressed, climbed up confidently, and walking to the extreme left-hand side of the scaffold, he said in quite a firm voice:

'Men of France, I die innocent. I forgive all my enemies, and I wish that my death be useful to the people.' He seemed to want to say more, the major general ordered the executioner to do his duty.

Louis' head fell at ten twenty in the morning. It was shown to the people. Immediately a thousand cries of: 'Long live the nation, long live the French Republic!' were heard. The body was taken away at once and left at the Madeleine church, where it was buried between the people who died on the day of his wedding, and the Swiss nationals who were massacred on 10 August. His grave was 12 feet deep and 6 feet wide; it was filled with lime.

Two hours later, nothing in Paris showed that he who once was the head of the nation had just suffered a criminal's execution. The public peace was not disturbed for a moment. If Louis' tragic end did not inspire all the interest that some people had counted on, his will is not likely to increase it: it shows that after having repeated so many times that he had sincerely adopted the Constitution, he regarded the constitutional king as merely a king stripped of his legitimate authority, and that he rejected it, down to the title that the Constitution had given him of king of the French, as he decorated himself, at least in the final act of his life, with that of king of France. The incontestable proofs of bad faith contained in this will dry up some of the sentiments of pity that compassionate souls like to feel. It is difficult to think that he could have been so happy with the belligerent powers, with his brothers, and with the nobility that was as obsequious as it was powerlessly rebellious, as to have sought only to deserve their approval. Indeed, what had they done for him once death came to hover over his head? Was there one gesture of interest, the least offer of sacrifice? They did not even have the hypocrisy of sensitivity, and they acted only in their own interests! . . .

But let us leave Louis under his crepe of mourning; from now on he belongs to history. There is something sacred for the moral and sensitive man in a victim of the law; all good citizens must turn their wishes, their talents and their strength towards the future. Divisions have hurt or have let enough hurt be done to France. All good citizens must sense the need for unity; and those who do not like its appeal still have their own self-interest in desiring it.

Source: *Gazette nationale ou le Moniteur universel*, no. 23, 23 January 1793, vol. 15, p. 242.

A provincial response

The divisions between Jacobins and Girondins were manifested across the country, not just in the Convention. Many people elsewhere in France agreed with the Jacobins about Louis' guilt. From Bordeaux, capital of the Gironde itself, the General Society of Citizenesses Friends of Liberty and Equality accused Louis of crimes against the nation. This was one of scores of women's political clubs established in Paris and about sixty provincial towns until they were closed down by the Convention on 30 October 1793.

Bordeaux, 7 February 1793, Year II of the Republic

Representatives of the French people
Too cowardly to resist the national will, the traitor Capet, plotting in the darkness the fatal dragnet in which he tried to entwine us . . . this generous nation that he had not hesitated to ruin. Soon, fearing that she might take back the power usurped by centuries of tyranny, he wanted to dissolve a sovereignty superior to his own, he surrounded with threatening bayonets the representatives of twenty-four million men. Their conviction was not at all shaken by this. Calm in the responsibility that had been entrusted them, they await death, and do not incline in any way to slavery. But the despot had relied too much on the blind obedience of the soldier. Enlightened by the love of homeland, they were no longer passive beings, but so many citizens ready to defend their brothers, their fellow citizens: the public will had been spoken.

No longer hoping to represent arbitrary power openly, the odious sceptre covered in the blood of the victors of the Bastille, he accepted the legal power which the deputies conferred on him. He promised to make the nation happy, by having laws carried out that had been made for it, while in secret striking down his enemies, with the same gold that he had from his munificence, protecting factious priests who sowed trouble and discord in the interior, and also paying the rebellious *émigrés*, the guards who had publicly been disbanded but still followed his orders and executed them too well on 10 August. Was it so as to point out new victims to them that, abandoning his bloodthirsty accomplices, he evaded the combat that he himself had ordered, and brought his guilty head into the sanctuary of the law; doubtless he thought he would soon see them appear dripping with the blood of Frenchmen, their hands put to use for crimes against the fatherland; to extinguish . . . liberty, equality and all the fruits of the revolution. . . .

For what crime can trouble he who turns his army against the fatherland! . . . he who orders the carnage of his subjects! And was dethroning enough for all the infamy? . . . and was reclusion or banishment enough for the one who made so much blood flow? Whose perfidious plotting has surrounded us with enemies? No: his head had to fall; Representatives, you have fulfilled the wish of the Republic, you have been just, and the tyrant is no more!

The General Society of Citizenesses Friends of Liberty and Equality of Bordeaux, sitting at the above intendancy
Elisabeth Oré, president

Source: Archives départementales de la Gironde, Series 12 L 19.

9

THE PEASANTRY AND THE RURAL ENVIRONMENT

The Rural Code, September 1791

The peasant revolution continued after 1789 because the National Assembly had not completely abolished feudalism. Also at stake were wider questions about ownership, control and use of rural resources. The legislators in the National Assembly believed in the sanctity of private property, but also recognised the strength of peasant attachment to collective practices, such as wood gathering in forests. This confusion was evident in a key piece of legislation passed in late September 1791. In the Rural Code the deputies decreed that collective practices such as *droit de parcours* (allowing livestock access across private land) and *vaine pâture* (sending livestock to graze on private fallow land) could not oblige owners of livestock to leave them as part of a communal herd, nor could individuals be prevented from enclosing their land for their private use. However, they also acknowledged the continued existence of collective practices.

TITLE 1   Of rural goods and customs

SECTION 1   On general principles of landed property
Article 1. The territory of France, in all its area, is free, as are the people who inhabit it; thus any landed property can only be subject, with regard to individuals, to taxes and charges whose agreement is not forbidden by the law, and, with regard to the nation, to the public contributions established by the legislative body, and to the sacrifices that the general good can demand, on condition of a just and previously agreed compensation.

Property owners are free to vary at their will the cultivation and management of their lands, to keep their harvests as they wish, and to dispose of all the products of their property within the kingdom and outside it, without harming the rights of others, and while conforming with the law.

Any property owner may oblige his neighbour to mark out the boundaries of their adjoining properties, at half of the cost. . . .

SECTION 5   On herds, hedges, pathways and infertile pastures
Article 1. All property owners are free to have on their property the quantity and type of livestock that they believe useful to the cultivation and running of their land, and to have them graze there exclusively, with the exception of the following ruling, with regard to pathways (*droit de parcours*) and to infertile pastures (*vaine pâture*).

Article 2. The reciprocal service between parishes, known as the *droit de parcours*, which has as a corollary the right of *vaine pâture*, will continue provisionally within the restrictions of the present section. . . .

Article 4. The right to enclose and to open inherited lands results essentially from that of property ownership, and cannot be denied to any property owner; the National Assembly repeals all those laws and customs that may impede this measure. . . .

SECTION 6   On harvests . . .
Article 2. Every property owner or farmer will be free to harvest his crop, whatever it may be, with the instruments and at the time that suits him, provided that he causes no damage to the neighbouring property owner.

However, in those areas where it is the custom to announce the beginning of the grape harvest, with regard to this a ruling may be made each year by the general council of the commune, but only for non-enclosed vineyards.

Source: *Gazette nationale ou le Moniteur universel*, no. 271, 20 September 1791, vol. 9, pp. 784–6.

The abolition of feudalism, 25 August 1792

Across most of rural France the response to the National Assembly's prevarication in August 1789 over the final abolition of seigneurialism had been an extension of non-compliance and rebellion against those practices which the Assembly seemed hesitant to abolish. Peasant communities effectively pressured successive assemblies towards a complete abolition. This lasted until the final abolition of seigneurialism in 1792–3. On 25 August 1792, a motion to end seigneurialism was passed by the Legislative Assembly. Seigneurial dues were now abolished without compensation, unless they could be proven to be derived from a legally valid contract. On 17 July 1793 this final proviso was removed. The feudal regime was dead.

The National Assembly, seeing the feudal regime as having been abolished, but that nonetheless its effects continue, and that nothing is more pressing than to make this debris of servitude, which covers and devours properties, disappear from French soil, decrees that the matter is urgent.

The National Assembly, having decreed an emergency, decrees the following:

Article 1. All outcomes that may be a product of the maxim, 'no land without its lord' (*nulle terre sans seigneur*), of that of enclaves, of statute-customs and rules, be they general or specific, will remain null and void.

All ownership of land is henceforth to be unequivocal and free of all dues, be they feudal or monetary, if those who lay claim to them cannot prove the opposite in the form set out below. . . .

Article 10. Arrears of dues abolished without compensation, even those that may be owing in accordance with judgements, agreements or covenants, are in no way payable.

Source: *Gazette nationale ou le Moniteur universel*, no. 239, 26 August 1792, vol. 13, pp. 527–8.

Land clearances in southern France, 1793

From the outset of the Revolution, the friction over the anti-seigneurial legislation of 1789 had been one aspect of a more general conflict over ownership and control of the 'wastelands', poorer or marginal land often used for grazing livestock. The deputies were horrified at the environmental damage in many parts of France as the poor cleared and cultivated these 'wastelands', especially on hillsides. Despite the Jacobins' willingness to restrict individual freedoms in the national interest, in the end they had had no more success in this matter than their liberal predecessors. In this report written from the southern department of the Aude on 8 December 1793, the Jacobin official Cailhava reported in his distinctively blunt fashion.

The shortage of wood is felt all along the coastline, and especially in Narbonne, due either to the drying up of the soil, or to the disdain that the inhabitants of Narbonne show for all those trees that produce only shade, of great necessity nonetheless in an area where the heat is excessive. . . . It is enough to drive you into a holy rage when, under a burning sky, you see destroyed in one minute the parasol that nature has spent fifty years perfecting. . . .

The terrain of the municipalities that make up the district of Lagrasse was once covered with wood thickets, mostly holm oak; but, during the Revolution, each individual used them up as though they were cabbages from his garden. Moreover, coal having become highly expensive, the charcoal burners used their neighbours' possessions all the less sparingly for that; the villagers who remove the bark from the holm oak in order to sell it to the tanners were no more sparing; add to that the shepherds who prefer to take their herds to the youngest thickets, and who fell the tall trees so that their animals can enjoy the tender leaves that grow on the stalks, and you will agree that it takes much less than this to destroy the largest forests.

Not far from Lagrasse, the former noble Dadvisard had the kindness—in emigrating—to leave 160 *seterées* [about 80 hectares] of wood to the nation. Well, they were left to be pulled out, destroyed, pillaged; goats graze there every day. . . .

The conservation of these woods is all the more necessary since, if they are destroyed, the Saint-Pierre forge, which belongs to the nation, can no longer work. . . . Why doesn't the nation nominate an inspector with responsibility for keeping watch on the woods, for ordering that they be replanted when they are thin; for having any shepherds punished if they go into thickets before they have grown tall enough to be safe from the fatal bite of livestock?

Source: Pierre Caron, *Rapport des agents du ministre de l'Intérieur dans les départements (1793–an II)*, 2 vols (Paris, 1913–51), vol. 1, pp. 138–9, 165–6.

10

A NEW CIVIC CULTURE

Divorce law, 20 September 1792

During the radical years of the Revolution a number of pieces of legislation were designed to improve family life, deemed hitherto to have been
cruel and immoral, like the *Ancien Régime* itself. Family courts were
instituted to deal with family conflict, penalties for wife beating were
introduced which were twice as heavy as for assaulting a man, and the
age of majority was reduced from 25 to 21. Of greatest importance was
a divorce law voted at the last session of the Legislative Assembly, on 20
September 1792. This gave women remarkably broad grounds for leaving an unhappy or violent marriage. Nationally, perhaps 30,000 divorces
were decreed under this legislation, especially in towns: in Paris, there
were nearly 6,000 in 1793–5.

The National Assembly, having decided that it is a matter of urgency, decrees
on the causes, the manner and the consequences of divorce, as follows: . . .

   Article 2. The divorce may occur through the mutual consent of the spouses.

   Article 3. One of the spouses may have the divorce issued on the simple alle-
gation of incompatibility of temperament or character.

   Article 4. Each of the spouses may equally have the divorce issued on specific
grounds, that is:

1.   the dementia, madness or violence of one of the spouses;
2.   the condemnation of one of them to corporal or serious punishment;
3.   the crime, cruelty or serious affront of one towards the other;
4.   the acknowledged dissoluteness of morals;
5.   the abandonment of the wife by the husband, or of the husband by the
     wife, for at least two years;
6.   the absence of one of them, without news, for at least five years. . . .

Source: *Gazette nationale ou le Moniteur universel*, no. 284, 10 October 1792, vol. 14, pp. 158–9.

The celebration of revolutionary heroes

The commemoration of the triumvirate of Jacobin 'martyrs of the Revolution' (Marat, Chalier, Le Peletier) was accompanied by the celebration of the heroism of individuals such as François Bara and Joseph-Agricol Viala, 13-year-old boys who had been killed fighting counter-revolution. These years were also a great age of political songs: one estimate is that the number of new songs increased from 116 in 1789 to 325 in 1792, 590 in 1793 and 701 in 1794. Most of these were exhortations to emulate the virtues of idealised *sans-culottes* or traded on caricatures of royalty, like the two below.

Follow in his [Le Peletier] works
The useful lessons
He gives on each page:
'Be just and good;
Hasten to take back
Your lost rights,
But cease laying claim to them
Without the necessary virtues.'

People, the great mass,
That obey only you,
Hear the thundering voice
That has proclaimed you king;
Marat, as long as he breathed,
Was your friend;
And through him your empire
Was strengthened. . . .

Let us place a double crown,
On the heads of these two mortals;
We owe them a throne,
Let us erect altars to them;
Let us consecrate the memory
Of their kindnesses;
And may their names, their glory
Live for ever!

Source: 'Civic Verses for the Unveiling of Busts of Francklin, Voltaire, Buffon, Jean-Jacques Rousseau, Marat and Le Pelletier, in the hall of the Popular and Republican Society of Avre-Libre (formerly Roye), Department of the Somme', by the Citizen Dourneau-Démophile, Member and Secretary of the Society. Printed in Paris, 8 Nivôse, Year II of the French Republic, one and indivisible. (Tune: 'Charming Gabrielle')

The Kings of France

In times past there were seen in France
Monsters who reigned without propriety,
Whose ambitious ignorance
Was the people's misfortune. (*Repeat.*)
In their palaces, these foolish despots,
Dressed in a shining doublet,
Maintained their portliness
From the purest blood of the *sans-culottes*.
Republican Frenchmen, conquerors of your rights,
Strike down (*repeat*) all these tyrants, profaners of the law. . . .

They have returned to the shadows,
Those great kings, cowardly and licentious,
Infamous drinkers, famous hunters,
Playthings of the vilest harlots.
Oh you, who are discouraged by nothing!
True lovers of Liberty!
Establish equality
On the debris of slavery.
Republican Frenchmen, conquerors of your rights,
Strike down (*repeat*) all these tyrants, profaners of the law.

Source: *Les Républicaines: chansons populaires des révolutions de 1789, 1792 et 1830* (Paris, 1848), pp. 34–6.

Uniform weights and measures, 1 August 1793

The imperatives of reason impelled the National Convention to accept proposals for sweeping reform of the systems of measuring weight, distance and volume. Previous systems were condemned as both bewilderingly irrational, varying as they did from district to district, and as tainted by their origins in the mists of *Ancien Régime* time. A uniform, decimal system of weights and measures, announced the Convention on

1 August 1793, would be 'one of the greatest benefits that it can offer to all French citizens'. It was followed in October by a new decimal calendar.

The National Convention, convinced that uniformity of weights and measures is one of the greatest benefits that it can offer to all French citizens . . . decrees the following:

Article 1. The new system of weights and measures, based on the measure of the Earth's meridian and on decimal division, will be uniformly used in the whole of the Republic.

However, to allow all citizens time to become acquainted with these new measurements, the provisions of the preceding article will only become compulsory in one year from the day of publication of the current decree. Citizens are merely invited to make use of it before this time.

Standards of the new weights and measures will be completed by artists chosen by the Academy of Science, and these will be sent to all administrative bodies of departments and districts. . . .

The Convention requires the Academy to put together a manual for the use of all citizens, containing simple instructions on the manner in which the new weights and measures should be used, and on the application of arithmetical equations concerning decimal division.

Instructions on the new measurements and their relationship to the most widely used old ones will be inserted into elementary arithmetic textbooks which will be created for national schools.

Source: *Gazette nationale ou le Moniteur universel*, no. 214, 2 August 1793, vol. 17, p. 287.

Dechristianisation in the provinces

The Catholic Church and thousands of deported French clergy looked to a victory of the counter-revolution as the only way to restore France to the fold. By late 1793, so high were the military stakes being fought for that the place of Christianity was called into question in many parts of France. Usually such 'dechristianisation' was the result of a mixture of initiative taken by a 'deputy on mission' from the National Convention and of local anticlericalism. In Saint-Quentin, in north-eastern France, the latter was present in uncompromising fashion, the result of antipathy to the Church's former wealth in the area and to the desperate military situation near the town.

THE DISTRICT OF SAINT-QUENTIN, TO THE MUNICIPALITIES IN ITS ENCLAVE

In execution of the orders of citizen André Dumont, representative of the people in the departments of the Nord, Pas-de-Calais, Somme, Aisne and others, the permanent and general council of the District of Saint-Quentin,

considering that the time has come when fanaticism and religious superstition must disappear for ever from the soil of liberty;

that it is urgent that the throne of error and falsehood be overthrown at the same time as that of the tyrant, to be replaced by the eternal reign of reason and philosophy;

that all individuals hitherto known under the general name of priests or ministers of public worship, disavowing the errors and prejudices to which they have been subjugated until now, and with the aid of which they have blinded and tyrannised the people for too long, must finally take in the social order the place which nature has assigned them . . .

that all churches and chapels, for too long the theatre of imposture, become today temples of reason and schools of republican virtue

decrees . . . the following:

Article 1. All municipalities, within twenty-four hours of receiving the present decree, will pull down and remove all crosses, whether in iron, copper, lead or other metal, which are to be found on or in churches, chapels, cemeteries or other public places in their municipality.

Article 2. In the place of crosses on churches, the municipalities will have flown the national colours, surmounted with the bonnet of liberty.

Article 3. In the next twenty-four hours, they will proceed with a detailed inventory of all objects in silver, copper, lead, iron and other metals; of all vestments in linen, surplices, chasubles and so on which were in their commune for the former use of public worship . . .

At Saint-Quentin, in public session, on 27 Brumaire of Year II of the one and indivisible French Republic.

Source: Archives départementales de l'Aisne, L 1506.

━━━◦◦◦◦━━━

Bouquier law on education, 19 December 1793

The central purpose of the Terror was to institute the emergency measures necessary at a time of grave military crisis. However, other decrees passed by the Convention and Committee of Public Safety went well beyond the needs of national defence and revealed a Jacobin vision of a society worthy of the grandeur of the Enlightenment and the Revolution. For example, Jacobin education policy, particularly the Bouquier law of December 1793, envisaged a system of free, compulsory education for children of 6–13 years with a curriculum emphasising patriotism and republican virtues, physical activity, field study and observation, and a role for schools in civic festivals. This would replace the primary education provided hitherto by priests and now in total disarray. The punitive provisions of the law below also highlighted the Jacobins' insistence on education as a duty as much as a right. The Jacobins had neither the time nor the funds to implement such a programme.

Bouquier, representative of the committee for public education, recalls the attention of the assembly to the deferred articles of his draft concerning schools of the elementary level, and has adopted the following measures:

Those fathers, mothers, guardians or trustees who have neglected to have their children or wards enrolled will be punished, on the first occasion, with a fine equal to a quarter of their taxes, and on the second occasion, will be relieved of their citizen's rights for ten years.

Male or female teachers teaching at the first level will receive, for each child attending their school: for male teachers, 20 livres, and for female teachers 15 livres, whatever be the population of the village.

They may neither take lodgers nor give private lessons outside their school, nor receive any gifts or bonuses.

Those young people who, reaching the age of 20, have not learnt a science, art or trade useful to society, will be deprived for ten years of citizen's rights. The same sentence will be upheld against fathers, guardians or trustees convicted of having contributed to this breach of the law.

The decree regarding the organisation of primary schools will be sent immediately to the departments, so that they may soon be brought into operation.

Source: *Gazette nationale ou le Moniteur universel*, no. 91, 21 December 1793, vol. 19, p. 6.

11

THE REPUBLIC AT WAR

Decree conferring French citizenship on foreigners,
26 August 1792

The Convention's sense that it was at the heart of a struggle of international significance was personified by the presence, as elected
deputies, of two foreign revolutionaries, Tom Paine from Britain and the
Dutchman Anacharsis Cloots. The British radical Joseph Priestley was
elected in two departments, but declined to take his seat. They were
three of eighteen foreigners who had already been made honorary
French citizens—among the others were heroes of the American
Revolution and Republic, British and European radicals and educa-
tors. The parliamentary reporter had some difficulty in transcribing their
names.

M. Guadet proposes, in the name of the special commission, and the Assembly
unanimously adopts the following decree.

The National Assembly, considering that those men who, through their
writings and through their courage, have served the cause of liberty and prepared the emancipation of peoples, cannot be seen as foreigners by a nation that
has been made free by their knowledge and their courage;

considering that, if five years of residence in France are sufficient for a foreigner to obtain the title of French citizen, this title is all the more
rightly due to those who, whatever the soil on which they live, have ded-
icated their strength and their vigilance to the defence of the cause of the
people against the despotism of kings, to the abolition of earthly prejudices; and to the extension of the limits of human knowledge;

considering that, if it is not possible to hope that men will one day form one
sole family, one sole association, before law as before nature, the friends of
liberty and of universal brotherhood should not be any the less dear to a

nation that has proclaimed its renunciation of any conquest, and its desire to fraternise with all people;

considering, finally, that at the moment when a National Convention is arranging the destinies of France, and preparing, perhaps, that of humankind, it is up to a generous and free people to call on all sources of knowledge, and to confer the right to work towards this great goal of reason on men who, through their feelings, their writings and their courage, have shown themselves to be so eminently worthy of it;

declares that it confers the title of French citizens on Priestly, Payne, Benthonn, Wilberforce, Clarkson, Makintosh, David Williams, Gornai, Anacharsis Clootz, Campe, Cormelle Paw, Pestalorri, Washington, Hamilton, Maddison, Klopsloc, Kosciusko, Gileers.

Source: *Gazette nationale ou le Moniteur universel*, no. 241, 23 August 1792, vol. 13, pp. 540–1.

The young republicans of La Rochelle, January 1793

On 16 January 1793 seven boys and eight girls aged about 13 years appeared before the municipal council of La Rochelle to present clothing for soldiers which they had bought by pooling their savings. One of them, Nanine Weis, made this statement on their behalf. Weis, like her friends, was from one of the wealthy Protestant families of the town. A fortnight later, following the execution of Louis XVI, France and England were at war. The ensuing English naval blockade spelt the ruin of these Protestant families whose wealth had been based on overseas trade, particularly in slaves and colonial produce. The Weis family departed for Paris having lost three-quarters of their wealth.

Citizen magistrates, you see before you a little society of young patriots, often brought together by the need our age has of fun, under the auspices of the friendship which unites our parents. Love of the homeland is already growing in our young hearts and we were worried to learn that the brave volunteers from our department who have leapt to our defence lack some of the necessities of their equipment. We took up a collection among ourselves, using our modest savings; we don't have much to offer. Our efforts have so far only been able to extend to the purchase of twenty-six pairs of shoes and twenty-nine pairs of socks, that we ask you to send to our generous compatriots on the frontiers. We will not stop offering prayers to heaven for the success of our arms against the enemies of our Republic.

Source: Archives municipales de La Rochelle, 1 D 1/5.

Decree conscripting 300,000 men, 24 February 1793

In early 1793 the Convention responded to the increasingly desperate military crisis by ordering a levy of 300,000 conscripts. This levy was easily implemented only in the south-east and east—two frontier regions—and around Paris. In the south, in the departments of the Aveyron and Lozère, it was the trigger for a short-lived revolt led by a small-town lawyer, Marc-Antoine Charrier. In the west it provoked a massive armed rebellion and civil war, known, like the region itself, as 'the Vendée'. This was to lead to huge loss of life on both sides: the Jacobins could not forgive a rebellion at a critical time in the war against foreign enemies; the Vendéans would not fight for a Revolution they believed had destroyed their Church.

The National Convention declares to all Frenchmen that the united despots threaten liberty. As a consequence, it decrees:

Article 1. All French citizens, from the age of 18 to 40 years, unmarried or widowed without children, are in a state of permanent conscription until such time as the full complement of recruitment of 300,000 men, decreed below. . . .

Law regarding the levying of 300,000 men, and on the method to be followed to implement this levy.

Article 1. The National Convention calls on 300,000 men who will, within as short a time as possible, rally to the armies of the Republic. . . .

Any citizen who is called on to march in defence of the fatherland, in conformity with what has been stated in the preceding articles, will be able to have himself replaced by another citizen in a condition to bear arms, and aged at least 18. . . .

Article 19. The following are not included in the general call for this levy:

1. Those whose incapacities put them in no state to carry arms.
2. Administrators making up the departmental and district directories. . . .
5. Mayors of communes, municipal officers and public prosecutors.

6. Members of the civil and criminal courts, clerks of court, national commissioners, justices of the peace.
7. District tax collectors.
8. Tax collectors and directors of registration.
9. Workers employed in the manufacture of arms and gunpowder.

Source: *Gazette nationale ou le Moniteur universel*, no. 57, 26 February 1793, vol. 15, pp. 549–50.

The Constitution of 1793

The Convention supported the Jacobins' harsh measures which they believed were necessary to secure the Republic to a point where the highly democratic Constitution of June 1793 could be implemented. This Constitution, largely the work of Robespierre, was remarkable for its guarantees of social rights and popular control over an assembly elected by direct, universal male suffrage. The results of a referendum on its acceptance were about 1.8 million 'yes' votes to 11,600 against, from an electorate of approximately six million males. Such was the degree of individual freedom guaranteed in the Constitution, however, that it was suspended until the peace, lest counter-revolutionaries abuse its freedoms. The Constitution is revealing of Jacobin political and social ideology.

DECLARATION OF THE RIGHTS OF MAN AND THE CITIZEN

The people of France, convinced that neglect and contempt for the natural rights of man are the sole causes of the world's misfortunes, have resolved to set out those sacred and inalienable rights in a solemn declaration, so that all citizens, being able to constantly compare the acts of government with the goal of any social institution, will never allow themselves to be oppressed and degraded by tyranny; so that the people may always have the basis of their liberty and happiness before their eyes, the magistrate the basis of his duties, and the legislator the object of his mission.

Consequently, it proclaims, in the presence of the Supreme Being, the following Declaration of the rights of man and the citizen.

Article 1. The goal of society is common happiness. The government is appointed to guarantee man the enjoyment of his natural and imprescriptible rights.

Article 2. These rights are equality, liberty, safety and ownership of property.

Article 3. All men are equal through nature and before the law.

Article 4. The law is the free and solemn expression of the general will; it is the same for all men, whether it protects or punishes; it can only order what is right and useful to society; it can only forbid what is harmful to it.

Article 5. All citizens are equally eligible for public employment. Peoples who are free know no grounds for preference other than virtues and talents.

Article 6. Liberty is the power belonging to man to do all that does not harm the rights of others: its principle is nature; its rule, justice; its safeguard, the law; its moral limits are in this maxim: do not do unto another what you would not have done to you.

Article 7. The right to express one's thoughts and one's opinions, whether through the press or in any other way, the right to assemble peacefully, the freedom to practise religion, cannot be prohibited. The need to state these rights assumes either the presence or the recent memory of despotism.

Article 8. Safety consists in the protection granted by society to each of its members, for the preservation of their person, their rights and their property.

Article 9. The law must protect public and individual liberty from the oppression of those who govern.

Article 10. No man may be accused, arrested or detained, other than in cases established by the law and according to the conventions that it has laid down; any citizen who is called upon or seized by the authorities must obey immediately; he makes himself guilty by resisting. . . .

Article 14. No man may be judged and punished until after he has been heard or legally summoned, and only in accordance with a law promulgated prior to the crime. A law that would punish crimes committed before it existed would be a tyranny; giving a retroactive effect to a law would be a crime.

Article 15. The law must only issue punishments that are strictly and clearly necessary; punishments must be proportionate to the crime and useful to society.

Article 16. The right of ownership of property is one that belongs to each citizen, to enjoy and to dispose at his will of his goods, his income, of the fruit of his labour and his industry.

Article 17. No type of work, cultivation or commerce may be forbidden to citizens' ingenuity.

Article 18. Any man may commit his services or his time; but he may neither sell himself nor be sold. His person is not alienable property. The law recognises no domestic service whatsoever; only an agreement of care and recognition between the working man and the employer may exist.

Article 19. No man may be deprived of the least portion of his property without his consent, unless it is when legally recorded public necessity demands it, and on condition of a just and prior compensation.

Article 20. No tax may be established unless it is for general use. All citizens have the right to be involved in the establishment of taxes, to watch over their use and to have an account given of them.

Article 21. Public assistance is a sacred debt. Society owes subsistence to unfortunate citizens, either by obtaining work for them or by providing means of existence to those who are unable to work.

Article 22. Instruction is the right of all men. Society must further the progress of public reason with all its power, and make instruction available to all citizens. . . .

Article 25. Sovereignty resides in the people. It is one and indivisible, imprescriptible and inalienable.

Article 26. No portion of the people may exercise the power of the entire people; but each section of the sovereign assembly must enjoy the right to express its will in complete freedom.

Article 27. Any individual who would usurp sovereignty should instantly be put to death by free men.

Article 28. A people always has the right to review, reform and change its Constitution. One generation may not subject future generations to its laws.

Article 29. Each citizen has an equal right to take part in the formation of the law and in the nomination of its mandatories or of its agents.

Article 30. Public offices are essentially temporary; they can be considered neither as honours nor as rewards, but as duties.

Article 31. Offences by the mandatories of the people and of their agents must never go unpunished. No man has the right to lay claim to greater inviolability than other citizens.

Article 32. The right to present petitions to the trustees of public authority may in no case be forbidden, suspended or limited.

Article 33. Resistance to oppression is the consequence of the other human rights.

Article 34. There is oppression against the social body when just one of its members is oppressed. There is oppression against each member when the social body is oppressed.

Article 35. When the government violates the rights of the people, insurrection is the most sacred of rights and the most indispensable of duties for the people and for each portion of the people.

CONSTITUTIONAL ACT

ON THE STATUS OF CITIZENS . . .
Article 4. Any man born and living in France, having reached the age of 20; any foreigner, having reached the age of 21, who, having lived in France for one year; lives there from his work; or acquires a property; or marries a French woman; or adopts a child; or supports an elderly person; finally, any foreigner who is judged by the legislative body as having truly earned humanity; is admitted to the exercise of the rights of a French citizen.

Article 5. The exercise of the rights of citizen is lost: through naturalisation

THE REPUBLIC AT WAR

in a foreign country; through the acceptance of duties or favours emanating from an unpopular government; through condemnation to penalties involving the loss of civil rights or corporal punishment, until personal rehabilitation. . . .

ON CIVIL JUSTICE

Article 85. The code of civil and criminal law is uniform for the entire Republic.

Article 86. The right of citizens to have a judgement made about their disagreements by arbiters of their choice may not be undermined.

Article 87. The decision of these arbiters is definitive, if citizens have not reserved the right to appeal.

Article 88. There are justices of the peace elected by the citizens of administrative districts determined by the law.

Article 89. They conciliate and judge at no cost. . . .

ON THE REPUBLIC OF FRANCE'S RELATIONS WITH FOREIGN NATIONS

Article 118. The people of France are the natural friend and ally of free peoples.

Article 119. It does not interfere in any way with the government of other nations. It does not allow other nations to interfere with its government.

Article 120. It gives asylum to foreigners banished from their homeland for the cause of liberty. It refuses it to tyrants.

Article 121. It does not make peace at all with an enemy that is occupying its territory.

ON THE GUARANTEE OF RIGHTS

Article 122. The Constitution guarantees equality, liberty, safety, ownership, national debt, the free exercise of religion, common education, public aid, the unlimited freedom of the press, the right to gather in popular societies, and the enjoyment of all the rights of man to all the French.

Article 123. The Republic of France honours loyalty, courage, old age, filial devotion, misfortune. It entrusts the guard of its Constitution to the virtues.

Source: *Archives parlementaires*, 24 June 1793, vol. 67, pp. 143–50.

12

REVOLT IN THE VENDÉE

The revolt breaks out, 5 March 1793

At the beginning of March 1793, riots broke out in the west of France. It was the beginning of a revolt that soon gained six departments, including the Vendée, the name by which the revolt is usually referred to. In the following extract from the memoirs of Jeanne Ambroise de Sapinaud (1736–1820), the widow of a local noble whose family was closely involved in the revolt, we clearly see not only some of the reasons for the uprising, but also the tendency of peasants in revolt to seek out nobles to 'lead' them. Note also the manner in which the rebels obtained weapons at the beginning of their struggle.

The war in the Vendée commenced on 5 March 1793. Peasants rose in revolt near Buffelière [we do not know which village she is referring to]; they then scattered into the neighbouring parishes and came to find M. Sapinaud de Bois-Huguet, better known by the name la Verrie. 'We take you', they told him, 'as our general, and you will march at our head.' Sapinaud tried to make them understand the misfortunes that they were going to bring down on themselves and the Vendée. 'My friends', he said, 'you will meet more than your match. What can we do? Only one department against ninety-two! We shall be crushed. I do not speak for myself; I hate life since I was witness to all the crimes and the barbarities which our unfortunate *patrie* has accumulated, and I would rather die at your head, fighting for my God and my king, than be dragged to some prison as they have done to all my peers. Believe me, go home, and do not destroy yourselves uselessly.' Those brave peasants, far from yielding to his reason, showed him that they could never submit to a government that had taken their priests away, and had imprisoned their king. 'They have deceived us', they said; 'why do they send us constitutional priests? They are not the priests who attended our fathers on their death beds, and we do not want them to bless our children.' My brother-in-law did not know what side

97

to take; he hesitated to give himself up to those good peasants, and expose himself to an almost certain death; but, seeing their obstinacy, he finished by ceding, put himself at their head, and left the same day for Les Herbiers. The peasants of La Gaubretière joined them. Passing by the château of Sourdy, they forced Sapinaud de La Rairie to march under the orders of his uncle. That same evening, that undisciplined troop, having for its defence nothing more than a few hunting rifles, sickles and sticks, arrived in front of Les Herbiers.

The inhabitants had been warned and had gathered as many patriots as they could. Two companies of Blues [revolutionary soldiers] had been sent to help them with four or five canons. Sapinaud de la Verrie, who was at the head of the badly armed troops, was willing to sacrifice his life and waited to be killed. Bullets whistled around him, he did not hear a thing. However, in less than two hours, the Vendéans had made themselves masters of the town and had chased the Blues. Not one of our own was killed, two men only had been wounded. The number of deaths on the side of the patriots was considerable and they abandoned a great quantity of rifles which were distributed among our peasants.

Source: *Mémoires de Madame de Sapinaud sur la Vendée* (Paris, 1824), pp. 31–4.

Guerrilla tactics

The groups of rebels which formed in the regions in revolt were not negligible from a military point of view. They numbered between 20 and 40,000, they very quickly learnt to use the terrain to their advantage, and they were adept at the use of firearms. This extract from the memoirs of General Turreau de Garambouville (1756–1816) outlines the tactics used by the guerrillas. Turreau was commander-in-chief of the Army of the West, and is best known for his *colonnes infernales* (see p. 102 below). His memoirs, first published in 1794, are full of praise for the manner in which the rebels fought. Of course, it was in his interest to depict the enemy as an almost invincible fighter. It helped explain the defeats suffered by the revolutionary forces at the beginning of the revolt and made his eventual victory over them that much more honourable.

The rebels, helped by the irregularity of nature, have a particular tactic which they know how to apply perfectly to their position and to local circumstances.

Assured of the superiority which their manner of attacking gives them, they never allow themselves to be anticipated: they only fight when they want, and where they want. Their skill in the use of guns is such that no other known people, no matter how warlike or clever they might be, fires so many shots as the hunter of Loroux or the poacher of the woodlands. Their attack is a terrible eruption, sudden, almost always unexpected, because it is very difficult in the Vendée to reconnoitre well, to keep watch, and consequently to defend oneself against a surprise. Their battle formation is the form of a crescent, and their flanks thus pointed are made up of their best sharpshooters, of soldiers who never fire a shot without first aiming, and who almost never miss a target at a reasonable distance. Before even realising it, you are crushed under a mass of fire such that our ordnance cannot achieve a comparable effect. They do not wait for the order to fire: they are not familiar with firing in battalions, lines or platoons, and yet they make you suffer a fire which is just as heavy, just as sustained and especially just as deadly as ours. If you resist their violent attack, it is rare for the rebels to dispute victory; but if you are then unable to draw any benefit, it is because they withdraw so rapidly that it is very difficult to reach them, especially since the terrain almost never allows for the use of cavalry. They scatter, they escape over the fields, woods, bushes, knowing all the paths, byways, glens, passes, knowing all the obstacles that oppose their flight and how to avoid them. If you are obliged to give way to their attack, you have as much difficulty in operating a retreat as they have the facility to flee when defeated. Victorious, they encircle you, cut you to bits; they pursue you with a fury, a bloodthirsty ferocity, an inconceivable rapidity. They run to the attack and to victory as they do in defeat, but they do not fire any less often for all that. They load their guns while walking, running even, and this constant state of mobility causes their fusillade to lose nothing of its energy and precision. In general, this war has such singular characteristics that you have to do it for a long time before getting to know it; and any educated general officer, formed by ten campaigns on the frontiers, would find himself very perplexed, on arriving in the Vendée, to operate successfully there.

Source: *Mémoires pour servir à l'histoire de la guerre de la Vendée par le Général Turreau* (Paris, 1824), pp. 26–8.

The massacre of prisoners

The war in the Vendée was particularly brutal. That is the nature of guerrilla warfare, but it also had something to do with the ideological passions aroused on both sides. The revolutionaries considered the insurgents to be traitors to the Republic at a time when it was beset by enemies on its borders, while the insurgents were largely inspired by religion as well as a desire to defend their own 'patrie' from the revolutionaries.

A report to the department of Maine-et-Loire, 1793

In this report, the commissaire for the department of Maine-et-Loire, Benaben, evokes a massacre of civilians that took place at Le Mans after the town was taken by republican forces.

I was witness to all the horror a town taken by storm can present. Soldiers spread out into the houses, and having taken the wives and daughters of the brigands who had not had time to flee, took them into the squares or the streets where they were crowded together and butchered on the spot; shot, bayoneted or slashed with swords. Ultimately, the fury of the soldiers was such that the general-in-chief, fearing that they would in the end turn on patriots, found no other means to cease the carnage than to sound the retreat.

If beauty and youth were given so little respect during this siege, even less was paid, as you can well imagine, to the position of great ladies whose heaving bodies were dragged in the mud. The hussars, who never lose their bearings on these occasions, took the richest prizes. . . .

The whole route to Mans, up to 5 or 6 leagues from Laval, was covered with the bodies of the brigands; it was a repetition of what I had seen between Angers and Mans. . . . Local peasants had made a general retreat into the woods and into the farms, and massacred more than we were capable of killing ourselves. Four or five leagues from Mans I saw on the side of the road about one hundred bodies, completely naked, piled one on top of the other, more or less like pigs ready to be salted. Those among us who did not know as well as the inhabitants of the countryside those who were foreign to the region, we contented ourselves with taking all the men and women who were not immediately claimed, and only killed those who could not walk, since we did not have carriages in which to transport them.

A letter from Benaben, 26 December 1793

At Savenay, a means was found to accelerate the execution of prisoners which was first used by Carrier at Nantes—mass drowning. In this extract from a letter by Benaben dated 26 December 1793, the use of this method is not only approved of but is the subject of a macabre joke.

I am writing to tell you that more than 1,200 brigands were shot at Savenay; but according to the information that I have since received and that I cannot call into question, it seems that more than two thousand were shot. They call that *sending to hospital*. An entirely different method is used here to get rid of this nasty lot. We put these scoundrels in boats which are then sunk to the bottom. We call that *sending to the water tower*. In truth, if the brigands have sometimes complained about dying of hunger, they at least cannot complain about dying of thirst. Today we made about 1,200 drink. I do not know who came up with this kind of punishment, but it is much more rapid than the guillotine which now appears destined to cut off the heads of nobles, priests and all those who, according to the rank they once held, had great influence over the multitudes.

Source: Claude Petitfrère (ed.), *La Vendée et les Vendéens* (Paris, 1981), pp. 58–60.

───────⊃◦◦◦⊂───────

Turreau to the Minister of War, 19 January 1794

Turreau was one of a number of generals (Westermann, Santerre, Ronsin, Rossignol) who came to the Vendée to advance their political-military careers. During the spring of 1794, after a series of military setbacks, the Vendée was declared 'public enemy number one'. Rather than attempt to understand why these departments had risen in the first place, there was a tendency to lump them all together as counter-revolutionaries. The Hébertist general, Turreau, was thus ordered to destroy all resistance. The following letter explains just how he went about doing so. A number of generals followed Turreau's example, letting their men terrorise the local populations.

My purpose is to burn everything, to leave nothing but what is essential to establish the necessary quarters for exterminating the rebels. This great measure is one which you should prescribe; you should also make an advance statement as to the fate of the women and children we will come across in this rebellious countryside. If they are all to be put to the sword, I cannot undertake such action without authorization.

All brigands caught bearing arms, or convicted of having taken up arms to revolt against their country, will be bayoneted. The same will apply to girls, women and children in the same circumstances. Those who are merely under suspicion will not be spared either, but no execution may be carried out except by previous order of the general.

All villages, farms, woods, heathlands, generally anything which will burn, will be set on fire, although not until any perishable supplies found there have been removed. But, it must be repeated, these executions must not take place until so ordered by the general.

I hasten to describe to you the measures which I have just put in hand for the extermination of all remaining rebels scattered about the interior of the Vendée. I was convinced that the only way to do this was by deploying a sufficient number of columns to spread right across the countryside and effect a general sweep, which would completely purge the cantons as they passed. Tomorrow, therefore, these twelve columns will set out simultaneously, moving from east to west. Each column commander has orders to search and burn forests, villages, market towns and farms, omitting, however, those places which I consider important posts and those which are essential for establishing communications.

Source: Richard Cobb and Colin Jones (eds), *The French Revolution: Voices from a Momentous Epoch, 1789–1795* (London, 1988), p. 206.

13

THE TERROR AT WORK

Law of Suspects, 17 September 1793

The Terror has often been seen as an attempt to institutionalise the violence that led to the massacre of prisoners and/or a response to a crisis situation brought about by threats to the Revolution. It was also, as the following decree shows, an integral part of the process of revolutionary government and the centralisation of the State. The Law of Suspects, along with the establishment of the Revolutionary Tribunals and Committees of Surveillance, was an important part of that machinery and the pursuit of those considered, for one reason or another, hostile to the Revolution.

Article 1. Immediately after the publication of the present decree, all suspected persons who are within the territory of the Republic and still at large shall be placed under arrest.

Article 2. The following are considered suspected persons: (1) those who, either by their conduct, relations, words or writings, have shown themselves to be partisans of tyranny, federalism and enemies of liberty; (2) those who cannot justify in the manner prescribed by the law of 21 March last [establishing Committess of Surveillance] their means of existence and their discharge of their civic duties; (3) those who have been refused certificates of patriotism; (4) public officials suspended or removed from their offices by the National Convention or its commissaries, and not reinstated, especially those who have been or shall be removed by virtue of the law of 12 August last; (5) those former nobles, including husbands, wives, fathers, mothers, sons or daughters, brothers or sisters, and agents of *émigrés* who have not constantly demonstrated their loyalty to the Revolution; (6) those who emigrated in the interval from 1 July 1789 to the publication of the law of 8 April 1792 [confiscating *émigré* property], although they may have returned to France in the period determined by that law or previously.

Article 3. The Committees of Surveillance established according to the law of 21 March last, or those substituted for them either by order of the representatives of the people sent to the armies and the departments, or by virtue of special decrees of the National Convention, are charged with preparing, each in its own *arrondissement*, a list of suspected persons, with issuing arrest warrants against them, and with affixing seals to their papers. Commanders of the public force to whom these arrest warrants shall be delivered shall be required to execute them at once, under penalty of dismissal.

Article 4. The Committee may not order the arrest of any person unless seven members are present, and only on an absolute majority of votes.

Article 5. Individuals arrested as suspects shall first be taken to jails in the place of their detention; in default of jails they shall be kept under surveillance in their respective places of residence.

Article 6. During the following week they shall be transferred into national buildings, which the departmental administrations shall be required, as soon as possible after receipt of the present decree, to designate and prepare for this purpose.

Article 7. The detainees may have their absolutely essential belongings taken into these buildings. They shall remain there under guard until the peace.

Article 8. The guard costs shall be borne by the detainees and divided among them equally. This guard duty shall be entrusted, preferably, to fathers of families and relatives of citizens who have gone or shall go to the frontiers. The salary is fixed, for each man of the guard, at the value of a day and a half of labour.

Article 9. Surveillance Committees shall forward without delay to the Committee of General Security of the National Convention the list of persons whom they have had arrested, with the reasons for their arrest, and the papers which they have seized with respect to them.

Article 10. The civil and criminal tribunals may, if there is occasion, hold under arrest as suspected persons, and send to the jails above mentioned, those accused of offences in respect of which it has been declared that there is no occasion for indictment, or who have been acquitted of charges brought against them.

Source: Philippe-Joseph-Benjamin Buchez and Prosper-Charles Roux, *Histoire parlementaire de la Révolution française*, 40 vols (Paris, 1834–8), vol. 29, pp. 109–10.

Robespierre on revolutionary government, 25 December 1793

On 10 October 1793, the government was declared 'revolutionary until peace', even though the structures and institutions had been put in place two months previously. A few months later, Maximilien Robespierre (1758–94), the person probably most associated with the Terror, defined the principles of 'revolutionary government' in this speech to the Convention. Revolutionary government had to be founded on terror, but a terror which was tempered by virtue.

We shall first outline the principles and the needs of revolutionary government; we shall then show the causes which tend to stifle them at birth.

The theory of revolutionary government is as new as the Revolution which brought it into being. One should not look for it in the books of political writers, who failed to foresee the Revolution, or in the laws of tyrants who, happy to abuse their power, are little concerned with seeking its legitimacy. Moreover, for the aristocracy, the phrase [revolutionary government] is an object of terror or a pretext for slander; for tyrants, scandal; for many people, an enigma. It needs to be explained to everyone so that at least those good citizens will rally in support of the principles of public interest.

It is the function of government to guide the moral and physical force of the nation towards the object for which it was established.

It is the function of constitutional government to maintain the Republic; the object of revolutionary government is to establish it.

Revolution is the war of liberty against its enemies; the Constitution is the government of a victorious and peaceful liberty.

The revolutionary government needs an extraordinary activity precisely because it is at war. It is subjected to less uniform and less rigorous rules because the circumstances in which it finds itself are tempestuous and shifting, and especially because it has been obliged to constantly deploy new and rapid resources to meet new and pressing dangers.

The principal concern of the constitutional government is civil liberty, and that of revolutionary government, public liberty. Under a constitutional government, it is almost enough to protect individual liberties against abuses from the State; under a revolutionary government, the State is obliged to defend itself against the factions which attack it.

Revolutionary government owes good citizens the protection of the State; to the enemies of the people, it owes only death.

Source: 'Rapport sur les principes du Gouvernement révolutionnaire fait au nom du Comité de Salut public par Maximilien Robespierre', in Jacques Godechot (ed.), *La Pensée révolutionnaire* (Paris, 1964), pp. 190–1.

Letter by a condemned prisoner, 2 March 1794

In December 1793, an insurrection broke out in the name of religious liberty in the communes of La Ferté-Gaucher, Maupertius and Meilleray, to the cry of 'Long live religion and the Catholic army! Down with the Clubs and the Jacobins!' A number of people, mostly artisans, were arrested, including the elementary school teacher Louis Prunelle. They were transported to Paris where they were condemned to death. Shortly before his execution, Louis Prunelle, one of the thousands of victims of the administrative machinery behind the Terror, wrote the following letter to his wife.

To citizeness Prunelle, school teacher, La Ferté-Gaucher in Brie, at Meilleray
Paris, 12 Ventôse, Year II of the Republic one and indivisible

My dear friend,
I have taken this moment to give you and your poor children some sad news. Of all that I ask you, the one thing is not to grieve. Put your confidence in the children and in the Supreme Being who must be your force and your support. It has already been two hours since I have suffered the news of my condemnation as a result of negligence on the part of a municipal officer from the commune of Meilleray, who did not send the documentation I asked him to.

Learn to console yourself, my dear friend, because I will never see you again. Look after the children and raise them well. I will suffer death as an innocent, accused of being one of the conspirators in the crowd from Meilleray when we were at La Ferté-Gaucher, which is not true, but then someone has to be punished. Throw yourself into the merciful arms of God. Show this letter to all my relatives and tell those from Champguion that they should look upon you and the children as if I were there, that they should not cause you any distress, and that they should always take care of you, as well as my poor children.

Goodbye, my friend, my dear heart, I leave you, reduced to tears, with kisses, as well as for my children, my father and mother and all my relatives whom I ask you to kiss goodbye for me. Pray to the Supreme Being for me; from the one leaving you for ever.

Your dear friend,
Prunelle

Source: Olivier Blanc, *La Dernière Lettre. Prisons et condamnés de la Révolution, 1793–1794* (Paris, 1984), pp. 209–10.

━━━━━⫷∘∘∘⫸━━━━━

Law of 22 Prairial, 10 June 1794

The Law of 22 Prairial was the most extreme of the series of measures introduced to protect the security of the State and punish those opposed to the Revolution. The calling of witnesses was no longer obligatory and was left to the discretion of the court. At the same time, those accused were denied the right to counsel. If the defendant was found guilty there was only one punishment—death. This is not to say that all defendants were found guilty; many were let off. The law was, nevertheless, the beginning of the second phase of the Terror during the spring and summer of 1794 when whole cartloads of suspects were sent to their death by guillotine on the Place de la Révolution.

The National Convention, having heard the report of the Committee of Public Safety, decrees:

Article 4. The Revolutionary Tribunal is established to punish the enemies of the people.

Article 5. The enemies of the people are those who seek to abolish public liberty, whether by force or by guile.

Article 6. Considered enemies of the people are those who have sought the re-establishment of royalty or sought to degrade or dissolve the National Convention and the revolutionary republican government of which it is the centre;

> those who have betrayed the Republic in the command of posts and armies, or in any other military function, maintained a secret correspondence with enemies of the Republic, or toiled to disrupt the provisioning or the service of the army;
>
> those who have sought to prevent the provisioning of Paris or to cause dearth in the Republic;
>
> those who have assisted the plans of the enemies of France, whether by promoting the sheltering and impunity of conspirators and aristocracy, by persecuting and slandering patriotism, by corrupting the representatives of the people, by abusing the principles of the Revolution, or the laws or measures of the government by false and treacherous applications;
>
> those who have deceived the people or the representatives of the people, to induce them into actions contrary to the interests of liberty;

those who have sought to spread despondency in order to promote the
enterprises of tyrants leagued against the Republic;

those who have spread false news to divide or disturb the people;

those who have sought to mislead opinion and to prevent the instruction of
the people, to deprave morals and corrupt the public conscience, to
impair the energy and purity of revolutionary and republican principles,
or to stop their progress, whether by counter-revolutionary or insidious
writings, or by any other machination;

untrustworthy suppliers who compromise the security of the Republic, and
peculators of the public wealth, other than those included under the
provisions of the Law of 7 Frimaire dealing with embezzlement;

those who, being charged with public office, misuse it to serve the enemies
of the Revolution, to harass patriots, or to oppress the people;

finally, all those who are designated in preceding laws relating to the punishment of conspirators and counter-revolutionaries and who, by
whatever means or by whatever outward appearances they assume, have
attacked the liberty, unity and security of the Republic, or toiled to prevent the enhancement of its strength.

Article 7. The penalty for all offences within the cognisance of the
Revolutionary Tribunal is death.

Source: Buchez and Roux, *Histoire parlementaire de la Révolution française*, vol.
33, pp. 193–8.

The Revolutionary Tribunal at work, June 1794

Nicolas Ruault, journalist and author, lived in Paris during the Revolution.
His letters to his brother, the Abbé Brice Ruault, *curé* at Evreux, written
between 1783 and 1796, constitute one of the most interesting accounts
of the period. Here he describes a chance encounter with a friend being
sent to the guillotine. His description of the workings of the
Revolutionary Tribunal in Paris at the height of the Terror is somewhat
exaggerated—of the 5,343 people who appeared before it, about 2,747
were condemned to death—but gives an insight into how moderate revolutionaries perceived the workings of the institutions of Terror.

Paris, 2 Messidor, Year II (21 June 1794)
. . . One of the things that has most distressed me during the terrible days that
I have just told you about is to have met an intimate acquaintance with whom

I was linked by friendship and whom you often saw at president Bonneuil's home, M. Annisson Duperron, director of the Royal Printing Works. I was coming back from the Tuileries when I saw in the distance going past the Louvre a tumbril full of condemned prisoners and I was surprised to see the extraordinary route they were being made to take. Whom did I see in that deadly carriage? The unfortunate Annisson! He recognised me, shrugged his shoulders, lifted his eyes to the heavens. Dumbfounded, unaware that he had been arrested, I wiped my eyes with my handkerchief and leant against a wall. I learnt that by a kind of refined barbarity, the order had been given to drive the tumbril to the Place de la Révolution by going past the Louvre, so that the unfortunate man would pass alive in front of his former home. . . . This type of sad and deadly encounter is very common and makes one feel all the more cruelly the horrible effects of revolutionary tyranny, the draconian laws of the Committee of Public Safety adopted by the Convention.

Condemned prisoners on their way to their place of execution are driven through the most populous and busy districts; hardly a day goes by that passers-by do not see among these numerous victims someone they know, a friend, a relative. For, unless one attends the sessions of the [Revolutionary] Tribunal every day, one is ignorant of the moment when the person one knows to be arrested is judged by this body that assassinates rather than condemns. The judges secretly choose whom they want to judge, or whom they have been ordered to judge. In the evening, prisoners at the Conciergerie are informed by a kind of extract from the indictment which warns them they are to appear before the Tribunal the next day. Indeed, they appear in numbers of fifty, sixty or seventy, seated on a rostrum of five or six rows. There they are asked their name, their age, their status, occupation, etc. . . . The indictment is then read to them as a group or in common. For the sake of appearances a few questions are asked of a few defendants who either reply or do not. The jury then deliberates in a small room where they remain about an hour talking among themselves, in order to do what they derisively call *deliberate*. They return to the hearing and declare *on their honour and their conscience* the defendants guilty. In two or three hours more than sixty to seventy people are thus condemned to death and executed the same day on the same scaffold.

For the sake of appearances again, a few people supposedly guilty of indiscreet utterances are mixed in with the accused and acquitted to give an outward show of clemency and generosity. During these rapid and murderous procedures, scenes sometimes occur which fill one's soul with a kind of dread: the accused, in trying to defend themselves, call an honest citizen, without reproach, to vouch for their innocence. Immediately the Tribunal orders that the witness invoked by the defendant be brought there. He arrives; if he talks too much in favour of the unfortunate person who has implored his testimony, if he speaks a few words that smack of royalism or the aristocracy, he is immediately indicted and thrown in the ranks of the accused. A few minutes later he is condemned to death with his friend. This dreadful experience has happened to several witnesses, among others to our notary Martin de L'Agenois. He was peacefully dining at home. At three o'clock, they came to take him as a witness before the Revolutionary Tribunal. He got up from the table and went to the palace with the gendarmes; he said a few words during the hearing, his replies were taken as an avowal of complicity; he was placed on the rostrum; at half past four he was tied up in one of those deadly tumbrils and was being driven to his death.

Such, my dear friend, and I say this without exaggeration, is the manner in which this terrible Tribunal proceeds. . . .

Source: Nicolas Ruault, *Gazette d'un Parisien sous la Révolution: lettres à son frère, 1783–1796* (Paris, 1976), pp. 353–5.

―――――◦◦◦◦―――――

The fall of Robespierre, July 1794

After an absence from public life that lasted about a month, Robespierre appeared before the National Convention on 8 Thermidor to attack all those who, according to him, had discredited the Revolution. Towards the middle of the speech, he made threats against a number of individuals but did not name names, thereby alarming many of his listeners. It gave those who opposed him the courage to come out into the open. The next day, 9 Thermidor, when Robespierre wanted to address the Convention again, he was refused a hearing and, with a number of followers, placed under arrest. Thousands of Parisians rallied to support Robespierre, but because none dared take the Convention head on, they very quickly lost the little initiative they had gained. Robespierre attempted to commit suicide by shooting himself but only succeeded in blowing away his lower jaw.

Paris, 12 Thermidor, Year II (31 July 1794)
Thank God! My dear friend! The decemviral tyranny was brought down three days ago. The rumour has undoubtedly reached you, since it was great and terrible as it should have been. It must be resounding throughout France at the moment. On the 10th [Thermidor, 29 July], Robespierre went to join Danton by the same route that he made his colleagues take to descend to the dead. Even the most ardent revolutionaries have found on this occasion the use of the admirable law of retaliation to be just: *Who lives by the sword . . . dies by the sword.* . . .

I will tell you how this great combat was fought in the Convention on the 9th [Thermidor, 28 July] while it is still fresh in my memory. Robespierre had not appeared either in the Committee of Public Safety or the Convention for several *décades* [a period of ten days]. . . . Since the death of Danton, discord has reigned in the Committee of Public Safety; Billaud-Varenne, Collot d'Herbois and Barère were together on one side, and on the other were Robespierre, Couthon, Le Bas and Saint-Just. Robespierre, who had a tendency to dominate his colleagues in the Committee and the Convention, and who aimed at a dictatorship, had completely isolated himself from them, but was nevertheless supported in his absence by Couthon and Saint-Just. . . . Robespierre did an about turn and on the 8th [Thermidor, 27 July] of this month in the National Convention gave a long, hypocritical speech, apologetic about his person, full of blame for a few members of the Committees of Public Safety and General Security, mixed with bitter reflections against a great number of other members, a speech in which he treated as an atrocious calumny the project attributed to him to aspire to a dictatorship, a speech which, finally, revolted the whole Convention and which he read that very evening to the Jacobins where he excited the most violent agitation for and against its author.

The members of the Convention attacked in this speech, numbering eleven, spied on by Robespierre's agents and threatened with the guillotine, gathered on the evening of the 8th in the gardens of the Tuileries and resolved to attack Robespierre during the session of the next day, the 9th, and to overthrow the kind of ideal throne on which he had placed himself. They did not fail; Tallien especially, who was the most violently threatened, formed the idea of killing Robespierre within the Assembly itself, at the tribune, if he came away victorious from the combat he had resolved to deliver. That is why Tallien never left the tribune and its steps as long as the stormy session lasted. He had left his house in the morning greatly agitated, refusing the chocolate drink his mother prepared for him each day. As she held him by the arm to force him to take his breakfast before leaving, she noticed a dagger hidden in his clothes; she was sick with fright. 'Mother,' he told her, 'either today is my last day or it is the last day of another. Let me go.' In effect, he went to the Convention and was the first to attack Robespierre. He was seconded by Billaud-Varenne, Bourdon, Vadier, Fréron, Louchet and a host of other members who all cried out 'Down with the tyrant' and demanded his arrest, as well as that of Saint-Just, Couthon, Lebas and Robespierre's brother. The decree was pronounced by Collot d'Herbois, president, after a unanimous vote and amid loud applause. . . . Robespierre was driven to the Luxembourg in a carriage; arriving at the door, the very patriotic concierge refused to receive him in the prison saying that there was no room. Robespierre demanded to be taken to the Hôtel de Ville, where he was transported with those who were guarding him in the carriage, and it was the municipality's bad luck that, seeing their hero among them, they took up arms against the

Convention. Hanriot [commander of the National Guard of Paris] immediately marched with his troops against the assembly and first invested the Committee of General Security; but he was stopped and taken tied to the Committee itself. He found the means to escape and quickly ran to the commune. In a short time, the Convention *outlawed* all the rebels. This decree terrified their followers; a few deputies ran on foot or on horseback, to the Hôtel de Ville, on the Place de la Grève, to harangue the riotous populace as well as the National Guard and managed to disperse them. The chaos then reached its peak among those in the municipality who were no longer in agreement and who had lost their heads. A pistol shot was fired at Robespierre's head [in fact, he attempted to commit suicide], Saint-Just was sabred, Coffinhal threw Hanriot into a cesspool, and Robespierre the younger jumped from a window and broke his leg, Lebas killed himself. Everybody at the municipality was arrested and led to the Conciergerie. Robespierre, kept in a room at the Hôtel de Ville with his brother and the two other members of the Committee of Public Safety, was arrested on the 10th by a few police, clerks and prosecutors and carried on a chair to the Committee of Public Safety and into the room called Liberty which serves as an ante-chamber to the Convention. He stayed there two hours on the floor, wounded in the jaw, unable to speak, and exposed to the sarcasm and insults of passers-by. From there, at around midday on the 10th, he was taken to the Conciergerie to join all the other rebels already locked up there. Couthon suffered another kind of martyrdom during the night of the 9th to 10th. He was thrown from a window onto the Place de la Grève. The poor legless cripple, paralysed in the lower half of his body, was the plaything of the populace from three o'clock until six o'clock in the morning. They took him by his arms and threw him into the air, letting him fall and laughing loudly at this. They led him thus up to the breastwork of the *quai* from whence they threw him alive or half dead into the river; but most cried out to keep him for the guillotine; he was consequently brought back to the Hôtel de Ville, still being belaboured and knocked about, and more or less carried to the Conciergerie to appear before the Revolutionary Tribunal where their friend Fouquier-Thinville was obliged to identify [the victims] and then to send them off to suffer execution. Around five in the evening, twenty-two of them were carried off in three tumbrils, in the same manner as twenty-two Girondins and Danton, with twenty-one others. Each of the tumbrils had in front of it a large tricolour flag which an executioner waved along the route. It was a day of rejoicing, the whole of good society was at the windows watching them pass; people applauded along the rue Saint-Honoré. Only Robespierre the elder showed any courage in going to his death in this manner, and indignation on hearing the cries of joy. His head was bandaged, his cold eyes, normally extinct, were alive and animated during his last moments. The other condemned prisoners did not move; they appeared overcome with shame and pain. Almost all of them were covered in blood and mud; one of Hanriot's eyes was hanging out of his head; they could have been mistaken for a group of bandits arrested in a forest after a violent combat. At seven in the evening they were dead; an immense crowd of men and women had come from all parts of the city to the Place Louis XV to see them decapitated.

Such was the end of Maximilien de Robespierre. . . .

Source: Ruault, *Gazette d'un Parisien sous la Révolution*, pp. 357–61.

Figure 4 A *muscadin*, with braided hair and stick for street fights. The ending of the economic and political constraints of the Terror in 1794 encouraged the sons and daughters of the well-to-do to mark themselves off by their clothing from the *sans-culottes* and Jacobins. The jeunesse dorée (Gilded Youth) also took physical revenge on those they blamed for their experiences during the Terror. Source: RMN-Bulloz.

14

THE THERMIDORIAN REACTION

The Gilded Youth attack the Jacobin Club, November 1794

The fall of Robespierre brought about a political reaction against the worst aspects of the Revolution, namely the Terror and Jacobinism. In the south of France this often led to political executions (see p. 120 below), but in Paris the 2–3,000 individuals who comprised what is known as the Gilded Youth, right-wing thugs, confined themselves to beating up their enemies, the Jacobins. Their headquarters was the Café de Chartres in the Palais Royal. Much like the *sans-culottes* had been used by the Jacobins, the Gilded Youth were used by the Thermidorians to terrorise their political opponents. This extract from the memoirs of Georges Duval (1772 or 1777–1853), a playwright who lived in Paris during the Revolution, gives an indication of who made up the Gilded Youth, and recounts their attack on the Jacobin Club in November 1794.

Fréron's Gilded Youth,* which was not in the least gilded, were called that because of their tone, their manners and the cleanliness of their dress which was in marked contrast with the language, the vulgar manners, and the official filthiness of the Jacobin costume. It was made up of all the young people who belonged to the upper classes of Paris society which had more or less suffered from the Revolution, several of whom had relatives or friends who had been drowned in that enormous shipwreck [that is, the Terror]. It was also made up of all the clerks of notaries, solicitors or appraisers, almost all the merchants' clerks, and finally all those who belonged to the honourable bourgeoisie. United, they formed in the middle of Paris a large enough army for the

---

* Stanislas Fréron (1754–1802), a Conventional, put himself at the head of a band of youths who were dubbed Fréron's Gilded Youth.

Convention to count on to oppose, if the occasion arose, the Jacobin masses who, in spite of the defeat of their leaders, were still solid and threatening. Up till then, however, the gilded youth . . . had limited themselves to teasing the Jacobins, to singing the 'Réveil du peuple' in the streets and the public promenades, and to making honourable amends to actors whose patriotic fervour had risen a few degrees too much during the course of the Revolution. But Barras, Fréron, Tallien, Goupilleau de Fontenay and Merlin de Thionville did not go to the trouble to train us, to discipline us, and to teach us the use of arms in order to carry out these vulgar exploits, or to parade in the streets crying out, 'Down with the Jacobins!' or to become the theatre police. The time was approaching when we were to be called upon to do great things, when our good will and our military talents were going to be seriously put to the test. Up till now I have told you about encounters that were hardly worth calling skirmishes; now let me tell you about sieges and combats.

[Duval goes on to say how Fréron stirred them up with a rousing speech at their general headquarters.]

This short harangue fired us up, made us enthusiastic, and we replied with the unanimous cry: 'To the Jacobin Club, to the Jacobins!' We crossed the rue Saint-Honoré in the greatest silence, Fréron and Tallien at our head. A few officers and a few soldiers devoted to the Convention joined us, and by the time we reached the courtyard of the Jacobin Club our gathering was all that more imposing. At our approach, [Jacobin] brothers and friends had closed all the doors and were singing the 'Marseillaise' at the top of their voices; we replied with the 'Réveil du peuple', and summoned them to open their doors. Their only reply was to throw at us benches, desks and fairly large stones which they had procured in advance, probably in the expectation of the siege which they were then subjected to. A few of us were wounded by these projectiles.

. . . in the meantime, the doors were still closed, the Jacobins shut up in their hall, and the siege dragged on. We were about to mount an assault by the windows when the besieged made a sortie. Then there really was a free for all, and prisoners were taken on both sides. The Jacobins took theirs into the hall; we locked ours, among whom were several sisters, in the former refectory of the order, and put guards on the door. Since new summonses proved useless, several assailants climbed through the windows. They penetrated into the rostrums occupied by the Jacobin sisters of the fraternal society. As they peaceably crossed the rostrums to get to the hall, the shrews attacked them, armed with knives, long knitting needles and open scissors with which they wounded a few of our men. After defending ourselves, we prepared to administer them a small punishment. Since we hesitated about what sort [of punishment], Martinville cried out: 'Good God, my friends, treat these hussies the same way they treated the venerable Sisters of the Charity of the Hôtel Dieu; let's whip them.' Fear took hold of them; they called their brothers for help, but these were occupied defending the entry to the hall which was about to be forced, and paid no attention to their cries, and the punishment was applied *in extenso*.

I must say, however, as a truthful narrator, that the flagellation was very light, and that only the modesty of these ladies suffered. And if one considers that these women were none other than those abominable Furies of the guillotine, whose sole daytime occupation was to accompany those unfortunate victims to the scaffold with their yells and shouts, and who came in the evening to the Jacobin Club to knit and applaud the propositions of massacres which succeeded each other daily, one could say that Fréron's Gilded Youth was far from giving them their just deserts.

The Jacobins were still holding out in their hall, and were not giving up. The Committees of Public Safety and General Security, which had ordered and directed the action, and to which we reported the state of affairs minute by minute, realised that the time had come to finish things off. To this end, they sent Barras, Goupilleau de Fontenay, Bourdon de l'Oise and Merlin de Thionville who arrived on the spot escorted by a few artillerymen to whom they gave the order to break down the doors. It took only a moment. We entered the hall at the double; and the brothers and friends, struck with the terror they had so long inspired in others, fled by all the exits, with no less agility than the representatives of the people assembled in the Orangerie at Saint Cloud, on 18 Brumaire, fled at the sight of Bonaparte and his grenadiers, abandoning their Carmagnoles and their red [phrygian] bonnets, as promptly as the deputies threw away their tricolour sashes and their senatorial cloaks in the bushes through which they ran to save themselves.

Source: Georges Duval, *Souvenirs thermidoriens*, 2 vols (Paris, 1844), vol. 2, pp. 10–12.

The de-martyrisation of Marat, February 1795

Jean-Paul Marat (1743–93) was deputy of the Convention and editor of the newspaper *L'Ami du peuple*, one of the most radical in Paris and which often called for the massacre of the enemies of the Revolution. He was more popular than Robespierre among the working classes of Paris. When he was assassinated by Charlotte Corday (13 July 1793) while in his bath, he became one of the martyrs of the Revolution. His remains were transferred to the Pantheon, the sepulchre of the great men of the Revolution. Less than one year later (8 April 1795), however, in the political reaction which followed Thermidor, his remains were removed. In the days leading up to this event, groups of people expressed their hatred of the man.

3 February

Yesterday, in the evening, there was commotion around the theatres, the Palais Egalité [the Palais Royal] and a few other places of which Marat was the pretext and the cause. At the theatre in the rue Feydeau, the public, basing itself on the order of the day passed by the Convention concerning the above-mentioned friend of the people, misinterpreted the law passed by the Committee of General Security, which had ordered the replacement of the bust on the stage. The curtain had hardly been raised than cries of 'Down with Marat! Down with Marat!' were raised. Someone tried to point to the law passed by the Committee but the Convention's decreed order of the day was brought up. 'As well', some-one added, 'Laignelot should come here. He will see if the will of the people has been well expressed, and whether it is a machine that has been put into move-ment by malicious people. . . .' After having smashed one of the busts at the theatre in the rue Feydeau, another was dragged with a rope tied round its neck into the gardens of Equality [the gardens of the Palais Royal], where it was then kicked and smashed to pieces with canes. Children picked up the debris and asked passers-by: 'Do you want some Marat? Here is a little piece of Marat.' People then marched to the kind of mausoleum which had been erected in honour of Marat at the Carrousel with the intention of destroying it. However, as there is still a guard at this place, it was respected, and the monument was not attacked. Three or four Jacobins, unhappy with the treatment that the royalists were handing out to Marat, allowed themselves to say that people who acted in this way were Muscadins, aristocrats, royalists, etc., and that they would drive their sabres through them. After making these remarks, they retired to a café near the Palais Egalité, but this café was soon surrounded. The [National] Guard arrived; they disarmed the four Jacobins who, amidst a strong escort, were led to the Committee of General Security. However, the Committee, fearing the consequences of this perturbation, informed the public, by a proclamation which appeared this morning, that the enemies of the inte-rior could take advantage of these manoeuvres, perhaps caused by good intentions, in order to calumny the French, to spread the view that France has no government, as Pitt [has convinced] the public in England. . . .

4 February

People were talking peaceably enough, in the various cafés of the gardens of Equality, about the law passed by the Committee of General Security of which we spoke yesterday. An ex-Jacobin was thrown out for having insinuated that in this law the Committee of General Security accused the anti-Maratists of inciting to pillage, and everybody praised the wisdom of the Committee which had wanted to assure public opinion about the monster which had bloodied our altars for such a long time. Suddenly, someone announced that the Titans [a reference to the Committee of Public Safety], who are not yet crushed under debris of the Mountain which their criminal pride had elevated in order to usurp the authority of the people and to reign as tyrants over France, had wanted to attack a representative in order to assassinate him. A single cry could be heard: 'We have sworn to make a rampart with our bodies around the Convention; the life of Legendre is threatened. Let us fulfil our oath.' More than 600 citizens were thus quickly assembled but, on their arrival the troubles were already over, and no representative was in danger; the citizens then dispersed. On their way, they bought busts of Jean-Jacques Rousseau and in several cafes substituted the real friend of the people for the debauched valet of Orleans; in others, having no more busts of Jean-Jacques, which have tripled in price, while busts of Marat are two a penny, they offered to reimburse the owners what they had paid for the hideous figure of the apostle of anarchy. Most victuallers were more than happy to accept that proposition to get rid of such a disgusting guest. . . . Arriving at the sewer of Montmartre, which is going to be renamed the sewer of Montmarat, the busts were broken, dragged in the mud, and dashed with the other Jacobin rubbish. The horrible mouth of our man eater had been covered in red paint, so that he looked like a Septembriseur [someone who had taken part in the September massacres], disgorging the blood he had drunk. . . .

6 February

The day before yesterday, a bust of Marat was found hanging at the entrance to a butcher's, on the corner of the rue de la Calande. Children who had seen it threw stones at it and smashed it, to the applause of the passers-by. A Jacobin woman, who wanted to defend her dear Marat, was booed by the crowd and escaped being whipped by a prompt flight.

Source: Extracts from the *Courrier républicain*, the *Messager du soir*, and the *Narrateur impartial*, cited in A. Aulard, *Paris pendant la réaction thermidorienne et sous le Directoire*, 4 vols (Paris, 1898), vol. 1, pp. 448, 451, 458.

⟩○◇○⟨

The White Terror in the provinces, 1795

Stanislas Fréron (1754–1802), an adversary of Robespierre and one of the instigators of 9 Thermidor (see 'The fall of Robespierre, July 1794' (p. 111), was sent on mission to the south of France to put an end to the massacre of revolutionaries by royalist gangs. He was later recalled to Paris and accused of orchestrating the massacres at Toulon and Marseilles. The account he wrote of those events is highly emotive and probably greatly exaggerated (Fréron was not an actual witness to any of the events he describes). In fact, the so-called White Terror was never as bloody, even if just as indiscriminate, as the Great Terror.

A new terror, far more productive of crime than that from which they claimed to be freeing themselves, now spread like a devouring lava flood in the departments of the Midi.

Marseilles, worthy rival of Lyons, disgraced itself by atrocities at which nature sickens. Its prisons, and those of Aix, Arles, Tarascon and almost all the communes of the Rhône delta, were soon crammed with prisoners, most of them detained with no charge specified on the arrest warrants. Royalism too had its 'suspects'. The *représentant en mission* here issued a decree ordering the arrest of all persons suspected of 'terrorism'. God knows what scope that gave to the relentless aristocracy and to private vengeance.

There was not one commune where, following Marseilles' example, daggers were not plunged with joy into republican hearts. Everywhere a kind of rivalry stirred up by the Furies, a contest for a prize to outdo all the rest in massacres. Neither age nor sex were spared. Women, children and old men were ruthlessly hacked to pieces in the name of humanity by cannibals who fought over the fragments. The département of the Vaucluse endured the same atrocities. That of the Basses-Alpes, whose people are naturally peaceful, hard-working and law-abiding, did not escape the contagion.

After this, it was not hard to excite the people's minds to a fury against anyone who could be called a terrorist. The image of the dangers Marseilles had just miraculously escaped obsessed everyone's thoughts. It was necessary in some way to turn the people into criminals. Popular hatred was directed against the ex-terrorists held in Fort Jean in Marseilles. Some of the people joined the gangs of hired murderers who went by the name of the compagnie de Jésus or compagnie du Soleil.

These vile and savage perpetrators of every kind of murder committed until then penetrated into the deepest cells, they rushed upon their defenceless and starving victims. Daggers and pistols, bayonets and stilettos were not enough—they loaded canon with grapeshot and fired it point-blank into the prison yards. They threw blazing sulphur in through the ventilators; they set fire to damp straw at the entrances to vaults where scores of prisoners were huddled and suffocated them in the thick smoke. They killed, slaughtered, they sated themselves on murder.

Bodies already pierced a thousand times were slashed and mutilated, their brains dashed out against the walls. The silence of death was only broken now and again by the murderers' savage cries or the victims' choking sobs. Knee-deep in blood, they could tread only upon corpses, and the last sighs of many a republican were breathed under the feet of the representatives of the people.

Source: Cobb and Jones (eds), *The French Revolution*, p. 236.

15

THE DIRECTORY

Boissy d'Anglas on the Constitution of 1795

After Thermidor the deputies now dominant in the Convention sought a political settlement that would stabilise the Revolution and end popular upheaval. The Constitution of Year III (August 1795) restricted participation in electoral assemblies by wealth, age and education as well as by sex. The social rights in the Constitution of 1793 were removed; indeed, the declaration of rights was replaced by a declaration of duties. The Constitution was put to the electorate: perhaps 1.3 million men voted in favour and 50,000 against, considerably fewer votes than for its predecessor in 1793. In this extract Boissy d'Anglas, one of the framers of the Constitution, outlines to an appreciative Convention the social bases of a stable political régime.

Finally the happy hour has arrived when, ceasing to be the gladiators of liberty, we can be its true founders. I no longer see in this assembly the villains who tarnished it; the archways of this temple no longer echo with their bloody vociferation, with their treacherous propositions. Our deliberations are no longer chained by the tyranny of the *décemvirs*, they will no longer be led astray by the demagogy of their accomplices. Their many and fierce satellites, disarmed, vanquished, imprisoned, will no longer have the insolence to bring their daggers here, and to point out their victims among you. Crime lives alone in the dungeons; industry and innocence have come out from there to revive agriculture, and to give their lives to commerce. . . .

You must offer to the French nation the republican Constitution that ensures its independence; you must, with its imminent establishment, finally guarantee the property of the rich man, the existence of the pauper, the enjoyment of the industrious man, the freedom and the safety of all. You must make the French people, in the midst of the nations that surround them, take the rank that their nature assigns them, and the influence that their strength, their knowledge, their

121

trade must give them; make tranquillity reign without oppression, liberty without unrest, justice without cruelty, humanity without weakness. . . .

We should be governed by the best among us: the best are the most learned and those most interested in maintaining the law: now, with very few exceptions, you will find such men only among those who, possessing property, are attached to the country where it is located, to the laws that protect it, to the tranquillity that preserves it, and who owe to this property and to the affluence that it brings the education that has made them able to discuss with wisdom and aptness the advantages and inconveniences of the laws that determine the fate of their fatherland. On the contrary, the man without property must constantly make virtuous efforts to interest himself in the order that holds nothing for him, and to oppose the movements that offer him some hope. . . .

If you give political rights to men without property unreservedly, and if they ever find themselves on the benches of the legislators, they will arouse unrest—or allow it to be aroused—without fear of its outcomes; they will establish—or allow to be established—taxes disastrous to trade and agriculture, because they will have neither felt nor feared nor predicted their deplorable results; and finally, they will lead us headlong into those violent convulsions from which we have barely emerged, and whose agonies will continue to be felt for such a long time across all of France. A country governed by property owners is in the social order; that where non-property owners govern is in the natural state.

Source: *Gazette nationale ou le Moniteur universel*, no. 281, 11 Messidor, Year III (29 June 1795), vol. 25, pp. 81, 92.

———◦◦◦—————

Mme de Staël on the the Directory, 1795–7

Until quite recently the Directory was usually portrayed as a corrupt and inefficient government that could not deal with the enormous social and economic problems, some of which are outlined below, that were the legacy of the Terror and Revolution. This was one of the reasons, it was argued, why Bonaparte was able to take power, or at least it was used as justification for his taking power. Historians, however, have gradually come to accept the real accomplishments of the Directory. Even contemporaries like Mme de Staël, the daughter of the Finance Minister, Jacques Necker, although critical of the Directory, recognised the real benefits that accrued to its rule.

One has to give credit to the Directory, and more still to the power of free institutions, no matter what form they are allowed under. The first twenty months which succeeded the establishment of the Republic constitute a particularly remarkable period of administration. Five men, Carnot, Rewbell [sic], Barras, Larevellière [sic], Letourneur, chosen in anger, came to power in the most unfavourable circumstances. They entered the Luxembourg Palace which they were designated without finding a table on which to write, and the State was no more in order than the Palace. Paper money was reduced to almost a thousandth of its nominal value; there was not as much as 100,000 francs in cash in the treasury; food supplies were so scarce that the discontent of the people in this respect was barely contained; the insurrection in the Vendée was still going on; civil unrest had given rise to bands of brigands, known by the name of *chauffeurs* [thieves who tortured their victims with fire], who committed horrible excesses in the countryside; finally, almost all the French armies were disorganised.

In six months, the Directory raised France from this deplorable situation. Coin smoothly replaced paper money; old proprietors lived in peace next to those who had acquired national goods; roads in the countryside had become perfectly safe; the army was very successful; the liberty of the press made a come-back; elections followed their legal course, and one would have been able to say that France was free, if the two classes of nobles and priests had enjoyed the same guarantees as other citizens. But the sublime perfection of liberty consists of the following, that it cannot do things by halves. If you persecute one single individual in the State, justice will never be established for all; all the more so when 100,000 individuals are placed outside the protective circle of the law. As soon as the Directory was established, revolutionary measures spoiled the Constitution: the second half of the existence of that government, which lasted four years in all, was so poor from every perspective that people easily attributed the disorder to the institutions themselves. . . .

Source: Germaine de Staël, *Considérations sur la Révolution française* (Paris, 1983), pp. 321–2.

━━━━◦◦◦◦━━━━

The *journées* of 12 and 13 Germinal, 1 and 2 April 1795

The Thermidorian Convention abandoned the economic restraints that had been introduced under the Terror as a result of popular pressure. The consequences, however, were the immediate collapse of the *assignats* and spiralling inflation. The peasantry no longer wanted to sell their goods for worthless paper money, thus causing high bread prices, hunger and distress. The *journées* of 12 and 13 Germinal were largely caused by those conditions and were some of the last popular demonstrations against the Convention. Unlike their Jacobin equivalents during the heyday of the Revolution, however, they were ineffectual.

Paris, 24 Germinal, Year III

Public affairs are a thousand times worse in Paris than with you, my dear friend; we are lost here in an immense chasm; we have become a hydra with 650,000 heads with as many empty stomachs that have been hungry now for a long time, and it is impossible, not necessarily to satisfy the hunger, but to half feed it. I dare not tell you all that is said, all the curses one hears in the long queues which form every evening, every night, at the bakers' doors, in the hope of getting, after five or six hours' wait, sometimes half a pound of biscuit per person, sometimes half a pound of bad bread, sometimes 6 ounces of rice or 6 ounces of biscuit per person. And yet the government treats the 4 or 5,000 men who lose half their working day waiting for this minuscule portion of wretched food, who complain about their poverty and the horror of their existence, as seditious. It has long been known that hunger is seditious by nature; it is *male suada* as the great poet Virgil energetically put it. Banish that, and these supposedly seditious people will disappear. They will not break into the august French Senate again, as they did on the 12th of this month (April), to cry, 'Give us bread! Give us bread!' People will no longer talk of *circenses* . . . It is no longer the time to laugh or jump around. The flour intended for Paris is stopped on the way and stolen by citizens even hungrier no doubt than ourselves, if such there be within the whole Republic. Yet there is no lack of flour anywhere! There is still plenty in store in the departments of the Nord, the Pas-de-Calais, the Somme, the Seine-Inférieure, etc. . . . . The farmers absolutely refuse to sell it for paper money; you have to go to them and take linen or table silver, jewellery or gold crosses to get a few bushels. The wretches! Brutal and grasping farmers! They are taking advantage of the absurd unlimited liberty of grain commerce in the country, and of the economists' régime introduced since 9 Thermidor, to strip the towns. . . . Discord is more firmly established than ever within its bosom [the Convention]; it returned triumphant with the seventy-three prisoners and the eighteen outlaws. Now we are back to where we were at the end of April '93; and a hundred times worse as far as financial matters go. Too many *assignats*, too much slacking in the government, too many favours shown to enemies of democracy, too much individual hatred among those we call legislators . . . What a situation! What a terrible perspective! . . .

Source: Ruault, *Gazette d'un Parisien sous la Révolution* (Paris, 1976), pp. 376–7.

———◦◦◦◦———

A complaint from the citizens of Besançon, 4 April 1798

Besançon in the south-east of France was both a manufacturing centre and a garrison town. The celebration of the Festival of the Sovereignty of the People (20 March 1798) the day before the electoral colleges were to meet led to a certain amount of unrest which was a prelude of the tactics to be used on election day: intimidation by troops, and rigging of the electoral lists by the municipality which admitted ineligible citizens while excluding eligible ones. Besançon also had a café run by a widow, citizeness Douhaint, whose husband had died defending the *patrie*. As the following extract shows, she became the centre of a farcical political quarrel that could have easily turned violent.

On the said Ventôse [28 February], several officers went to citizeness Douhaint's place. Amid the insults, and threatening to bring her before a Military Commission to condemn her to death by firing squad, they sang a song whose chorus went: 'Thrust with a sabre, ah! the elections, an aristocrat on each lamp-post, ah! the brilliant festival, the beautiful lamp-post!' [It was probably sung to the tune of the 'Carmagnole'.] . . . They declared that her [street] sign displeased them and that if she did not take it down that very evening, they would come back the next day and tear it down. . . The 30 Ventôse was the day set by the anarchists to bring to the height of exasperation soldiers who had been deceived, and thereby strengthen the terror. The Festival of the Sovereignty of the People was meant to be a drunken revel for the exclusives . . . The great exploits were reserved for the next afternoon, at a moment when people, excited by wine, could be more easily pushed into excesses. A civil banquet for 600 people was prepared by the new administrators according to the established custom . . . At the end of the banquet, the guests spilled into the streets, insulting and striking citizens who had not taken the wise precaution of locking themselves at home . . . Around ten o'clock, the crowd headed for the Café of 9 Thermidor . . . The assailants attempted to tear down the sign, but since it was too high and well attached, they were unable to do so . . . It is worth noting that all the rotten disease-ridden soldiers who were in the military hospital had received unlimited leave and were not to return until the festivities were entirely over [that is, until the next day]. . . . In front of the buildings where the [electoral] assemblies were going to open, there was a crowd of armed soldiers waiting for the signal to lend a strong hand and carry out more confidently the exclusions the anarchists were meditating . . . In the 6th section, which was meeting in an old church, at least one hundred citizens, almost all of them cultivators, were violently chased out . . . nevertheless those unfortunates were expelled only after being threatened with the most horrible death: the scoundrels, instigators of these excesses, had removed the top stone of a grave into which they wanted to throw them to bury them alive . . . On 1 Germinal, at two in the afternoon, a crowd of individuals, mostly made up of soldiers, went to the town hall, took a ladder from the fire depot, and put it up against the house of citizeness Douhaint to take down the sign . . . [it was] immediately taken to the public square in front of the town hall, broken in pieces and burnt under the noses of the municipal officers, amid dancing and the cries of the unbridled mob. . . .

Source: Archives nationales, AFIII 244, in *La Révolution française à travers les archives* (Paris, 1988), p. 410.

A police report on the climate of fear and uncertainty

New elections in April 1797 brought about a swing in the electorate to the right. The resulting conflict between the executive, the Directory and the right-wing majority in the chambers led to a political stalemate that was overcome when the Directory annulled the elections and expelled 177 royalist deputies. The coup of 18 Fructidor (4 September 1797) thus threatened to undermine the Constitution of 1795 and led to a lack of confidence in the electoral process. This extract from a police report highlights the climate of uncertainty which seemed to dominate public opinion after the coup.

A great amount of anxiety caused by the actual financial situation prevails in the public. Investors, especially those with a modest debt, are profoundly and painfully touched by the subject of the resolution which concerns them. Violent grumblings can be commonly heard against public poverty, and the detractors of the *journée* of 18 Fructidor say that the cause of poverty is due to that event. The sensation which the resolution produced relative to investors is considerable, even among those individuals who have interests among themselves; debtors who pretend to follow closely the market deny all other arrangements.

The number of workers without employment has increased in Paris, and there are rumours that unemployment is just as great in the departments; the great distress to which they will be reduced at the beginning of winter raises the fear of unfortunate consequences. The spirit of malevolence sows alarm everywhere; the vast majority of the public has once again given itself up to fear; rumours are rife that another 18 Fructidor is going to take place any time.

The 13 Vendémiaire is cited; people also say, and in the following phrases, that it is certain the Directory is going to purge the two Councils once again. Some fear it, while others express the desire to see it occur sooner rather than later. Then people announce the impending arrival of 50,000 men from Paris; 10,000 have already arrived, it is said. In the groups which have formed in the Tuileries, it is said, speaking of the present Constitution, that it is not at all popular and that it is an aristocratic government, that if the Constitution was put in the hands of men who were in no way republican it would become a monarchy as in 1791; that the only difference between the Constitution of '91 and that of '95 is that the execution of the laws, instead of being confided in one person, is confided in five. People have also expressed fears that the government will let itself be circumvented by the friends of Carnot and Cochon, and people were remarking that royalists sought to raise their heads and to inspire doubts in the Directory about the intentions of patriots, one of which people astutely assumed was to re-establish the Constitution of '93. Fears about the future in political terms, complaints and even grumblings about financial matters, and the desire for peace: such was the mood and the character of public opinion yesterday and yet again today. An exterior calm nevertheless continues to exist without change.

Source: Archives nationales, AFIV 1478, cited in Charles Ballot, *Le Coup d'état du 18 fructidor an V* (Paris, 1906), pp. 188–9.

16

BONAPARTE

Proclamation to the Army of Italy, 26 April 1796

Seven days before his marriage with Josephine (2 March 1796), Napoleon was nominated commander-in-chief of the Army of Italy. He was only 27. He was given a limited objective—to contain the Austrians in Italy—while the main thrust of the campaign was to be carried out by Hoche in Germany. Legend has it that Napoleon went about transforming the Army of Italy, which was demoralised and lacking in *matériel* and discipline, into an outstanding fighting force, making Italy the main theatre of operations. This is true up to a point. As the following documents show, his troops were far less heroic than the image of the grenadiers portrayed in official propaganda and were largely motivated by plunder. Bonaparte's famous appeal supposedly launched on 27 March 1796 ('Soldiers, you are naked and badly nourished'), was an invitation to pillage and loot, but is probably apocryphal. More interesting from a political point of view is the proclamation of 7 Floréal which Bonaparte made before attacking the Austrians with only 30,000 troops. Bonaparte appealed to their sense of honour and glory to perform ever greater feats. At the same time, however, he attempted to reassure the Italian civilian population by pointing out how severely he would deal with looters. The French army had been looting indiscriminately and Bonaparte's orders two days previously to try and stem the pillage (Order of the Day, 24 April 1796) had proved ineffective.

Soldiers, in fifteen days you have won six victories, taken twenty-one flags, fifty-five pieces of canon, several fortresses, and conquered the richest part of Piedmont; you have taken 15,000 prisoners, killed or wounded more than 10,000.

Until now you have fought over barren rocks, distinguished yourselves by your bravery, but useless to the *patrie*. Today, your services are equal to those of the Army of Holland and the Army of the Rhine, and have compensated for everything. You have won battle without canon, crossed rivers without bridges, conducted forced marches without boots, bivouacked without alcohol and often without bread. The Republican phalanx, the soldiers of liberty, were the only ones capable of suffering what you have suffered. Thanks be to you, soldiers! The grateful Republic owes you its prosperity, and if, victors of Toulon, you were able to predict the immortal campaign of 1794, your present victories foretell an even better campaign.

The two armies which audaciously attacked you a short time ago now flee terrified before you; those perverse men who laughed at your misery and delighted in the thought of your enemies' triumphs are now confounded and trembling.

But, soldiers, you have accomplished nothing since there is still so much to do! Neither Turin nor Milan is yet yours . . .

At the beginning of the campaign you were destitute; today you are abundantly provided for; you have taken numerous stores from your enemies; siege artillery has arrived. Soldiers, the *patrie* has the right to expect great things from you. Can you fulfil its expectations? The most difficult obstacles have undoubtedly been overcome, but you have more battles to deliver, towns to take, rivers to cross. Are there any among you whose courage is failing? Are there any among you who prefer to return across the summit of the Apennines and the Alps, to patiently endure the insults of those slave soldiers? No, there are none among the victors of Montenotte, Millesimo, Dego and Mondovi. All of you are burning to carry the war far from the French people; all of you want to humiliate those proud kings who dare dream of putting us in irons. All of you want to dictate a glorious peace which will indemnify the *patrie* for the enormous sacrifices it has made. All of you, on returning to your villages, will be able to say with pride: 'I was a soldier in the conquering Army of Italy!'

Friends, I promise you this conquest, but there is one condition you have to swear to fulfil, and that is to respect the people you deliver, and to suppress the horrible pillage to which scoundrels encouraged by our enemies deliver themselves. Without it, you will not be the liberators of the people, you will be their scourge. You will not honour the French people, you will disavow them. Your victories, your courage, your success, the blood of our brothers who died in battle, all will be lost, even honour and glory. As for me and the generals who have your confidence, we would be ashamed to command an army without discipline, without bridle, which knows no other law than force. But, invested with the national authority, strengthened by justice and the law, I will know how to impose respect for the laws of humanity and honour which that little group of men without courage and without hearts trample underfoot. I will not tolerate that brigands soil our laurels; I will ensure that the rules I have passed are strictly observed. Looters will be shot without pity; several have been already. I have had occasion to note with pleasure the zeal with which good soldiers have executed these orders.

People of Italy, the French army has come to break your chains; the French people is the friend of all peoples. Come to meet them with confidence; your property, your religion and your customs will be respected.

We are making war as a generous enemy, and we only begrudge the tyrants who have reduced you to slavery.

General Headquarters, Cherasco, 7 Floréal, year IV

Source: *Correspondance de Napoléon Ier publiée par ordre de l'Empereur Napoléon III*, 32 vols (Paris: 1858–69), vol. 1, pp. 187–8.

Two accounts of the battle of Arcola, November 1796

The most celebrated image of the Italian campaign was Gros' painting of Bonaparte crossing the bridge at Arcola. Despite the fact that neither Bonaparte nor Augereau actually succeeded in storming his way across the bridge, the battle was almost immediately transformed into one of the major themes of Napoleonic propaganda. The cowardice of the troops was discreetly overlooked in the official reports and disappeared entirely with the legend that portrayed the French grenadiers in heroic posture. So too was the fact that Bonaparte ended up being pushed or thrown off the bridge into the swampy waters below.

Letter from Bonaparte's aide-de-camp, Joseph Sulkowski

Joseph Sulkowski (1770–98) was a Pole in the service of the Revolution. After joining the French army, he was sent to Italy where he was noticed by Bonaparte who made him one of his aides-de-camp. He was later killed during the expedition to Egypt. His account of the attack on the bridge of Arcola on 15 November confirms that Bonaparte did actually seize the flag and rush onto the bridge, but also points out how the attack was a complete failure.

. . . In the morning, I found myself with Verdier; he was entrusted with this important attack, and he commanded the élite of Augereau's division. He marched, first knocking over the forward posts that the enemy had on the embankment, pushing them back under the cannon in the village. The latter stopped our troops. Verdier ordered the charge on two occasions, he advanced up to that dangerous spot I mentioned, but, having reached there, his grenadiers stopped again, profiting from the slope of the embankment to take cover, and that first ardour, so precious in battle, evaporated into insignificant rifle fire. Seeing this, Augereau ordered the rest of his division to advance in order to support the advance guard; the movement took time; the enemy, who felt the importance of the post, sent three battalions to support the village, we saw them arrive at the double, dragging their cannon after them. From that moment on the danger increased, the posts were reinforced, in Arcola all the windows crowded with soldiers had been transformed into loopholes, two cannon took us from the points, and two howitzers, placed on the embankment itself, unleashed death by ricocheting [cannon balls] in the middle of our tightly formed ranks marching into combat. Our position became critical, we were to die for nothing, to retreat or to take the village, the latter being the preferred option. Our most valiant generals put themselves at the head [of the troops], had the charge sounded, marched, pleading with us not to retreat, even hitting us, but no-one followed, the enemy got them in sight, and they fell under fire. Bon, Lannes, Verdier, Verne returned shot through with bullets and drowning in their blood. At that disheartening sight, Augereau, the intrepid Auguereau, rushed forward, went through the ranks of frightened soldiers, tore the flag from the flag bearer and advanced towards the enemy; a courageous few followed him, the others hesitated; but unlucky shots having killed five or six, they retreated and again took refuge behind the embankment.

Augereau, although abandoned, returned without being wounded. Fate, after having struck down all the generals in his division, wanted to preserve this warrior so useful to our armies. In the meantime, the general-in-chief [Bonaparte], learning of the state of affairs, had already advanced himself half way. He was told about the irreparable losses that had just occurred, the enemy's obstinacy, the discouragement of our soldiers; the battle was engaged. It was victory or death, and he took a role deserving of his glory. We saw him suddenly appear on the embankment, surrounded by his general staff and followed by his guides, he dismounted, drew his sword, took the flag and rushed onto the middle of the bridge amid a rain of fire. The troops saw him but none of them imitated him. I was present at that incredible cowardice and can hardly believe it. Were the victors of Lodi to cover themselves in infamy? The moment was brief, but fatal for all those who surrounded Bonaparte, his aide-de-camp Muiron, General Vignolle, the lieutenant of the guides, and two of Belliard's adjutants fell by his side. I myself was hit by shot, right in the chest, the rolled-up coat I was wearing round my neck saved my life; but at the same time a shell exploded at my feet and I was hit in the head with the earth it threw up; the blow was so violent that I lost consciousness, and when I came to I was already far from the scene, carried by troops.

I was told afterwards that the general-in-chief, seeing that his efforts were to no avail, withdrew and, this time, the grenadiers rushed to follow his example; all fled, everybody was crushed together, the throng was so great that he [Bonaparte] was thrown into a ditch full of water; without his general staff, he would have drowned, because the fugitives did not even think to give him the slightest help. The soldiers stopped when they were out of range of the cannon, when we succeeded in stopping and rallying them all the more easily that the enemy was not pursuing them. . . .

Source: Marcel Reinhard, *Avec Bonaparte en Italie. D'après les lettres inédites de son aide de camp, Joseph Sulkowski* (Paris, 1946), pp. 177–9.

Louis Bonaparte and the state of the Army of Italy, 24 November 1796

This letter, written by Louis Bonaparte to a friend, Cuviller, known as Fleury, aide-de-camp of General Clarke, gives a good indication of the state of morale of the Army of Italy towards the end of 1796, after eight months of constant fighting. There is an enormous disparity between the very real despair and evident fatigue felt by Louis on the one hand, and his brother's official proclamations on the other.

At general headquarters in Verona, 4 Frimaire, Year V of the French Republic one and indivisible
To the aide-de-camp of the general-in-chief, at Cuviller

I haven't received any news from you for a long time. What is the reason for this my dear Fleury?
There have been a lot of battles over the last few days, I thought for a moment that we would all succumb to them. It is a war of officers, we have lost a considerable number. All the brave are dead or wounded, there are regiments commanded by lieutenants and battalions commanded by quartermaster sergeants. All the brave are dead, and you can count those who remain. The troops are no longer the same and loudly demand peace. No more energy, no more ardour among them. If we hold out against the enemy, it is only because of the officers. But in vain, they hit them with the flat of their swords, they are abandoned and perish alone. Take the affair in front of the village of Arcola the other day, if it had been left to the same officers, it would have been an easy task to take the village, but the courageous from the various corps have been cut off in their prime and only the brats are left. Imagine, my dear Fleury, that they even abandoned the general-in-chief. He was at their head, all the officers with him had been killed, and the cowards who were behind had

fled. The enemy who saw their movements better than us came up before us, really I don't know how my brother did not succumb. The brave General Lannes was wounded three times in this battle. Generals Verdier, Vignolle, Vernes, Gardanne, Robert, Lebon fell as well. One or two of his aides-de camp were killed, and we greatly miss them, they were Muiron, major in the artillery, aide-de-camp, and the young Elliot. My older brother is torn by pain in naming them, but you probably know already. It is a tribute that every man owes his country. He who does not know how to die is not French. To die is nothing, but one at least has to die usefully. It is tiredness which worries everyone. For the last eight months we have always fought against new troops. As soon as we beat them at Como, we turned to defeat them at Rivoli. All those forced marches whose combinations the enemy admires are tiring. We count ourselves lucky to be able to resist 50,000 savages with 10,000 or 12,000 men.

In Paris, people reason well but they are mistaken. One should undoubtedly not exaggerate one's political opinions, but what is certain is that only republican enthusiasm can lead to victory. At the moment it is destroyed, I believe the time for peace has come. You know my friend what would happen if we were beaten back to our frontiers?

Nevertheless we have beaten them. Six to seven thousand prisoners in all, 12,000 enemy troops out of action, are the fruit of the fighting which has just taken place.

Adieu. Comfort General Clarke for the loss of his cousin [Elliot]. He died bravely and is missed by the whole army, even more by his comrades.

Your friend,
L. Bonaparte

Source: Archives nationales, AFIII 72, in *Annales historiques de la Révolution française* 9 (1932), p. 354.

Proclamation to the people of Egypt, 2 July 1798

Shortly before disembarking on the shores of Egypt, Bonaparte, with the help of one of the Orientalists who had accompanied him, Venture de Paradis, wrote the following proclamation to the people of Egypt. There are two versions: one in Arabic and the other in French, the latter being a watered-down version of the proclamation, especially the passages touching on religion and Bonaparte's Islamic demands. The expedition involved Bonaparte's personal and military prestige, but the campaign was also transformed into a civilising mission, entirely in keeping with the revolutionaries' rhetoric of the Grande Nation. Bonaparte thus attempted to present himself as someone who had come to restore the legitimate authority of the Ottomans. This translation is closer to the Arabic version of the text.

In the name of God the beneficent, the merciful, there is no god but God, he has no son nor associate in his reign.

On behalf of the French Republic founded on the basis of Liberty and Equality, General Bonaparte, head of the French army, lets it be known to the people of Egypt that for too long the Beys who govern Egypt have insulted the French nation and have snubbed our merchants: the hour of their punishment has arrived.

For too long this pack of slaves bought in Georgia and the Caucasus have tyrannised most of the world; but God, the Lord of the Universe, the all powerful, has ordered that their empire come to an end.

People of Egypt, you will be told that I have come to destroy your religion; it is a lie, do not believe it! Reply that I have come to restore your rights, to punish the usurpers; that I respect God, his prophet and the glorious Coran more than the Mamelukes.

Tell them that all men are equal before God; wisdom, talent and virtue are the only differences between men.

Now, what wisdom, what talent, what virtues distinguish the Mamelukes so that they have exclusively all that makes life pleasant and agreeable? Are there good lands? They belong to the Mamelukes. Are there beautiful slaves, beautiful horses and beautiful homes? They belong to the Mamelukes. If Egypt is their farm, let them show the lease God has given them. But God is just and merciful towards the people; and with the aid of the All Powerful, from this day on, no Egyptian will be prevented from acceding to an eminent post: the wisest, the most educated and the most virtuous will govern, and the people will be happy.

Once there were great towns among you, large canals, great commerce. Who destroyed all this, if not the greed, the injustice and the tyranny of the Mamelukes?

Cadis [Mohammedan judges], Sheiks, Imams, Tchorbadjis, tell the people that we are the friends of true Muslims. Did we not destroy the pope who said that we have to make war on Muslims? Did we not destroy the Knights of Malta, because those madmen believed that God wanted them to make war on Muslims? Have we not, throughout the centuries, been friends of the Sultan (may God fulfil his desires!) and the enemy of his enemies? Have not the Mamelukes, on the contrary, always rebelled against the authority of the Sultan, whom they still repudiate? They do as they like.

Three times happy those who are with us! They will prosper in fortune and rank. Happy are those who remain neutral! They will have the time to learn to know us, and they will side with us. But misfortune, three times misfortune, to those who take up arms with the Mamelukes and fight us! There will be no hope for them: they will die.

Article 1. Every village situated within a radius of 3 leagues from the place where the army will pass through will send a deputation in order to let the commanding general of the troops know they will obey, and to inform him that they have raised the red, white and blue flag of the army.

Article 2. Any village which takes up arms against the army will be burnt to the ground.

Article 3. Any village which submits to the army will raise, with the flag of our friend, the Sultan, that of the army.

Article 4. The Sheiks will put seals on the goods, houses and property which belong to the Mamelukes, and will take care that nothing is misappropriated.

Article 5. The Sheiks, Cadis and Imams will continue the functions of their posts. Each inhabitant will remain at home, and prayers will continue as usual. Each inhabitant will thank God for the destruction of the Mamelukes and will cry: Glory to the Sultan! Glory to its friend, the French army! Curses on the Mamelukes, and happiness to the people of Egypt.

General headquarters, Alexandria, 14 Messidor, Year VI
18th of the month of Muharrem, in the year 1213 of Hegira
Bonaparte

Source: Henry Laurens, *L'Expédition d'Egypte, 1798–1801* (Paris, 1989), pp. 75–7.

Bonaparte as the Jewish Messiah, 28 February 1799

This letter from a *commissaire* addressed to the director of the department of the Nord, Merlin de Douai, shows how, even without the use of propaganda, Bonaparte's military victories touched people in milieux where one would not normally expect him to have made an impact. In 1798, when Bonaparte made a raid into what was then known as Syria (present-day Israel), he undertook nothing in favour of the Jews. Nevertheless, the rumour spread throughout the ghettos of central Europe that Bonaparte was going to create a Jewish state.

I cannot resist the temptation to tell you about a conversation I had recently with a Jew, coming back from Lille to Douay, and as it is good to kill time while travelling, one might just as well talk with an Israelite as examine cloud formations, or curse against the roughness of the stones which give you a constant mobility as disagreeable as it is involuntary. In short, I entered into conversation with the person sitting opposite me, and much like the fox of the fable, I more or less held the following language:

Q. Well, Hebrewer (this is how they are called in Germany), what do you think of our Revolution?

A. It was made to astound the world.

Q. Are you of German or Portuguese extraction?

A. I am German.

Q. Are you still waiting for the Messiah?

A. No, he has arrived.

Q. I have not read the news in any gazette.

A. You did not see then that Bonaparte has seized the Holy Land?

Q. Yes, I know that, but what does our general, who eats bacon and sausages, have in common with the Messiah? Did not Godefroi de Bouillon also seize Palestine without the Temple of Jerusalem rising from its ruins?

A. Well, this time it will rise. There are 1,500,000 Jews in Europe who, if they must, will sacrifice their fortunes and their lives for such a glorious enterprise.

As the child of Abraham uttered these last words with passion, I feigned approval of his ideas. He told us about his hopes at great length and repeated that Bonaparte was the Messiah.

I do not know if my companion was more fanatic than the rest of his brothers, those who practise religion are all more or less so, but I have to admit that the unction with which he spoke, and even more the 1,500,000 Hebrews he put forward, singularly tickled my thoughts, especially when I thought about how one could greatly profit from these people by caressing their religious prejudices.

I will leave it to your wisdom to think about whether this idea has any value, or to laugh about it as a joke.

Source: Archives nationales, AFIII, 21 b, letter from the *commissaire* of the Nord to Merlin de Douai, 28 February 1799, in *La Révolution française à travers les archives* (Paris, 1988), pp. 426–9.

Justifying the coup of Brumaire, 10 November 1799

The proclamation, posted in Paris and reprinted in the *Moniteur*, constituted the official version of the coup. The events of 19 Brumaire which took place at Saint-Cloud were thus twisted and contorted—the angry scene in the Council of Five Hundred was portrayed as a plot

Séance du Corps-Législatif à l'Orangerie de S. Cloud(.,
Apparition de Bonaparte et Journée libératrice du 19 brum.* an 8. (10. 9.* 1799.)
A Paris chez Decourtis, Rue des Grands Degrés N. 12.

Figure 5 The appearance of Bonaparte at the Orangerie, 19 Brumaire. In order to justify the coup of Brumaire, the myth of an assassination attempt against Bonaparte was circulated both in the print media and in anonymous popular engravings that could be bought on the streets. The attack on Bonaparte's person was meant to be equated with an attack on liberty. Source: Bibliothèque nationale de France.

against Bonaparte's life and the deputies were made out to have been armed with stilettos: 'twenty assassins threw themselves on me and aimed at my chest.' Moreover, there was no mention made of Sieyès or Lucien Bonaparte who both played significant roles leading up to and during the coup. The proclamation is revealing not only for how Bonaparte perceived himself but for how he wanted to be perceived. He posed as someone who was above party politics, as the restorer of moderation, as a representative of the conservative wing of the Revolution.

On my return to Paris, I found division among all the authorities and agreement only on one truth, that the Constitution was half destroyed and could no longer save liberty.

Every faction came to me, confided their plans in me, and asked me for my support: I refused to be the man of one faction.

The Council of Elders summoned me; I replied to its call. A plan for a general restoration had been decided on by men whom the nation is accustomed to see as the defenders of liberty, equality and property: this plan demanded calm and independent scrutiny, free from all influence and fear. The Council of Elders resolved to transfer the Legislative Body to Saint-Cloud; it gave me the responsibility of organising the force necessary for its independence. I believed it my duty to my fellow citizens, to the soldiers perishing in our armies, and for the national glory acquired at the cost of their blood, to accept the command.

The Councils assembled at Saint-Cloud; republican troops guaranteed their safety from without, but assassins created terror from within. Several deputies from the Council of Five Hundred, armed with stilettos and firearms, circulated death threats.

The plans which should have been developed were held up, the majority were disorganised, the most intrepid speakers were disconcerted, and the futility of every wise proposition evident.

I took my indignation and grief to the Council of Elders. I asked it to guarantee the execution of its generous plans. I presented it with the evils besetting the fatherland which they were able to imagine. They united with me through new testimony of their steadfast will.

I then went to the Council of Five Hundred; alone, unarmed, head uncovered, just as the Elders had received and applauded me. I came to remind the majority of its wishes, and to assure it of its power.

The stilettos which threatened the deputies were immediately raised against their liberator; twenty assassins threw themselves on me and aimed at my chest. The grenadiers of the Legislative Body, whom I had left at the entrance to the hall, ran to put themselves between me and the assassins. One of the brave grenadiers (Thomé) was struck and had his clothes torn by a stiletto. They carried me out.

At the same time, cries of outlaw were heard against the defender of the law. It was the fierce cry of the assassins against the force destined to put them down.

They crowded around the president, uttering threats, arms in hand; they ordered him to declare me an outlaw. I was informed of this, and I ordered that he be snatched from their fury, and six grenadiers of the Legislative Body carried him out. Immediately afterwards, grenadiers from the Legislative Body charged into the hall and had it evacuated.

The factions, thus intimidated, dispersed and fled. The majority, freed from their attacks, returned freely and peaceably to the meeting hall, heard the propositions which were made for public safety, deliberated, and prepared the salutary resolution which is to become the new and provisional law of the Republic.

Frenchmen, you will undoubtedly recognise in this conduct the zeal of a soldier of liberty, of a citizen devoted to the Republic. Conservative, tutelary and liberal ideas have been restored to their rightful place by the dispersal of the rebels who oppressed the Councils and who, having become the most odious of men, have not ceased to be the most contemptible.

Signed BONAPARTE

Source: *Correspondance de Napoléon Ier*, vol. 6, pp. 6–8.

17

LAW AND ORDER

Crushing the rebels in the Vendée, 14 January 1800

In order to consolidate his régime, it was important to bring the civil unrest
that had torn the country apart for so many years to an end. Measures of
repression were thus carried out in the provinces where 'Military Tribunals'
were used to put an end to what was commonly referred to as 'brigandage'. In the Vendée, General Brune (1763–1815) was charged with
annihilating the last of the Chouans. It was, of course, a continuation of the
policy already adopted by the Directory, but it also fell within the logic of
Bonaparte's attitude towards peoples in insurrection first expressed in
Italy: an exemplary punishment had to be meted out.

To General Brune, commander-in-chief of the Army of the West
. . . The government will do no more than it already has done for the departments of the west.

The Army of the West is made up of 60,000 men under arms. You will
pursue the brigands with energy, you will put yourself in a position to quickly
end this war. The peace of Europe is dependent on its end.

. . . The suspension of hostilities concluded between General Hédouville and
the Chouans will only last until 1 Pluviôse [21 January]. Georges, who com-
mands the rebels in the Morbihan, is not included.

I calculate that on the evening of the 27th [Pluviôse, or 16 February] you
will arrive in Angers; only remain there long enough to order the 60th half-
brigade and the troops you can relieve from this department to march for the
Morbihan, and then leave for Nantes.

From there, march to the Morbihan where you will find the 22nd and the
72nd. Disperse Georges's assemblies. Take his cannon, his stores of grain (he
has a great quantity on the coast which he sells to England). Finally, begin to
make the whole weight and horror of war come down on the rebels of the
Morbihan. At the beginning of Pluviôse, make sure:

1   that English ships anchored off the coast of Morbihan no longer commu-
    nicate with Georges;
2   that they see from the top of their masts the flags of the Republic disperse
    the brigands and destroy their hope.

Diplomatic reasons of the greatest importance make it necessary for the
English to learn that considerable French forces are pursuing Georges within
the first five days of Pluviôse, so that they send the news to England.
. . . Welcome any individual who submits, but do not tolerate any meeting
of leaders; do not enter into any further diplomatic negotiations.
   [Have] a great tolerance for priests; but act severely against the larger communes in order to oblige them to protect themselves and to protect the smaller
ones. Do not spare communes that behave badly. Burn a few farms and a few
large villages in the Morbihan, and start to make a few examples.
   Do not let your troops want for either bread, meat or pay. There are enough
guilty [people] in the departments to maintain your troops. It is only by
making war terrible for them that the inhabitants themselves will unite
against the brigands and will at last feel that their apathy is dangerous. . . .

Source: *Correspondance de Napoléon Ier*, vol. 6, pp. 109–12.

<hr />

Decree limiting the French press, 17 January 1800

Military repression was followed by an attempt to censor those who
opposed Bonaparte's policies. As early as February 1800, fifty newspapers were closed down, leaving only thirteen in circulation. By 1811, this
number had been further reduced to four. The same thing occurred for
the theatre. Bonaparte repressed both the left and the right and called
on the French people to forget their differences and to think instead of
the unity of the French nation.

The Consuls of the Republic, considering that a part of the newspapers printed
in the Department of the Seine [Paris] are instruments in the hands of the enemies of the Republic, and that the government is especially charged by the
French people to watch over their security, decrees the following.
   Article 1. The Minister of Police will allow, during the entire course of
the war, the printing, publication and distribution of the newspapers hereby
designated: [the names of thirteen papers follow], and newspapers *exclusively*
devoted to the sciences, arts, literature, commerce, announcements and
public notices.

Article 2. The Minister of General Police will immediately report on all newspapers printed in the other departments.

Article 3. The Minister of Police will make sure that no new newspapers are published in the department of the Seine as well as in other departments of the Republic.

Article 4. The owners and editors of the newspapers retained by the present decree will present themselves to the Minister of Police in order to prove their qualifications as French citizens, their residence and their signature, and they will promise loyalty to the Constitution.

Article 5. All newspapers which include articles contrary to the social order, to the sovereignty of the people and to the glory of the armies, or which publish abuse against governments and nations friendly to or allied with the Republic, even when those articles are taken from foreign periodicals, will be suppressed immediately.

Source: Buchez and Roux, *Histoire parlementaire de la Révolution française* (Paris, 1834–8), vol. 38, pp. 331–2.

Bonaparte's speech to the priests of Milan, 5 June 1800

Another facet of restoring order in France was to mend the broken bridges with the Catholic Church. The following eulogy to Catholicism and the condemnation of the anticlerical policies of the Directory before a gathering of priests in Milan reveals that Bonaparte was already seriously thinking of a reconciliation between Church and State well before the process of the Concordat was set in motion.

I wanted to see you assembled here in order to have the satisfaction of telling you myself about the feelings which move me on the subject of the apostolic, Catholic and Roman religion. Persuaded that Catholicism is the only religion which can procure true happiness for a well-ordered society, and strengthen the basis of a good government, I assure you that I will apply myself at all times and by every means to its protection and defence. You, the ministers of this religion, which is of course also mine, I regard you as my dearest friends; I declare that I will consider as disturbing public peace and as an enemy of the common good, and that I will punish as such in the most severe and obvious manner, and even, if I have to, with the death penalty, anyone who in the least insults our common religion, or who dares commit the slightest outrage against your sacred persons.

My formal intention is that the Christian, Catholic and Roman religion be maintained in its entirety and that it be practised publicly, and that it enjoy this public exercise with a freedom as full, extensive and inviolable as during the period when I entered these fortunate regions for the first time. All the changes which then took place, mainly in discipline, were done against my inclinations and my way of thinking. Simple agent of a government that was not in the least concerned with the Catholic religion, I was then unable to prevent all the disorders they wanted to stir up at any price, with the aim of overthrowing it. At the moment when I have been provided with full powers, I have decided to make use of every means I believe to be appropriate to assure and guarantee this religion.

Modern philosophers have endeavoured to persuade France that the Catholic religion was the implacable enemy of every democratic system and of every republican government. Hence the cruel persecution the French Republic carried out against the religion and its ministers; hence all the horrors which that unfortunate people were delivered up to. The diversity of opinion which, during the revolutionary era, reigned in France on the subject of religion has been one of the sources of this disorder. The experience opened the eyes of the French and convinced them that of all religions there was none that adapted itself, like the Catholic religion, to diverse forms of government, which more greatly favours, in particular, democratic republican government, better establishes rights and throws more daylight on principles. I too am a philosopher and I know that, no matter what the society, no man can pass for just and virtuous if he does not know where he comes from and where he is going. Reason alone will not give us any definite information about that. Without religion, we walk constantly in the shadows and the Catholic religion is the only one which gives man certain and infallible enlightenment about his nature and his final end. No society can exist without morals; there are no good morals without religion; only religion, then, can give the State a firm and lasting support. A society without religion is like a ship without a compass. A ship in that case can neither assure its route nor hope to enter port. A society without religion, always agitated, perpetually rocked by the shock of the most violent passions, itself experiences all the furies of a civil war which precipitates it into the abyss of evil, and which, sooner or later, infallibly leads to its ruin.

France, learning from its misfortune, has finally opened its eyes; it has recognised that the Catholic religion is like an anchor which alone can fix it in its agitations and save it from the efforts of the tempest. It has, as a result, recalled religion to its bosom. I cannot deny that I have contributed a good deal to this great work. I can assure you that churches have been opened in France, that the Catholic religion is regaining its former brilliance, and that the people look with respect on those sacred pastors who return, full of zeal, amid the abandoned flock.

Do not let the manner in which the late pope was treated inspire you with fear. Pius VI owed his misfortune in part to those to whom he had given his confidence and in part to the cruel policies of the Directory. When I am able to get in touch with the new pope, I hope that I will have the fortune to remove all the obstacles that may yet oppose the complete reconciliation of France with the head of the Church. I am aware of what you have suffered, as individuals as well as in terms of property. As individuals you will be, once again, sacred in the future and respected by everybody. As for your property, I will take care to give the necessary orders so that it is returned to you at least in part, and I will act in such a way that you will be assured for ever of the means of existing honourably.

This is what I wanted to communicate to you on the subject of the Christian, Catholic and Roman religion. I hope that the expression of these sentiments remains etched on your minds, that you put into order what I have just said, and I will make sure that the public is informed through the printed word, so that my arrangements are known not only in Italy and France but in all of Europe.

Source: Roger Dufraisse, *Napoléon. Correspondance officielle* (Paris, 1970), vol. 1, pp. 93–4.

Senatus Consultum on the 'Infernal Machine' plot, 5 January 1801

On Christmas Eve 1800, while Bonaparte was on his way to the Opera, a bomb exploded in the rue Saint Niçaise after his carriage had already driven past. It nevertheless killed two people and wounded six others. Although the Minister of Police, Joseph Fouché, discovered that the assassination attempt was royalist in origin, Bonaparte nevertheless used the 'Infernal Machine' plot as a pretext to do away with potential political rivals, and to eliminate what remained of the revolutionary left—a mixture of Jacobins, Enragés and Hébertistes. One hundred and thirty-two people were thus deported to either French Guyana or to the Seychelles Islands to suffer what was known as the 'dry guillotine'.

Bonaparte, First Consul, in the name of the French people, proclaims the Senatus Consultum the terms of which follow.

SENATUS CONSULTUM—15 NIVÔSE, YEAR IX
The Conservative Senate, assembled with the number of members required by Article 90 of the Constitution;

deliberating on the government's message of the 14th of this month, transmitted to it by three Councillors of State, the said message relative to the assassination attempt of 3 Nivôse, and to the precautionary act of the superior police which it necessitates;

After a second reading of the diverse documents with this message, to wit:

1 the speech of the government spokesman;
2 the deliberation of the Council of State of 11 Nivôse;
3 the report from the Minister of Police of 11 Nivôse;
4 the decree of the Consuls of the Republic of the same day which places the citizens whose names are on the said decree under special surveillance outside the European territory of the Republic;

after having heard the report of the Special Commission, named in yesterday's session, to render an exceptional account of the said documents;

considering that it has been well known for several years that, within the Republic and in particular in the city of Paris, a number of individuals exist who, at different periods of the Revolution, have sullied themselves with the greatest crimes;

that these individuals, taking the name and the rights of the people, have been and continue to be at all times the source of every plot, the agents of every assassination attempt, the venal instrument of every foreign and domestic enemy, the perturbers of every government, and a curse on the social order;

that the amnesties accorded these individuals in different circumstances, far from bringing them back to obey the law, have only emboldened them by habit, and encouraged them by impunity;

that their plots and assassination attempts recently repeated, by the very fact that they have failed, become a new reason to attack the government whose justice threatens them with a last punishment;

that as a consequence of the documents submitted to the Conservative Senate, that the presence of these individuals in the Republic, and in particular in this great capital, is a constant cause of alarm and secret terror for peaceful citizens, that they fear the chance success of some conspiracy by these violent men and the return of their vengeance;

considering that the Constitution has not determined the security measures necessary to take in a case of this nature; that, as a result of the silence of the Constitution and the law on the means to oppose the dangers which every day threaten the commonwealth, the desire and the will of the people can only be expressed through the authority which it has specially charged to preserve the social contract, and to maintain or to annul acts favourable or contrary to the constitutional charter;

that, according to this principle, the Senate, interpreter and guardian of this charter, is the natural judge of the measure proposed on this occasion by the government;

145

that this measure has the advantage of uniting the two characteristics of
firmness and leniency in that, on the one hand, it removes from society
the trouble-makers which put it in danger, and on the other leaves them
a last means of making amends;

finally, considering that, according to the very expression of the Council of
State, that provisional order of the government to the Conservative
Senate, to call for the examination of its own acts and the decision of the
tutelary body, becomes, by force of example, a safeguard capable of reas-
suring the nation for what will follow, and of securing the government
itself against any dangerous act to public liberty;

For all these reasons, the Conservative Senate declares:

that the Act of Government dated 14 Nivôse is a protective measure of the
Constitution.

Signed Laplace, President; Clément de Ris de Rousseau, Secretary

ACT OF GOVERNMENT DATED 14 NIVÔSE, YEAR IX
PROMULGATED ON THE 18TH (AS BEING PART OF THE SENATUS
CONSULTUM OF THE 15TH)

The Consuls of the Republic, based on the report of the Minister of Police, the
Council of State having heard, order the following.

Article 1. The citizens whose names follow will be placed under special surveillance, outside the European territory of the Republic: [a list of 132 names
follows.]

Article 2. The Ministers of Marine and General Police are charged with the
execution of the present order, which will be published in the *Bulletin des lois*.

Source: Buchez and Roux, *Histoire parlementaire de la Révolution française*, vol.
38, pp. 375–8.

Report by the sub-prefect of Nyons (Drôme), 23 January 1802

Great strides were made by Bonaparte in restoring law and order in the
countryside, and especially in those regions that had been in revolt.
Nevertheless, banditry, partly as a result of conscription and desertion,
could not be eliminated entirely, as this sub-prefect from the department
of the Drôme in the south of France complains. Note the presence of
deserters in brigand bands, and desertion as a cover for true brigands.

REPORT ON THE SITUATION IN THE 3RD *ARRONDISSEMENT* OF
THE DEPARTMENT OF THE DRÔME, DURING THE MONTHS OF
VENDÉMIAIRE, BRUMAIRE AND FRIMAIRE, YEAR X
[SEPTEMBER–DECEMBER 1801]

Brigandage, that destructive curse which has devastated this region for such a long time, which exiled peace and security for several years, being almost completely defeated, its impure remains have dared, during this last trimester, to make new attacks against the public security of this *arrondissement*. The presence of a few of these bandits who, sometimes, are still seen, no longer alarm citizens assured of rapid and effective protection, and who are full of confidence in the wisdom, activity and zeal of the higher authorities of the department. If the inhabitants of the countryside removed from the provincial capital have not come out strongly against the brigands, and suffer them in their midst, it is the result of ignorance which renders their coarse spirits more susceptible of impressions of fear and terror, or of a simplicity which it is easy to take advantage of. The surest and most customary means is to pass oneself off as a deserter. It is by means of this disguise that the brigands find shelter in the mountains of this *arrondissement*, without arousing mistrust or suspicion. One cannot nevertheless deny that there are always a few individuals who are cowardly and criminal enough to secretly help and protect them.

In a region whose area is considerable, and whose population is not very great, where the most general occupation is the cultivation of the land, which offers, in all seasons, constant and uninterrupted work, where the produce suffices the needs of the inhabitant, begging and vagrancy are almost unknown. Also, very few beggars are ever seen. Women, children and disabled men of the *arrondissement*, leaving their commune every now and then, go into the prosperous towns to solicit the generosity of its citizens, and then return home with the money of help and pity which enables them to subsist for a time. We almost never see foreign beggars arrive here.

The conduct and the surveillance of travellers does not take up much of the police's time. This *arrondissement* is not particularly frequented and that is because its commerce is limited, and because it is, by its position, far from the large communication routes. Those who are under surveillance are very few. No complaints and no unfavourable information about them has been received.

As much as the position of this *arrondissement* is satisfactory from the point of view of the civil police, it is distressing from the point of the view of the rural police. Rural offences and the night-time stealing of fruit have been common and multiple. The disorder has been such that proprietors have been obliged to come together to defend their harvests, and one individual who was stealing olives at night was killed in Frimaire in the region of the town of Nyons. The authors of this murder have escaped prosecution. But in condemning what is criminal about his action, one has to admit that it has been useful for the security of the countryside.

It would be appropriate to develop here the causes, to propose a few remedies for the ills about which everyone complains, but when the former are known, when everything proves that the latter are being looked into, it would be a waste of time to go on about this subject; which leads me to bring this letter to an end.

Written at Nyons, 3 Pluviôse, Year 10
For the sub-prefect
[illegible signature]

Source: Archives nationales, F^7 8428.

18

RULE BY PLEBISCITE

The Concordat, 10 September 1801

One of Napoleon's first priorities was to re-establish good relations with the Papacy, which had fought the revolutionary Church settlement tooth and nail. Napoleon gained everything he desired in the Concordat: he appointed the bishops and archbishops of the French Church, and all bishops had to swear an oath of fidelity to the French Republic.

CONVENTION BETWEEN THE FRENCH GOVERNMENT AND HIS HOLINESS PIUS VII

The government of the French Republic recognises that the Roman, Catholic and apostolic religion is the religion of the great majority of French citizens.

His Holiness likewise recognises that this same religion has derived and at this moment again expects the greatest benefit and grandeur from the establishment of Catholic worship in France and from the personal profession which the Consuls of the Republic make of it.

In consequence, after this mutual recognition, as much for the benefit of religion as for the maintenance of internal tranquillity, they have agreed on the following.

Article 1. The Catholic, apostolic and Roman religion shall be freely exercised in France. Its worship shall be public, and in conformity with the police regulations which the government shall deem necessary for the public tranquillity.

Article 2. The Holy See, in concert with the government, will make a new division of the French diocese.

Article 3. His Holiness declares to the holders of French bishoprics that he expects from them, with firm confidence, for the good of peace and unity, every sacrifice, even that of their sees.

After this exhortation, if they refuse the sacrifice demanded by the good of the Church (a refusal that His Holiness nevertheless does not expect), he will

Figure 6 Napoleon Bonaparte, First Consul, upholder and restorer of the Catholic faith in France. The policies of religious and social reconciliation carried out during the Consulate enabled Bonaparte to restore a degree of political stability in France. In this engraving, Bonaparte, with his hand literally supporting the cross and standing next to the Papal Nuncio, Cardinal Caprara, is portrayed as the upholder and restorer of the Catholic faith in France. Source: Bibliothèque nationale de France.

be provided, by new office holders, to the government of the bishoprics of the new divisions, in the following manner:

Article 4. The First Consul of the Republic will make appointments, in the three months following the publication of the bull of His Holiness, to the archbishoprics and bishoprics of the new divisions. His Holiness shall confer canonic institution, following the forms established in relation to France before the change of government [that is, before the Revolution].

Article 5. The First Consul shall also make nominations to bishoprics that fall vacant in the future; canonic institution shall be granted by the Holy See, in conformity with the preceding article.

Article 6. Before entering upon their functions, the bishops shall directly swear, at the hands of the First Consul, the oath of loyalty which was in use before the change of government, expressed in the following terms:

> I swear and promise to God, upon the holy scriptures, to obey and remain loyal to the government established by the Constitution of the French Republic. I also promise not to have any correspondence, nor to assist by any counsel, nor to support any league, either within or without, which is contrary to the public tranquillity; and if, within my diocese or elsewhere, I learn that anything to the prejudice of the State is going on, I will make it known to the government.

Article 7. Ecclesiastics of the second order shall swear the same oath at the hands of the civil authorities designated by the government.

Article 8. The following prayer shall be recited at the end of divine service, in all the Catholic churches in France:

> *Domine, salvam fac Republicam;*
> *Domine, salvos fac Consules.*

Article 9. Bishops shall make new divisions of parishes within their diocese, which will only come into effect after the consent of the government.

Article 10. Bishops will name their parish priests. The choice can only be made from people approved by the government.

Article 11. Bishops may have a chapter in their cathedrals, and a seminary for their diocese, without the obligation of the government to endow them.

Article 12. All metropolitan churches, cathedrals, parishes and other non-alienated property necessary for worship, shall be placed at the disposition of the bishops.

Article 13. His Holiness, for the good of peace and for the successful re-establishment of the Catholic religion, declares that neither he nor his successors will trouble in any manner the purchasers of alienated ecclesiastical goods, and in consequence, the ownership of these same goods, the rights and revenues attached to them, shall remain untransferable in their hands or those of their relatives who are entitled to them.

Article 14. The government assures a suitable salary to bishops and parish priests whose dioceses and parishes are comprised with the new division.

Article 15. The government shall likewise take measures so that French Catholics may, if they so desire, give donations to Church foundations.

Article 16. His Holiness recognises in the First Consul of the French Republic the same rights and prerogatives enjoyed by former governments.

Article 17. It is agreed by the contracting parties that, in case one of the successors of the current First Consul is not Catholic, the rights and prerogatives mentioned in the above article, and the nomination of bishoprics, shall be regulated, in relation to him, by a new convention.

Ratifications shall be exchanged at Paris within forty days.

Done at Paris, 26 Messidor, Year IX of the French Republic

Source: Buchez and Roux, *Histoire parlementaire de la Révolution française*, vol. 38, pp. 465–70.

The Consulate for Life, 1802

The referendum was a means used by Napoleon to give his régime an air of popular support and was used on four separate occasions to approve a change in the Constitution. It was first used in 1799 when the Constitution of Year VIII was submitted for approval. We now know as a result of Claude Langlois' research carried out in the 1970s that the results were largely falsified. Napoleon again used a referendum in 1802, this time asking for approval for appointment as Consul for Life. Approximately 3.5 million people voted for, and about 8,300 voted against the proposition. Once again there was some falsification of the vote, but not on the levels that took place previously. Electors did not always answer with a simple 'Yes' or 'No'; they often wrote long comments justifying their choices. These comments, even if they were restricted to the élite of society, nevertheless offer a rare insight into what people thought of Bonaparte, both from the perspective of the opposition, as well as those who were taken in by the régime's propaganda.

A hostile response from the Aube

I would vote in the affirmative on the question proposed above if the history of the [world's] peoples did not teach me that placing for life the supreme magistrature in any state, [even] in the hands of the most just, has often changed the heart and the commendable frame of mind of the person who has been invested and that the office has almost always, I say, been dangerous for the liberty of the public and the individual. I admire, like so many others, Bonaparte's military and political talents, but my enthusiasm does not lead me to believe that he is infallible, or to number him among the gods. Guided by these considerations, I am not of the opinion that Napoleon Bonaparte should be designated Consul for Life.

Source: Archives nationales, BII 483A.

A favourable response from the Var

This reply uses a little more poetic licence, something that was not uncommon for the day.

The favourite of Mars and the friend of Minerva!
The terror of Europe and the friend of the French!
Bonaparte! . . . Great God, may your hand preserve him!
May he be our Consul and may he be it for ever!

Source: Archives nationales, BII 629A.

Founding the Empire, 1804

The referendum submitted to the French people in May 1804 asking for approval of the transformation of the life consulate into a hereditary empire gave similar results to that of 1802: about 3.5 million in favour and about 2,500 against. The comments contained in the plebiscite of 1804 are, however, much thinner on the ground than in 1802, and are mostly favourable to Napoleon. The little opposition which is expressed is not against the creation of the title emperor, which people generally seemed to think Napoleon deserved, but against the creation of a hereditary title.

Some reservations in Paris

Yes, on condition that Napoleon's heirs are like him.

I vote yes—to the exclusion of women and their descendants.

Yes, a hundred times yes, for the title, because one cannot honour and love too much our leader, but no, for ever no, to heredity which for me renders power odious.

Source: Archives nationales, BII 815A and B.

A hostile response from Troyes

I consider the reign of law like the reign of people whose will the law expresses, but the reign of one man seems to me irreconcilable with the reign of the whole. Napoleon Bonaparte deserves all possible honours. I even believe him to be worthy of the title emperor, but will his successors, in inheriting his glory, also inherit his character, his courage, his virtues? I say then no and I will not say otherwise, unless the immutability of the laws which constitute the Republic one and indivisible, equality before the law, civil liberty, the liberty of the press, the liberty of conscience, in one word Liberty, can be demonstrated without any possible doubt and unless an institution which is wise, strong and immutable can guarantee the inviolability of these laws. I mean to strongly oppose everything that tends to violate them, an opposition to the idea of despotism. Such is my wish.

Source: Archives nationales, BII 683A.

19

GOVERNING THE EMPIRE

The Civil Code, March 1803–March 1804

Napoleon brought to completion a project dear to the hearts of the revolutionaries, the drafting of new law codes. The Civil Code was the most important of a number of codes (civil procedure, commercial, criminal, penal, rural) because it institutionalised equality under the law (at least for adult men), guaranteed the abolition of feudalism and, not least, gave the nation one single code of law replacing the hundreds in effect in 1789. Although not of his making, Napoleon nevertheless presided over more than half of the one hundred sessions of the Council of State that took place over the three years it took to finalise the code, thereby imprinting it with his own personal values. There was nothing unusual about them, however. They were widely accepted throughout France. The Code thus institutionalised the subservience of women in marriage and of workers in their places of employment. Divorce was still allowed (it had been established in 1792), but under conditions that were very unfavourable to wives.

BOOK I OF THE RIGHTS AND RESPECTIVE DUTIES OF
HUSBAND AND WIFE

212 Husband and wife mutually owe each other fidelity, succour and assistance.

213 The husband owes protection to his wife, the wife obedience to her husband.

214 The wife is obliged to live with her husband, and to follow him wherever he may think proper to dwell: the husband is bound to receive her, and to furnish her with everything necessary for the purposes of life, according to his means and condition.

215 The wife cannot act in law without the authority of the husband, even where she shall be a public trader, or not in community, or separate in property. . . .

217 A wife, although not in community, or separate in property, cannot give, pledge or acquire by free or chargeable title, without the concurrence of her husband in the act, or his consent in writing. . . .

TITLE VI   OF CAUSES OF DIVORCE

The husband may demand divorce for cause of adultery on the part of his wife.

The wife may demand divorce for cause of adultery on the part of her husband, where he shall have kept his concubine in their common house.

SECTION II   OF THE PROVISIONAL MEASURES TO WHICH THE DEMAND OF DIVORCE FOR CAUSE DEFINED MAY GIVE CAUSE

267   The provisional administration of the children shall remain with the husband plaintiff or defendant in divorce, unless it shall be otherwise ordered by the tribunal, at the request either of the mother, or of the family, or of the imperial proctor, for the greater benefit of the children. . . .

SECTION III   OF EXCEPTIONS AT LAW AGAINST THE SUIT FOR DIVORCE FOR CAUSE DETERMINATE

272 The suit of divorce shall be extinguished by the reconciliation of the parties, whether occurring subsequently to the facts which might have authorized such suit, or subsequently to the petition for divorce. . . .

297 In case of divorce by mutual consent, neither of the parties shall be allowed to contract a new marriage until the expiration of three years from the pronunciation of the divorce.

298 In the case of divorce admitted by law for cause of adultery, the guilty party shall never be permitted to marry with his accomplice. The wife adulteress shall be condemned in the same judgement; and, on the request of the public minister, to confinement in a house of correction, for a determinate period, which shall not be less than three months, nor exceed two years. . . .

302 The children shall be entrusted to the married Party who has obtained the divorce, unless the court, on petition of the family, or by the commissioner of government, gives order, for the greater benefit of the children, that all or some of them shall be committed to the care either of the other married party, or of a third person.

Source: Bryant Barrett (ed.), *The Code Napoleon*, 2 vols (London, 1811), vol. 1, pp. 47, 49, 57; vol. 2, p. 358.

Napoleon on governing Italy, 5 June 1805

Napoleon's son-in-law, Eugène de Beauharnais (1781–1824), was named Viceroy of Italy at the age of 23. He is considered to be one of Napoleon's most capable and enlightened rulers. Napoleon's instructions to Eugène on how best to govern the Italian people give an interesting insight into his attitudes towards politics. The key word seems to be mistrust.

By entrusting you with the government of Our Kingdom of Italy, We have given you proof of the respect your conduct has inspired in Us. But you are still at an age when one does not realise the perversity of men's hearts; I cannot therefore too strongly recommend to you prudence and circumspection. Our Italian subjects are more deceitful by nature than the citizens of France. The only way in which you can keep their respect, and serve their happiness, is by letting no-one have your complete confidence, and by never telling anyone what you really think of the ministers and high officials of your court. Dissimulation, which comes naturally at a maturer age, has to be emphasised and inculcated at yours. If you ever find yourself speaking unnecessarily, and from the heart, say to yourself: 'I have made a mistake', and do not do it again. Show respect for the nation you govern, and show it all the more as you discover less grounds for it. You will come to see in time that there is little difference between one nation and another. The aim of your administration is the happiness of My Italian peoples; and the first sacrifice you will have to make will be to fall in with certain of their customs which you detest. In any position but that of Viceroy of Italy you may boast of being a Frenchman: but here you must forget it, and count yourself a failure unless the Italians believe that you love them. They know there is no love without respect. Learn their language; frequent their society; single them out for special attention at public functions; like what they like, and approve what they approve.

The less you talk the better: you are not well enough educated, and you have not enough knowledge to take part in informal debates. Learn to listen, and remember that silence is often as effective as a display of knowledge. Do not be ashamed to ask questions. Though a viceroy, you are only 23; and however much people flatter you, in reality they all know your limitations, and honour you less for what they believe you to be than for what they hope you will become.

Do not imitate me in every respect; you need more reserve.

Do not preside often over the State Council; you have too little experience to do so successfully—though I see no objection to your attending it, while an assessor acts as president, from his ordinary seat. Your ignorance of Italian, and of legislation too for that matter, is an excellent excuse for staying away. Anyhow, never make a speech there: they would listen to you and not answer you back: but they would see at once that you are not competent to discuss business. So long as a prince holds his tongue, his power is incalculable; he should never talk unless he knows he is the ablest man in the room.

Do not trust spies. They are more trouble than they are worth. There is never enough unrest in Milan to bother about, and I expect it is the same elsewhere. Your military police make sure of the army, and that is all you want.

The army is the one thing you can deal with personally, and from your own knowledge.

Work with your ministers twice a week—once with each of them separately, and once with them all together in Council. Half the battle will be won when your ministers and councillors realise that your only object in consulting them is to listen to reason, and to prevent yourself being taken by surprise.

At public functions, and at fêtes, whenever you have Frenchmen and foreigners together, arrange beforehand where they are to be, and what you are to do. It is better never to form a following; and you must take the greatest care not to expose yourself to any sort of affront. If anything of the kind occurs, do not stand for it. Prince, ambassador, minister, general—whoever it may be, even if it is the Austrian or Russian ambassador—have him arrested on the spot. On the other hand, such incidents are always a nuisance; and what matters little in my case might have troublesome results in yours.

Nothing is so advisable as to treat the Italians well, and to get to know all their names and families. Do not show too much attention to foreigners; there is nothing to gain by it. An ambassador will never speak well of you, because it is his business to speak ill. Ministers of foreign countries are, in plain words, accredited spies. It is well to keep them at arm's length. They always think better of those they seldom see than of their professed friends and benefactors.

There is only one man here at Milan who really matters—the Minister of Finance: he is a hard worker, and knows his job well.

Although they know I am behind you, I have no doubt they are trying to gauge your character. See that your orders are carried out, particularly in the army: never allow them to be disobeyed.

The public decree that I have signed defines the powers I am delegating to you. I am reserving for myself the most important of all—the power of directing your operations. Send me an account of your doings every day. It is only by degrees that you will come to understand how I look at everything.

Do not show my letters to a single soul, under any pretext whatsoever. It ought not to be known that I write to you, or even that I write at all. Keep one room to which no-one is admitted—not even your private secretaries.

You will find M. Méjan useful, if he does not try to make money; and he will not do that if he knows that you are watching him, and that a single act of this kind will ruin him in my eyes as well as yours. He should be well paid, and have good prospects of promotion. But in that case he must be available at all hours, and amusing himself the rest of the day. And you will have to rebuke him for a tendency he shares with all Frenchmen to depreciate this country—all the more so as it is accompanied by melancholia. Frenchmen are never happy out of France.

Keep my household and stables in order, and make up all my accounts at least once a week; this is all the more necessary as they have no idea how to manage things.

Hold a review in Milan every month.

Cultivate the young Italians rather than the old: the latter are good for nothing . . .

You have an important position, and will find it pretty hard to work. Try to get to know the history of all the towns in My Kingdom of Italy; visit the fortresses, and all the famous battlefields. It is likely enough that you will see fighting before you are 30, and it is a tremendous asset to know the lie of the land.

Source: *Correspondance de Napoléon Ier*, vol. 6, pp. 488–91.

The Imperial Catechism, April 1806

The Imperial Catechism, which did not in fact appear in print until August 1808, was a logical extension of the Concordat. It was put together by Napoleon's Minister of Religion, Jean-Etienne-Marie Portalis (1745–1807) and the abbé Etienne Bernier (1762–1806). Pius VII rejected the first draft because of its obvious subordination of religion to Napoleon. Nevertheless, the Papal Legate to Paris, Cardinal Caprara (1733–1810), was willing to overlook the pope's objections and authorised acceptance of the document. Along with the Concordat, it was one of the instruments used by Napoleon to assure himself of the support of French Catholics. Note the association of Napoleon with God who thereby becomes His instrument on earth.

LESSON VII

Q. What are the duties of Christians towards the princes who govern them, and what in particular are our duties towards our emperor, Napoleon I?

A. Christians owe the Princes who govern them, and in particular we owe our emperor, Napoleon I, love, respect, obedience, loyalty, military service, the taxes ordered for the preservation and the defence of the Empire and his throne. We also owe him our fervent prayers for the salvation and spiritual and temporal prosperity of the State.

Q. Why are we obliged to carry out these duties towards the emperor?

A. First, because God who creates empires and distributes them according to His will, in showering our emperor with gifts, both in peace and in war, has established him as our Sovereign, and has made him the minister of His power and image on earth. To honour and to serve our emperor is then to honour and to serve God Himself. Second, because Our Lord Jesus Christ, both by His teaching and His example, has taught us Himself what we owe to our Sovereign. He was born obeying the laws of Caesar Augustus; He paid the prescribed taxes; and He even ordered to render unto God that which belongs to God, and to Caesar that which belongs to Caesar.

Q. Are there not particular reasons which should attach us more strongly to Napoleon I, our emperor?

A. Yes, for he is the one God created in difficult circumstances in order to re-establish public worship and the holy religion of our fathers, and in order to become its protector. He has restored and preserved public order, by his profound and active wisdom; he defends the State by his powerful arm; he has become the anointed of the Lord, by the consecration he received from the Sovereign Pontiff, head of the universal Church.

Q. What should we think of those who fail in their duty towards our emperor?

A. According to the apostle Saint Paul, they would be resisting the order established by God Himself, and would render themselves worthy of eternal damnation.

Q. Should the duties that we owe our emperor equally bind us to his legitimate successors, in the order established by the Constitutions of the Empire?

A. Yes, without a doubt, for we read in the Holy Scriptures that God, Lord of heaven and earth, by command of His supreme will and by His providence, gives empires not only to one person in particular, but also to his family.

Q. What are our duties towards our magistrates?

A. We should honour, respect and obey them because they are the depositories of the authority of our emperor.

Q. What is forbidden by the fourth Commandment?

A. We are forbidden to be disobedient towards our superiors, to harm them or to speak ill of them.

Source: André Latreille, *Le Catéchisme Impérial de 1806. Études et documents pour servir à l'histoire des rapports de Napoléon et du clergé concordataire* (Paris, 1935), pp. 80–1.

━━━━━━━━━◦◦◦◦━━━━━━━━━

The Continental Blockade

Since 1793, the French government had carried out policies intended to ruin British commerce; it hoped in this way to eliminate or at least dampen the British will to join, and its ability to finance, military coalitions against the French. Napoleon systematised the policies he inherited from the Revolution by introducing measures to enforce the blockade of British goods throughout Europe. At the same time as he tried to exclude Great Britain from all commerce with the continent, he attempted to impose French commercial hegemony (the Continental System).

The Berlin decrees, 21 November 1806

The formal pretext for the economic measures instituted by Napoleon was the British naval blockade of 16 May 1806. The Berlin decrees, so called because they were issued while Napoleon was in that city after the defeat of Prussia, declared Britain and its possessions in a state of blockade and forbade all communications with them.

The imperial camp at Berlin, 21 November 1806
Napoleon, emperor of the French and king of Italy, etc., considering:

1. That England does not recognise the law of nations universally followed by all civilised peoples;
2. That she considers an enemy any individual belonging to the enemy's state, and consequently makes prisoners of war not only the crews of armed ships of war, but also the crews of merchant ships and ships of commerce, and even commercial agents and merchants travelling on business;
3. That she extends to the vessels and commercial merchandise and to the property of individuals the right of conquest, which is only applicable to that which belongs to the enemy's state;
4. That she extends to unfortified towns and commercial ports, to harbours and the mouths of rivers, the right of blockade which, in accordance with reason and the customs of all civilised peoples, is only applicable to fortified towns; that she even declares in a state of blockade places before which she has not even a single ship of war, even though a place may not be blockaded except when it is so completely besieged that no attempt to approach it can be made without imminent danger; that she even declares in a state of blockade places which all her united forces would be incapable of blockading, entire coasts and whole empires;
5. That this monstrous abuse of the right of blockade has no other aim than to prevent communication among nations, and to build the commerce and industry of England on the ruins of the commerce and industry of the continent;

6. That, since this is the obvious aim of England, whoever deals on the continent in English merchandise thereby favours her designs and renders himself her accomplice;

7. That this behaviour of England, worthy of the earliest stages of barbarism, has profited that power to the detriment of all others;

8. That it is a natural right to oppose the enemy with such arms as it makes use of, and to fight it in the same way as it fights, when it has disregarded all ideas of justice and all liberal sentiments, a consequence of civilisation among men:

We have resolved to apply to England the practice which she has consecrated in her maritime legislation.

The provisions of the present decree shall constantly be considered as the fundamental principle of the Empire until such time as England has recognised that the rights of war are one and the same on land and sea; that they cannot be extended to either private property, no matter what kind, or to the persons of

Figure 7 The Giant Commerce overwhelming the Pigmy Blockade. Napoleon's attempt to prevent English goods from entering the Continent met with a similar response from the English. They attempted to prevent what they called 'contraband', that is, anything that could help the French war effort, from reaching the Empire by blocking access to European ports. The clash was an unequal one since the English controlled the high seas. Source: British Museum.

individuals unconnected with the profession of arms, and that the right of blockade should be restricted to fortified places actually invested by sufficient forces.

We have consequently decreed and do decree the following:

Article 1. The British Isles are declared to be in a state of blockade.

Article 2. All commerce and all correspondence with the British Isles is forbidden.

Consequently, letters or packages directed to England or to an Englishman, or written in the English language, shall not pass through the post and shall be seized.

Article 3. Every individual who is an English subject, of whatever state or condition he may be, found in any country occupied by Our troops or by those of Our allies, shall be made a prisoner of war.

Article 4. All warehouses, merchandise or property of whatever kind belonging to a subject of England shall be regarded as a lawful prize.

Article 5. Trade in English goods is prohibited, and all goods belonging to England, or coming from her factories or her colonies, are declared a lawful prize.

Article 6. Half the product of the confiscation of goods and property declared a lawful prize by the preceding articles shall be used to indemnify the merchants for the losses they have experienced by the capture of merchant vessels taken by English cruisers.

Article 7. No vessel coming directly from England or from the English colonies, or having visited these since the publication of the present decree, shall be received in any port.

Article 8. Any vessel which, by means of a false declaration, contravenes the above provisions shall be seized; and the vessel and cargo shall be confiscated as if it were English property.

Article 9. Our Court of Prizes in Paris is charged with the final judgment in all disputes which may arise in Our Empire or in the countries occupied by the French army relating to the execution of the present decree. Our Court of Prizes in Milan is charged with the final judgement in the said disputes which may arise within the territory of Our Kingdom of Italy.

Article 10. The present decree shall be communicated by Our minister of foreign affairs to the King of Spain, Naples, Holland and Etruria, and to Our other allies whose subjects, like Ours, are the victims of the injustice and the barbarity of English maritime legislation.

Article 11. Our ministers of foreign affairs, war, the navy, finance and the police, and Our directors general of the post office are charged, each with that which concerns him, with the execution of the present decree.

Source: *Correspondance de Napoléon Ier*, vol. 13, pp. 682–5.

The decree of Milan, 17 December 1807

The British replied to the Continental Blockade with the Orders in Council passed on 11 November 1807. They thereby announced their intention of seizing any ship that may have sailed from or was sailing to a French-controlled port. Given the superiority of the British on the high seas, this was a real blow to Napoleon's bid for economic supremacy on the continent. His response was the decree of Milan, a tit-for-tat measure that extended the terms of the Berlin decrees to all neutral ships that complied with the orders. Eventually, merchants and other enterprising individuals found ways of circumventing the various blockades: smuggling became rife in spite of the threat of the death penalty on those caught bringing in British goods.

At the Royal Palace of Milan, 17 December 1807
Napoleon, Emperor of the French, King of Italy, Protector of the Confederation of the Rhine;

> in view of the measures adopted by the British government on 11 November last, which obliges the vessels of neutral powers, friends and even allies of England, not only to a visit by English cruisers, but even to an obligatory stay in England and to an arbitrary tax of so many per cent of their cargo, to be regulated by English legislation;
>
> considering that, by these acts, the English government has denationalised the vessels of every nation of Europe; that it is in the power of no government to compromise its independence and its rights, all the sovereigns of Europe being jointly liable for the sovereignty and independence of their flags; that if, by an inexcusable weakness which would be seen as an indelible stain in the eyes of posterity, such tyranny should be admitted in principle and consecrated by custom, the English would take this into consideration to establish it in law, as they have profited from the tolerance of governments to establish the infamous principle that a flag does not cover the merchandise, and to give to their right to blockade an arbitrary extension which threatens the sovereignty of all states;
>
> we have decreed and do decree the following:

Article 1. Any vessel, of whatever nationality, which suffers the visit of an English vessel or is subjected to a voyage to England, or has paid any tax whatsoever to the English government, is, as a matter of fact, declared denationalised and shall lose the guarantee of its flag and shall become English property.

Article 2. Should such vessels, denationalised in this manner by the arbitrary measures of the English government, enter Our ports or those of Our allies, or fall into the hands of Our vessels of war or Our privateers, they shall be declared good and lawful prizes.

Article 3. The British Isles are declared to be in a state of blockade by sea and by land.

Any vessel, of whatever nationality, no matter what its cargo, that sails from an English port or from an English colony or from a country occupied by English troops, or sailing to England or an English colony or to a country occupied by English troops is, by violating the present decree, a lawful prize: it may be captured by Our vessels of war or by Our privateers, and adjudged to the captor.

Article 4. These measures, which are nothing more than a just reciprocity for the barbarous system adopted by the English government, which puts its legislation in the same category as that of Algiers, shall cease to have effect for any nation that obliges the English government to respect its flag. They shall remain in force as long as that government does not return to the principles of the law of nations which govern relations between civilised peoples in a state of war. The provisions of the present decree shall be repealed and void, as a matter of fact, as soon as the English government returns to the principles of the law of nations, which are also those of honour and justice.

Article 5. All ministers are charged with the execution of the present decree, which will be printed in the *Bulletin des lois*.

Source: *Correspondance de Napoléon Ier*, vol. 16, pp. 227–9.

Imposing the Code Napoléon on the Empire

The debate about whether Napoleon attempted to unify Europe under a common code, or whether he even attempted to apply the Code Napoléon systematically, are questions which have preoccupied historians in recent times. The selection of documents in this section highlight what was a general trend, namely Napoleon's desire to create a system which would facilitate the extraction of men and money from the territories incorporated within the Empire.

Napoleon to Louis, King of Holland,
13 November 1807

Louis Bonaparte (1778–1846) was made king of Holland in 1806. He proved to be a popular monarch, largely because he did his best to serve his new subjects, and often ignored advice from Napoleon. He enraged Napoleon by refusing to implement the Code Napoléon, which he considered to be 'un-Dutch', or enforce the Continental Blockade, which he considered immoral. The following extracts from Napoleon's correspondence highlights the practical difficulties involved in implementing a system that was not universally accepted. The emperor's frustration at the lack of cooperation is apparent.

Fontainebleau, 13 November 1807

I have received your letter of 9 November. If you meddle with the Code Napoléon, it will no longer be the Code Napoléon. I do not know what time you need, or what changes there are to make, or how it will harm individual fortunes. You are inexperienced in administration if you think that the establishment of a definitive code can trouble families and cause disastrous disorder in the country. You are being told fairy stories because the Dutch are jealous of everything that comes from France. However, a nation of 1,800,000 souls cannot have a separate legislation. The Romans gave their laws to their allies: why should France not have its laws adopted in Holland? It is equally necessary for you to adopt the French monetary system; this is what Spain, Germany, all of Italy have done. Why should you not do so? To have the same civil laws and the same money tightens the bonds between nations. When I say 'the same money' I mean that your money will carry the arms of Holland and the effigy of the king, but the type of money and its organisation must be the same. . . .

Source: *Correspondance de Napoléon Ier*, vol. 11, p. 161.

Napoleon to Jérôme, King of Westphalia,
15 November 1807

Fontainebleau, 15 November 1807

Dear brother, you will find enclosed the Constitution of your kingdom. This Constitution contains the conditions on which I renounce all my rights of conquest and the rights I have acquired over your country. You must follow it faithfully. The happiness of your people is important to me, not only because of the influence they may have over your glory and mine, but also from the point of view of the whole European system. Do not listen to those who tell you that your people, accustomed to servitude, will receive your kindness with ingratitude. People are more enlightened in the kingdom of Westphalia than some would have you believe and your throne will not be truly established without the confidence and love of your people. What the people of Germany impatiently desire is that individuals who are not noble and who are men of talent will have an equal claim to your consideration and to employment; that all types of servitude and intermediate links between the sovereign and the lowest class of people be entirely abolished. The benefits of the Code Napoléon, the publicity of procedures, the establishment of juries, will be the distinctive features of your monarchy. And to tell you the complete truth, I am counting more on their effect for the extension and the consolidation of your monarchy than on the results of your greatest victories. Your people need to enjoy a certain liberty, equality and a well-being unknown to the peoples of Germany, and this liberal government will produce, one way or another, the most salutary changes for the system of the Confederation [of the Rhine] and the power of your monarchy. This manner of governing will be a more powerful barrier separating you from Prussia than the Elbe, the fortresses and the protection of France. What people would wish to return to the arbitrary government of Prussia when they have tasted the benefits of a wise and liberal adminis-tration? The peoples of Germany, as well as those of France, Italy and Spain, desire equality and demand liberal ideas. I have been managing the affairs of Europe long enough to be convinced that the burden imposed by the privileged classes is contrary to the wishes of the general opinion. Be a con-stitutional king. . . .

Source: *Correspondance de Napoléon Ier*, vol. 16, pp. 166–7.

Napoleon to Joachim Murat, 27 November 1808

Aranda, 27 November 1808

I read with attention the memorandum submitted by your minister, secre-tary of state of Justice, on the Code Napoléon. The most important consideration in the Code is that of divorce; it is its foundation. You should not touch it in any manner whatsoever; it is the law of the State. I would prefer Naples to belong to the former king of Sicily than to see an expur-gated Code Napoléon. Divorce is not contrary to religion; its provisions have in any case been greatly modified. Moreover, those whose consciences have been offended by it will never use it. I cannot consent, in my capacity as guarantor of the Constitution, to modifications to the Code Napoléon. It has been adopted throughout the kingdom of Italy; Florence has it, Rome will have it soon, and priests will have to cease nurturing prejudices and look to their own affairs.

Keep to the middle road. It is not in cajoling priests that something will happen; if they think that you need them badly, they will fail you. . . .

Source: Maximilien Vox, *Correspondance de Napoléon. Six cents lettres de travail (1806–1810)* (Paris, 1948), pp. 374–5.

20

RESISTANCE AND REPRESSION

Conscription under Napoleon

The French revolutionary armies were largely made up of recruits. When, however, the number of men volunteering to join the ranks of the army began to dwindle, the government had recourse to the Jourdan Law of 5 September 1798 introducing conscription. All men between the ages of 20 and 25 were eligible to be called up. Those with money could buy their way out by paying for a replacement; the average price was about 2,000 francs. Those who could not afford a replacement or who did not want to leave their villages were, as the following report shows, obliged to find more imaginative means of avoiding conscription.

Conscription frauds in the Ariège, 5 October 1806

The registers of the certificates of births, marriages and deaths of most of the communes of the department of the Ariège are in a deplorable state.

These registers, and in particular those of marriage, have been shamefully defaced or falsified in order to procure for an infinite number of young men the means of avoiding military service.

The origins of these forgeries go back to the end of Year VI, that is to the period when the provisions of the laws of 19 and 23 Fructidor were known in the department of the Ariège. These exempted those requisitioned men married before 1 Germinal in Year VI from the draft and exempted conscripts married before 23 Nivôse of the same year from the ballot.

At that time, certain intriguers united in order to sell false acts of marriage to requisitioned men and conscripts of the department, and they have succeeded in their criminal aims, either by abusing the rusticity of public officers of some of the smaller communes situated in the mountains, or by sharing with them their culpable traffic, or by imposing on the good faith of the administrative corps of Viba extracts of false acts inscribed in the registers of the communes.

There are crimes the possibility of which one can only suspect; the administrative bodies countersign with confidence the extracts of the false acts which are presented to them because they undoubtedly cannot suspect that functionaries charged with the preservation of the registers of births, marriages and deaths are capable of violating the sacred trust confided in them, and of compromising in this manner the state of the men and the Constitution of families which are the fundamental basis of the social order. The military authorities consequently have no difficulty in receiving the objections supported by the above-mentioned extracts, because they cannot without the least bit of information suspect as forgeries that which the administrative corps has, so to speak, authorised by authenticating with their signatures; the rusticity of the claimants, their countenance assured, the custom by which the inhabitants of the countryside marry very early; everything contributes to prolonging the error of the military authorities by sparing them questions or verifications which could destroy it.

Encouraged by their success, the authors of these odious machinations lose all sense of moderation; the draft of conscripts provides them each year with a new occasion to satisfy their insatiable cupidity; they make themselves masters of the registers of births, marriages and deaths of almost all of the rural communes of the *arrondissement* in the mountains; they profit from all the blank spaces which can be found in the marriage registers for the Years II, III, IV, V and VI and add pages to these registers in order to procure false acts of marriage, not only for the conscripts of the department of the Ariège, but also for the conscripts of the neighbouring departments.

They deface the marriage registers for Year VII and subsequent years, so that they can place at a date before the 23 Nivôse of Year VI acts of marriage of conscripts married after that period.

Widows of 50, 60 and 80 years old, or women whose husbands are still alive, or girls aged for the most part under 14 (who in large part have since contracted new marriages with others, as well as young people falsely married), are named, often without their knowledge, on false acts inscribed on the registers.

The same woman appears on up to eight or nine different acts.

Sometimes the names of women who are long since dead, or who have never existed, are inscribed on false acts.

They do not limit themselves to defacing and falsifying the marriage registers. They deface and falsify the death registers, either in order to procure for the falsely married conscripts death certificates of the deceased woman they have been given as a wife, or to testify as dead conscripts who, protected by the local authorities, cannot be sought by higher authorities, or in order to procure for conscripts the means of profiting from the birth certificate of a deceased brother.

They alter, deface and suppress whole registers of births in order to procure for conscripts the means to get crossed off the lists by proving through a false birth certificate, or through a false investigation (which have unfortunately become very common in the department), that they are not of conscription age, or to procure for conscripts for the years after Year VII the advantages of the amnesty accorded to conscripts for the years before Year VII, or in order to diminish or render null in certain communes the quota they must supply for conscription. We have even discovered birth registers for conscription where all the boys have been transformed into girls.

Finally, such is the greed of the forgers (especially during Years XI and XII) that they employ with great recklessness all sorts of roundabout means to perpetrate their infamous speculation; they circulate the rumour in the countryside that there is an infallible means of getting out of conscription, and that one can with ease speak with such individuals who can procure these means;—they adapt the price of the forgeries according to the fortunes of the conscripts; they produce them for about 24 francs;—they visit the houses of conscripts to offer their forgeries;—they are so audacious as to traffic marriage registers in the markets and fairs and even on the public squares of the provincial capital of the *arrondissement* of St-Girons;—sometimes they approach groups which form in these public places, turn the conversation to conscription, express pity for the parents who are obliged to send their children to the army, discover by that stratagem those who may have need of their offices, take them to one side or lead them either to a tavern or to the house of an accomplice, propose documents which they call legal in return for a certain sum, and succeed all the more easily in deceiving the credulity of these wretches by citing numerous successes they have obtained of the same sort; they only demand the price agreed upon after having countersigned the false acts they have inscribed or get inscribed in the registers.

Such is the faithful portrait of the schemes which have been practised in the department of the Ariège in order to paralyse the execution of the laws on requisitions and conscription. . . .

Signed: Judge Darmaing

Source: Archives nationales, F⁷ 8743.

Administrative corruption, 18 July 1807

This report from the Prefect of the Gironde shows another example of fraud, but also that even local notables were not immune from prosecution for evading conscription.

That mayor represented his son during the nominations. He asked for his discharge before the Council of Recruitment on the grounds of infirmities which rendered him unfit for service. An illness attested to by medical certificates prevented him from appearing before the meetings of the Council. It was decided that he should appear as soon as his health permitted. I did not hear any more about him until the 16th of this month (July 1807) when I learnt that the young man was walking about his commune and was in good health. I gave orders to the Gendarmerie to arrest him at his father's house and to indict him before the Council. This example was necessary in order to prove to the poor classes, who are always ready to complain about acts of justice which concern them, that there are no exceptions. It was also fitting to punish by a kind of humiliation a functionary who, by sleight of hand, wanted to arrange the departure of the reserve before a decision had been made about his son, who has been declared in good health and is going to be sent after the rest of the reserve.

Source: Jean Tulard, *La Vie quotidienne des Français sous Napoléon* (Paris, 1978), pp. 142–3.

⟫◦◦◦⟪

Dealing with the rebels in Italy, 7 February 1806

Towards the end of 1805, General Andoche Junot was sent to Parma to suppress a rebellion. The following instructions to Junot are not only an invitation to loot, pillage and massacre peasants probably guilty of nothing more than living in the area of the revolt, but clearly demonstrate that Napoleon did not tolerate any opposition to his will. He was not in the slightest bit interested in the particulars surrounding the origins of the revolt. He was only interested in punishment. In this, at least, his approach was consistent with the prevailing attitudes of those in power towards peasants in revolt.

General Junot,
I received your letter from Parma, of 30 January, and that from Plaisance, of 1 February. I am not satisfied with the spirit which reigns there.

I am certain that M. Moreau has badly administered, and you will see that I have recalled him and replaced him with a prefect. But that does not justify the rebellion. The report from the major of the 42nd is from a man who does not know the Italians, who are false. Seditious under a weak government, they only respect and fear a strong and active government.

My wish is that the village which rebelled so as to give itself over to Bobbo should be burned, that the priest who is in the hands of the Bishop of Plaisance be shot, and that three or four hundred of the culprits be sent to the galleys. I do not have the same notions of clemency as you. One can only be merciful by being severe, without which that unfortunate country and Piedmont would be lost, and torrents of blood would be needed to assure the tranquillity of Italy.

We have known rebellion; it must be met with vengeance and punishment. . . . As for the rest, I do not share your opinion about the innocence of the peasants of Parma. They are great rascals who carried out the worst excesses; and I am surprised that one of my most experienced soldiers thinks that resisting my arms, and disrespecting my flags is a misdemeanour. My wish is that they be revered with religious sentiment.

You yourself should march into every village; always be on horseback and write to me every day about what you see and what you do. I will not disapprove of any rewards that you might decide to make, but punishments should be numerous and severe; spare no-one. Do not rot away in the towns. Speak to me only of the abuses of the administration. Every abuse, even the tyrannical excesses of my agents, even if they are as numerous as those of Carrier, shall be excused in my eyes the day the rebels, like those of Parma, take up arms and carry out justice themselves.

Believe my long experience of Italians. In one month's time your conduct will have greatly influenced the respect of my Italian peoples for my government. Burn one or two large villages so that no trace of it remains. Say that it is by my order.

Large states can only be maintained by acts of severity. Nothing absolves the inhabitants of the State of Parma. Support the Gendarmerie and purge the country of these brigands.

Source: Vox, *Correspondance de Napoléon*, pp. 312–14.

———————<>———————

A response to pillage in Spain, 12 December 1808

Spain proved to be a constant drain on the manpower and resources of the empire. It is estimated that between 1808 and 1813, the Grande Armée lost at least 260,000 men, a great many of them to guerrilla warfare. In contrast to the orders to Junot to set an example by burning villages, here Napoleon desperately seeks to pacify and quell popular discontent against the régime by instructing his troops to maintain the strictest discipline. It not only reveals an apparent contradiction in Napoleon's approach to governing people, but highlights the importance of and the apparent difficulty in maintaining open communications with Spain.

ORDER OF THE ARMY

Chamartin, 12 December 1808

The emperor is unhappy with the disturbances which are taking place. Pillage destroys everything, even the army which practises it. Peasants desert; it has the double inconvenience of turning them into irreconcilable enemies who get their revenge on isolated soldiers, and who swell enemy ranks as we destroy them; and of depriving us of all information, so necessary to make war, and of all means of obtaining subsistence. Peasants who used to come to the markets are kept away by the troops who arrest them, plunder their goods and beat them.

The emperor orders his marshals, generals and officers to take the firmest measures in order to put an end to these abuses and to these excesses which compromise the safety of the army. Consequently, it is ordered that:

1   Any individual who stops or mistreats an inhabitant or peasant carrying goods into the city of Madrid will be immediately tried before a military tribunal and condemned to death;
2   Any individual who pillages and prevents the establishment of order will be tried before a military tribunal and punished with death.

The emperor orders his marshals, generals and other officers to give special protection to the establishment of posts, either post offices or relays; safety measures will be introduced.

Consequently, it is forbidden to: lodge any individual in post offices or relays; take fodder or any other subsistence from relays; to take horses, either from the stables of relays or on the roads; to mistreat messengers and thus cause delays.

Any soldier found guilty of the above offences will be arrested and tried before a military tribunal in order to be judged as he would be for pillage or for having compromised the safety of the army.

Source: *Correspondance de Napoléon Ier*, pp. 131–2.

21

THE RUSSIAN CATASTROPHE

Napoleon to Alexander I, 1 July 1812

The idea of invading Russia was considered as early as 1810 when it became obvious that Alexander I was no longer adhering to the Treaty of Tilsit. He could no longer afford to do so; the blockade was badly hurting both the Russian economy and the tsar's reputation at home.

Four days after crossing the frontier into Russia, Napoleon met with the Russian emperor's aide-de-camp, General Alexander Balashov. He had been sent to explain to Napoleon that there could be no negotiations as long as French troops were on Russian soil. Napoleon's reply was a personal indictment against Alexander. It is obvious that Napoleon felt betrayed, but also that he had misjudged him. It also shows that Napoleon, who was looking for a knock-out blow and who probably had no intention of advancing so far into Russian territory, was still unsure as to what he wanted from Alexander.

I have received Your Majesty's letter. The war which divided our states was ended by the Treaty of Tilsit. I went to the Niemen conference with the resolution not to make peace unless I obtained all the advantages that circumstances promised me. Consequently, I refused to see the king of Prussia there. Your Majesty said to me, 'I will be your second against England'. This remark from Your Majesty changed everything; the Treaty of Tilsit was its corollary. Since then, Your Majesty has wished that modifications be made to the Treaty; you wished to keep Moldavia and Wallachia, and to carry your boundaries forward to the Danube. You had recourse to negotiations. This important modification of the Treaty of Tilsit, so advantageous to Your Majesty, was a result of the Erfurt Conference [September 1808]. It appears that, towards the middle of 1810, Your Majesty wished new modifications to the Treaty of Tilsit. There were two means of arriving at that, negotiation or war. Negotiation had been successful for you at Erfurt; why, this time, did you take a different course? You rearmed on a large scale, declined the path of negotiations, and appeared to wish to obtain modifications to the Treaty of Tilsit only by the protection of your numerous armies. The relations established between the two powers, after so many events and blood spilled, found themselves broken; war became imminent.

I also took up arms, but six months after Your Majesty had done so on your part. I have not raised a battalion, I have not drawn a million from my treasury for the emergency of war, without letting Your Majesty and your ambassador know about it. I have not missed a single opportunity to explain myself. Your Majesty has made before all of Europe a declaration such as powers usually make only in wartime and when they no longer expect anything from negotiations; I have not replied to it. Your Majesty was the first to assemble his armies and to threaten my frontiers. Your Majesty was the first to leave for field headquarters. Your Majesty, after having constantly refused for eighteen months to explain yourself, has finally had delivered to me by your minister a summons to evacuate Prussia as a prior condition of any explanation. A few days later, this minister requested his passports and repeated his demand three times. From that moment, I was at war with Your Majesty. However, I wanted to preserve the hope that Prince Kourakine had wrongly understood his instructions, and that he was not authorised to make this demand that Prussia be evacuated a sine qua non condition for further discussion, which was clearly to place me between war and dishonour; inappropriate language on the part of Russia which neither past events nor the respective strengths of the two states authorised him to address me, and which was opposed to Your Majesty's character, to the personal esteem which you have sometimes shown me and finally to the memory that you cannot have lost that, in the most critical circumstances, I have honoured you and your nation enough to propose nothing to you that could be in the least contrary to delicacy and honour. I thus charged Count Lauriston to approach Your Majesty and your Minister of Foreign Affairs to explain all these circumstances and to see if there would not be a means of bringing about the opening of negotiations by considering as nullified the arrogant and inappropriate summons of Prince Kourakine. A few days later, I learned that the court of Berlin had been advised of this course of action on the part of Prince Kourakine, and that even it was quite surprised by such extraordinary language. I was not long in learning that at Petersburg, too, this *démarche* was known and that sensible men disapproved it; finally, the English newspapers apprised me that the English knew of it. Prince Kourakine had thus only followed his instructions literally. Still, I wanted to preserve hope, and I awaited the answer of Count Lauriston, when I received at Gumbinen the Legation Secretary, Prevost, who advised me that, against the law of nations, against the duties of sovereigns in like circumstances, without regard to what Your Majesty owed to me and to himself, not only had you refused to see Count Lauriston, but even, something without precedent, that you even forgot that the minister had also refused to hear and confer with him, though he made known the importance of the letter and the intent of his orders. I understood then that the lot had been cast, and that this invisible Providence whose rights and empire I recognise, had decided this affair as so many others. I marched on the Niemen with the deep-seated feeling of having done all to spare humanity these new misfortunes, while satisfying my honour, that of my people, and the sanctity of treaties.

There, Sire, is the explanation of my conduct. Your Majesty may have many things to say, but you should say to yourself that for eighteen months you refused to explain anything; since then, you have declared that you will not hear anything unless I have previously evacuated the territory of my allies. You thus hope to deprive Prussia of the independence which you appeared to wish to guarantee; at the same time you point out to me the Caudine Forks [site of a Roman defeat in 321 BC]. I pity the spitefulness of those who could give such advice to Your Majesty. Whatever might be, never has Russia been able to use this language with France; it is at best that which the Empress Catherine could have used to the last kings of Poland.

War is thus declared between us. Even God cannot cause that which has been done to be undone. But my ear will always be open to peace negotiations; and when Your Majesty seriously wishes to rid yourself of the influence of men hostile to your family and to your glory and that of your Empire, you will always find in me the same feelings and true friendship. A day will come when Your Majesty will acknowledge that if, from the end of 1810, you had not changed, that if, wanting modifications to the Treaty of Tilsit, you had had recourse to honest negotiations, which is not to change, you would have had one of the most beautiful reigns over Russia. After terrible and repeated disasters, you had by your wisdom and policies healed all the wounds of the state, joined to your Empire immense provinces, Finland and the mouth of the Danube. But I would have also gained a great deal; the Spanish business would have been ended in 1811, and probably peace would have been concluded with England at that time. Your Majesty lacked perseverance, confidence and, if I am permitted to say so to you, honesty; you have spoiled all your future. Before crossing the Niemen, I would have sent an aide-de-camp to Your Majesty, according to the custom that I followed in preceding campaigns, if the men near you who direct the war and who appear to me, in spite of the lessons of experience, to be so eager to wage war, had not shown so much dissatisfaction with the mission of Count Narbonne, and if I had not had to consider as the result of their influence the rejection of my ambassador. It then appeared unworthy of me to let anyone suspect that, under pretext of procedure, by sending someone else to Your Majesty, I could have had any other goal.

If Your Majesty wants to end the war, you will find me so disposed. If Your Majesty is determined to continue it and if you wish to establish a truce on the most liberal grounds, such as not considering men in hospital as prisoners— so that neither side has to hurry evacuations, which involves heavy losses—such as the return every two weeks of prisoners made by either side, using a rank for rank exchange system, and all other stipulations that the custom of war between civilised nations has allowed: Your Majesty will find me ready for anything. Even if, in spite of hostilities, Your Majesty wants to establish some direct communications, the principle as well as the formalities could also be negotiated in the truce.

It remains for me to end by begging Your Majesty to believe that, while complaining of the direction that you have given your policies, which has so sad an influence on our lives and nations, the private feelings that I bear for you are not in the least affected by these events and that, if fortune should again favour my arms, you will find me, as at Tilsit and Erfurt, full of affection and esteem for your fine and great qualities and desirous of proving it to you.

Source: *Correspondance de Napoléon Ier*, vol. 24, pp. 1–5.

Conditions during the Russian campaign, 1812

The weather was obviously an important factor. In this extract we see that it was not only the Russian summer which took its toll on men and horses, but also the freak storms which caught many unawares. Jean-Roch Coignet, promoted to lieutenant and placed in charge of a battalion of stragglers, gives an impression of the enormous logistical difficulties involved in moving so many men, and the complete breakdown in discipline, well before the army had reached Moscow.

The march to Moscow

On the 26th June, 1812, we crossed the Niemen. Prince Murat formed the advance guard with his cavalry; Marshal Davoust, with sixty thousand men, marched in column, together with the whole guard and his artillery, on the high road to Wilna. It is impossible to give any idea of such a spectacle as those columns, moving over those arid plains, with no habitations except some wretched villages devastated by the Russians. Prince Murat caught up with them at the bridge of Kowno; they were obliged to fall back upon Wilna. The weather, which up to that time had been very fine, suddenly changed. On 29th June, at three o'clock, a violent storm arose, just before we came to a village, which I had had the greatest possible difficulty in reaching. When we reached the shelter of this village, we could not unharness our horses; we had to take off their bridles, cut grass for them, and light our fires.

The storm of sleet and snow was so terrible that we could scarcely keep our horses still; we had to fasten them to the wheels. I was half dead with the cold; not being able to stand it any longer, I opened one of my wagons, and crept inside. Next morning a heartrending sight met our gaze: in the cavalry camp nearby, the ground was covered with horses frozen to death; more than ten thousand died during that dreadful night. When I got out of my wagon, all numbed with the cold, I saw that three of my horses were dead. I at once harnessed those that were left to my four wagons. The wretched animals were shaking and trembling enough to break their bones; they threw themselves into their collars in desperation; they were half mad, and plunged violently in harness. If I had been an hour later, I should have lost them all. It took all our strength to master them.

When we reached the highway, we saw the dead bodies of a number of soldiers who had succumbed before the terrible storm. This demoralized a great many of our men. Fortunately, our forced marches caused the Emperor of Russia to leave Wilna, where he had established his headquarters. In this large city it was possible to reduce the army to order. The Emperor arrived on 29th June, and immediately gave orders to arrest stragglers of all arms, and quarter them in an enclosure outside of the city. Here they were closely confined, and their rations were distributed to them. Military police were sent out in every direction to pick them up. They were formed into three battalions of seven or eight hundred men; all of them were still in possession of their arms.

After a short interval of rest, the army marched forward into immense forests, where it was necessary to be constantly on the watch, for fear of being surprised by the enemy in ambush. An army must march carefully when there is a danger of being cut off. Before he started himself, the Emperor sent the chasseurs of his guard on ahead, and we remained with him. . . .

After leaving Wilna, we found ourselves surrounded by great forests. I left the head of my battalion, and went to the rear, making the stragglers keep up by placing my little bandsman on the right to mark time. Night came on and I saw some of the deserters steal away into the depths of the forest without being able to bring them back to the ranks, on account of the darkness. I could do nothing but curse. What was to be done with such soldiers? I said to myself, 'They will all desert'.

. . . At dawn I had the assembly beaten; at broad daylight I made my drummer beat to arms, and started once more on our route, telling them that the Emperor was going to have all deserters arrested. I marched until noon, and, as we emerged from a wood, I came upon a herd of cows grazing in a meadow. My soldiers immediately took their bowls, and went off to milk the cows, and we had to wait for them. When the evening came, they would camp before nightfall, and every time we came across any cows, we had to stop. It may be imagined that this was not much fun for me. At last we came to a forest, very far from the towns, a considerable portion of which had been destroyed by fire. This burnt forest extended along the way on my right, and I saw a party of my troops turn to the right into these charred woods. I galloped off after them, to make them come back to the road. To my surprise, these soldiers faced about and fired at me. I was obliged to let them go. This was a plot got up among the soldiers of Joseph Napoleon, who were all Spaniards. There were a hundred and thirty-three of them, and not one single Frenchman had joined the brigands.

That same evening we emerged from the forest, and came to a village where there was some cavalry stationed, with a colonel who was guarding the forks of the road, and showing troops which to take. I went to him and made my report; he ordered my battalion to camp, and, upon suggestions from me, he sent for some Jews and his interpreter. He judged, from the distance, the village to which my deserters must have gone, and sent off fifty chasseurs, with the Jews to guide them. About half-way they met some peasants who had been unjustly treated, and were coming to ask for protection. They reached the village at midnight, surrounded it, and surprised the Spaniards while they were asleep; seized them, disarmed them, and put their muskets in a wagon. The men were tied and put into small wagons with a strong guard. At eight o-clock in the morning the hundred and thirty-three Spaniards arrived, and were set free from their shackles. The colonel ordered them into line and said to them, 'Your conduct has been disgraceful. I am going to form you into sections. Are there any sergeants or corporals among you to form your sections?' At this two sergeants showed their stripes, which had been concealed by their cloaks. 'Stand out! Are there any corporals?' Three came forward. 'Stand out! Are there any more among you? All right! Now, the rest of you will draw lots.' Those who drew white tickets were placed on one side, and those who drew black ones, on the other. When all had drawn, he said to them, 'You have run away, you have acted as incendiaries, you have fired upon your officer; the law condemns you to death, and you must submit to your punishment. I could have you all shot, but I will spare half of you. Commander, order your battalion to load. My adjutant will give the command to fire.' They shot sixty-two of them. My God! What a scene it was. I left the spot immediately with a bursting heart, but the Jews were highly delighted.* Such was my first experience as lieutenant.

Source: Captain Jean-Roch Coignet, *The Note-Books of Captain Coignet. Soldier of the Empire, 1799–1816* (London, 1998), pp. 207–15.

---

* They had the spoils of the men who were shot [note in original].

The crossing of the Berezina

Following the French example, the German states of the Confederation of the Rhine also introduced conscription. In Württemberg, Jakob Walter was conscripted first in 1806 and was then recalled to arms on two other occasions, in 1809 and again in 1812. He thus became one of the hundreds of thousands of men making up the Grande Armée which invaded Russia, and one of the very few to survive the campaign. This extract from Jakob's memoirs describes the crossing of the Berezina by the 50,000 men who had survived thus far. The river, which was normally covered by ice during this period, unexpectedly thawed, obliging Napoleon's engineers to hastily construct two bridges to get across.

It was November 25, 1812, when we reached the Borissov. Now the march went towards the Berezina River, where the indescribable horror of all possible plagues awaited us. On the way I met one of my countrymen, by the name of Brenner, who had served with the Light Horse Regiment. He came toward me completely wet and half frozen, and we greeted each other. Brenner said that the night before he and his horse had been caught and plundered but that he had taken to flight again and had come through a river which was not frozen. Now, he said, he was near death from freezing and starvation. This good, noble soldier had run into me not far from Smolensk with a little loaf of bread weighing about two pounds and had asked me whether I wanted a piece of bread, saying that this was his last supply. 'However, because you have nothing at all, I will share it with you.' He had dismounted, laid the bread on the ground, and cut it in two with his sabre. 'Dear, good friend,' I had replied, 'you treat me like a brother. I will not forget as long as I live this good deed of yours but will rather repay you many times if we live!' He had then a Russian horse, a huge dun, mounted it, and each of us had to work his way through, facing his own dangers. This second meeting, with both of us in the most miserable condition because no aid was available, caused a pang in my heart which sank in me unforgettably. Both of us were again separated and death overtook him.

When we came nearer the Berezina River, there was a place where Napoleon had ordered his pack horses to be unharnessed and where he ate. He watched his army pass by in the most wretched condition. What he may have felt in his heart is impossible to surmise. His outward appearance seemed indifferent and unconcerned over the wretchedness of his soldiers; only ambition and lost honour may have made themselves felt in his heart; and, although the French and Allies shouted into his ears many oaths and curses about his own guilty person, he was still able to listen to them unmoved. After his Guard had already disbanded and he was almost abandoned, he collected a voluntary corps at Dubrovna which was enrolled with many promises and received the name of 'Holy Squadron'. After a short time, however, this existed in name only, for the enemy reduced even them to nothing.

... After a time, from about two till four o'clock in the afternoon, the Russians pressed nearer and nearer from every side, and the murdering and torturing seemed about to annihilate everyone. Although our army used a hill, on which what was left of our artillery was placed, and fired at the enemy as much as possible, the question was: what chance was there of rescue? That day we expected that everyone must be captured, killed, or thrown into the water. Everyone thought that his last hour had come, and everyone was expecting it; but, since the ridge was held by the French artillery, only cannon and howitzer balls could snatch away part of the men. There was no hospital for the wounded; they died also of hunger, thirst, cold, and despair, uttering complaints and curses with their last breath. Also our sick, who had been conveyed to this point in wagons and consisted almost entirely of officers, were left to themselves; and only deathly white faces and stiffened hands stretched towards us.

When the cannonade had abated somewhat, I and my master set out and rode down the stream for about half an hour to where there was a village with several unburned houses. Here was also the general staff of Württemberg. In the hiding places here, I sought for something to eat at night; with this purpose I lighted candles that I had found; and I did find some cabbage ('Kapusk') which looked green, spotted, and like rubbish. I placed it over a fire and cooked it for about half an hour. All at once cannon balls crashed into the village, and with a wild cheer the enemy sprang upon us. With all the speed we succeeded in escaping, since we mounted and rode away as fast as possible. I couldn't leave my pot of cabbage behind, to be sure, but held it firmly in my arms on the horse, and the fear that I might lose my half-cooked meal made me forget entirely the bullets which were flying by. When we were a little distance from the place, my master and I reached our hands into the pot and ate our cabbage ('Kapusk') in haste with our fingers. Neither could leave his hands bare because of the cold, and because of our hunger and the cold we vied for each other in grabbing swiftly into the warm pot, and the only meal for the entire day was at an end again in short time.

When it became day again, we stood near the stream approximately a thousand paces from the two bridges, which were built of wood near each other. These bridges had the structure of sloping saw-horses suspended like trestles on shallow-sunk piles; on these lay long stringers and across them only bridge ties, which were not fastened down. However, one could not see the bridges because of the crowd of people, horses, and wagons. Everyone crowded together into a solid mass, and nowhere could one see a way out or a means of rescue. From morning till night we stood unprotected from cannonballs and grenades which the Russians hurled at us from two sides. At each blow from three to five men were struck to the ground, and yet no one was able to move a step to get out of the path of the cannonballs. Only by the filling up of the space where the cannonball made room could one make a little progress forward. All the powder wagons also stood in the crowd; many of these were ignited by the grenades, killing hundreds of people and horses standing about them.

I had a horse to ride and one to lead. The horse I led I was soon forced to let go, and I had to kneel on the one I rode in order not to have my feet crushed off, for everything was so closely packed that in a quarter of an hour one could move only four or five steps forward. To be on foot was to lose all hope of rescue. Indeed, whoever did not have a good horse could not help falling over the horses and people lying about in masses. Everyone was screaming under the feet of the horses, and everywhere was the cry, 'Shoot me or stab me to death!' The fallen horses struck off their feet many of those still standing. It was only by a miracle that anyone was saved.

In the crowd the major and I held fast to one another; and, as far as it was possible, I frequently caused my horse to rear up, whereby he came down about one step further forward. I marveled at the intelligence with which this animal sought to save us. Then evening came and despair steadily increased. Thousands swam into the river with the horses, but no one ever came out again; thousands of others who were near the water were pushed in, and the stream was like a sheep dip where the heads of men and horses bobbed up and down and disappeared.

Finally, toward four o'clock in the evening, when it was almost dark, I came to the bridge, the second having been shot away. Now it is with horror, but at that time it was with a dull, indifferent feeling, that I looked at the masses of horses and people which lay dead, piled high upon the bridge. Only 'Straight ahead and in the middle!' must be the resolution. 'Here in the water is your grave; beyond the bridge is the continuation of a wretched life. The decision will be made on the bridge!' Now I kept myself constantly in the middle. The major and I could aid one another; and so amid a hundred blows of sabres we came to the bridge, where not a plank was visible because of the dead men and horses; and, although on reaching the bridge the people fell in masses thirty paces to the right and to the left, we came through to firm land.

Source: Marc Raeff (ed.), *The Diary of a Napoleonic Foot Soldier* (Windrush Press, Moreton-in-Marsh, 1991, copyright © The Orion Publishing Group Ltd and Doubleday Publishing Inc.), pp. 80–9.

29th Bulletin of the Grande Armée: The retreat from Moscow, 3 December 1812

Although this Bulletin was dated 3 December, it was actually dictated on the night of 5 December, after Napoleon had abandoned what was left of his army. It appeared in the *Moniteur* on 17 December, the day before he arrived back in Paris. It was written after the Malet affair (see pp. 187–9). Note the last line—'His Majesty's health has never been better'—which may appear egotistical after the loss of hundreds of thousands of men, but it was important to scotch rumours of his death and to reassure his subjects that he was indeed alive and well. Note also Napoleon's tendency to blame everything else—the cold weather, bad generals—for the defeat. The Bulletin is one of the elements responsible for the myth of 'General Winter' and its role in the defeat of the Grande Armée. Note also the absence of any reference to the loss of men. Instead, the Bulletin concentrates on the loss of horses, probably as a means of preparing public opinion for the inevitable. There is no mention either of the horrific hardships suffered during the crossing of the Berezina. Instead, in true Napoleonic form, the heroic feats of a few individuals are mentioned.

Molodcheno, 3 December 1812

The weather was perfect until 6 November, and the troop movements were executed with the greatest success. It began to get cold on the 7th; from that time on, each night we lost several hundred horses which died at Bivouac. After arriving in Smolensk, we had already lost a considerable amount of cavalry and artillery horses. . . . The cold, which started on the 7th, suddenly increased, and from the 14th, 15th and 16th the thermometer reached minus 16 and 18 degrees [Celsius]. The roads were covered in black ice; horses of the cavalry, artillery and baggage train died every night, not by hundreds but by thousands, especially the horses from France and Germany. More than 30,000 horses died in a few days; our cavalry found itself on foot; our artillery and our transport wagons found themselves without teams. We had to abandon and destroy a large part of our cannon as well as our munitions and food supplies.

The army, so magnificent on the 6th, was very different from the 14th on, almost without cavalry, without artillery, without transport. Without cavalry, we could not reconnoitre more than a quarter of a league; for all that, without artillery we could not stand firm and risk battle; we had to march so as not to be forced into battle, which the lack of munitions made undesirable; we had to occupy a certain space so as not to be outflanked, and this without cavalry to reconnoitre and to link the columns. This difficulty, combined with an excessive cold which came upon us suddenly, made our situation difficult. Men whom nature had not made hard enough to rise above the accidents of fate and fortune appeared shaken, lost their good humour, and dreamed only of misfortunes and catastrophes; those whom nature had created superior to everything retained their good humour and their normal composure, and saw new glory in surmounting the different difficulties.

The enemy, who saw on the roads the traces of this terrible calamity which had struck the French army, sought to profit from it. It surrounded all our columns with Cossacks, who carried off, like Arabs in the desert, baggage trains and carriages that had been separated. That contemptible cavalry, which is full of bluster and which is not capable of breaking through a company of light infantry, made itself feared by the force of circumstances. Nevertheless, the enemy had reason to regret all serious attempts they wanted to undertake; they were knocked head over heels by the Viceroy [Eugène de Beauharnais], in front of whom they had taken position, and they lost many men.

The duc d'Elchingen [Marshal Ney], who with 3,000 men made up the rear guard, had the ramparts of Smolensk blown up. He was surrounded and in a critical situation; he got out of it with the intrepidity which characterises him. After having held the enemy at a distance during the whole 18th and after having constantly driven them back, [Ney] moved on the right flank during the night, crossed the Dnieper and foiled the enemy's calculations. On the 19th, the army crossed the Dnieper at Orsha, and the Russian army, tired, having lost a lot of people, ceased its efforts.

. . . Meanwhile, the enemy occupied all the crossing points of the Berezina: that river is 40 *toises* [about 250 feet] wide; it was carrying a reasonable quantity of ice; and its shores were made up of marshland 300 *toises* [about 2,000 feet] long, which made it a difficult obstacle to cross. The enemy general had placed his four divisions at different points where he assumed the French army would try to cross.

On the 26th, at the break of day, the emperor, after having deceived the enemy by different movements carried out during the 25th, proceeded to the village of Studentka and immediately, in spite of an enemy division and in its presence, had two bridges thrown over the river. The duc de Reggio [Marshal Oudinot] crossed, attacked the enemy and kept them on the run for two hours; the enemy withdrew to the bridgehead at Borisov. General Legrand, an officer of the highest merit, was badly wounded, but not mortally. The army crossed throughout the 26th and 27th.

. . . The whole army having crossed on the morning of the 28th, the duc de Bellume [Marshal Victor] guarded the bridgehead on the left bank; the duc de Reggio, and behind him the whole army, was on the right bank.

[A description of a battle which took place on the 28th follows]. The next day, on the 29th, we remained on the field of battle. We had to choose between two routes, that of Minsk or that of Vilna. The road to Minsk passes through a forest and wild marshlands, and it would have been impossible for the army to feed itself. The road to Vilna, on the contrary, passes through very good country. The army, without cavalry, low on ammunition, terribly tired from fifty days of marching, dragging its sick and wounded from so many battles after it, needed to reach its stores. . . .

To say that the army needed to re-establish discipline, to reorganise itself, to refit its cavalry, artillery and its supplies, is the result of the events that have just been described. Rest is its first need. Supplies and horses are arriving. General Bourcier already has more than 20,000 remounts in various depots. The artillery has already made up its losses. Generals, officers and soldiers have greatly suffered from fatigue and lack of food. Many have lost their baggage as a result of losing their horses; a few through Cossack ambushes. The Cossacks have taken a number of isolated men, surveyors who were mapping positions, and wounded officers who were marching without taking any precautions, preferring to run risks rather than calmly marching in convoy.

The reports of the general officers commanding the corps will identify those officers and soldiers who have most distinguished themselves, and will [furnish] the details of all those memorable events.

Throughout all of these movements, the emperor has always marched in the middle of his Guard, the cavalry was commanded by Marshal [Bessières], duc d'Istria, and the infantry was commanded by the duc de Danzig [Marshal Lefebvre]. His Majesty is satisfied with the morale his Guard has shown: it has always been prepared to go wherever circumstances demanded, but circumstances have always been such that its simple presence is enough not to engage it.

. . . Our cavalry had lost so many mounts that it was necessary to bring together the officers who still had a horse to form four companies of 150 men each. Generals served as captains, colonels as non-commissioned officers. This Holy Squadron, commanded by General Grouchy and under the orders of the king of Naples [Murat], never lost sight of the emperor in all these movements.

His Majesty's health has never been better.

Source: *Correspondance de Napoléon Ier,* vol. 24, pp. 377–82.

22

COLLAPSE

The Malet Affair, October 1812

While Napoleon was absent in Russia, General Claude-François de Malet (1754–1812) made a vain attempt to overthrow the régime in Paris by persuading the Prefect of the Seine to believe that Napoleon had died in Russia. As the following letter from a conscript to his parents shows, he also managed to convince most of the garrison commanders in Paris, who obediently followed his orders. When he shot a general who asked to see his credentials, he was seized and imprisoned. He was tried that night, along with seventeen other conspirators, and shot the next day. Although the plot never seriously threatened the régime, it had a bad impact on public opinion, demonstrating just how precarious the dynasty was.

Paris, 25 October 1812
M. Pourcelle, Bailiff at Breteuil (Oise)

My dear Papa,
At the moment I am writing to you, I am at my cousin's from whom I asked a bed and supper, our cohort having left Versailles today. We received our marching orders this morning and that prevented me from informing you about them.

On the 23rd of this month at three in the morning we were suddenly awoken and received the order to immediately take up arms, without any exceptions.

In the blink of an eye the cohort had assembled in the courtyard of the barracks with rifles and baggage.

A general in full uniform [that is, Malet], appeared among us and read out a proclamation which in substance said that His Majesty the emperor had died under the walls of Moscow on the 7th of this month; that in order to replace

187

him it had been considered appropriate to create a Council with General Moreau as president; that these measures had been taken to save what remained of the army; that the cohorts would be disbanded; that in the meantime troops would receive 20 sous a day; then followed a great number of promotions to superior ranks and the destitution of several people of the highest rank, notably General Count Hullin, commander of the 1st Military Division and of Paris and General Doucet, chief of the general staff.

The news of the death of our emperor made such an impression on us that we remained stupefied and speechless for several minutes. This silence was only interrupted by the almost unanimous cry of: what a tragedy!

The reading of the proclamation had hardly come to an end than the general put himself at our head and led us to several streets in Paris.

On the way, he opened the prisons of the Force and released three personalities who had long ago been proscribed and rejected by society, one of whom had been General Moreau's aide-de-camp.

The latter then took command and led us to Their Excellencies the Prefect [Pasquier] and the Minister of Police [Savary] who were arrested and escorted to prison after they had been beaten around, without any respect for their rank.

For his part, the general [Malet] had left with a detachment of the cohort for Count Hullin's, undoubtedly with the intention of murdering him; and in effect he fired a shot to his head and leaving him for dead retired to do the same to General Doucet, but the latter had the presence of mind to rush at him at the moment he fired and called his dragoons who ran to him, disarmed the general and chained him up.

The detachment from our cohort made no effort to defend the general.

Soon the general's other accomplices were arrested and we have just been told that this morning's proclamation was false and that the emperor was alive.

We received this happy news with repeated acclamations of 'Long live the emperor', exclamations which proved our love for our sovereign.

We were also told that we had been deceived by conspirators and we were advised to return immediately to our barracks.

During this time the Imperial Guard had received thirty cartridges each man with orders to attack us on the Place de Grève if we showed the least delay in returning, but since we were neither rebels nor conspirators they did not need to resort to violence to make us obey; we returned to the barracks satisfied to have learnt that our emperor was well, but sorry to have been led into error by scoundrels who wanted to make us the victims of their ambitious projects; for if they had succeeded in the murders they had wanted to commit we would have seen those terrible times reappear when anarchy reigned and France would have been prey to factions and the most bloody revolution.

Fortunately the crime was discovered in time and the police was re-established. Our cohort was the only one whose name has been marked by an ineffaceable stain. Most of our leaders have been arrested. They are accused of taking part in the plot. As for us we simply obeyed, and even though we have nothing to reproach ourselves, it is nonetheless true that fingers will always be pointed at us; the truth is, our innocence remains intact and we do not fear for one minute being reproached with unfaithfulness to our emperor and the *patrie*.

It is as a result of these unfortunate circumstances that we are leaving Paris only too happy if a more disagreeable punishment is not inflicted on us.

Count Hullin has not been mortally wounded. I will give you more details later; from now on write to me at Versailles.

I am well and embrace you all. M. and Mme Barthélemy and your god-daughter and her husband have asked me to tell you a thousand things.

My cousin is doing wonderfully.

My respects to mama.

[Signed] Pourcelle

Source: Jacques Godechot (ed.), 'Lettres de conscrits de 1812 et 1813', in *Annales historiques de la Révolution française* 44 (1972), pp. 627–30.

———≡◦◦◦≡———

The state of opinion in the countryside, 30 November 1813

Despite some local opposition to the draft, conscription was a largely uneventful process by this stage of the Empire. Nevertheless, as this report from the Prefect of the department of the Finistère shows, there was a general longing for peace that was prevalent throughout French society.

The financial sacrifice necessitated by the decree of the 11th of this month relative to the supplementary contribution for 1813 seems very light, and a new demand is expected. Money is nothing compared to the loss of so many hands for agriculture and industry, of so many children raised and cherished by their parents. People say how much this last sacrifice is all the more painful and at the same time more regrettable in view of the real interests of the government. It is the countryside especially that the last call-up has tapped into. It is also in the countryside that the most profound sorrow is joined with the most profound resignation, which feeds anxiety about the future. Already farmers are saying that from now on, in certain cantons, they will hardly be able to cultivate half their lands. Already several farmers have announced as much to their proprietors who in turn are upset and worried about the depopulation which circumstances have forced on them. People ardently desire an end to so many sacrifices, less for any regrets they may have at the moment than out of fear of the consequences. For, it is said, what good is the most fertile soil, if there are no hands to cultivate it?

. . . After having read an article in the *Gazette de France*—'The nation wants peace, the monarch does also!'—people are asking themselves 'Are the nation and the monarch in agreement over the conditions [of peace]?' Public opinion continues against the maintenance of conquests so that, if on the one hand people ardently desire to see our enemies beaten, people appear on the other hand to fear the successes of the emperor who could still, they say, let himself go too far and finish by leading France to an inevitable destruction.

The Prefect of the department of the Finistère, 30 November 1813

Source: Bertaud, *Le Consulat et l'empire, 1799–1815* (Paris, 1989), p. 112.

The deposition of Napoleon, 3 April 1814

The occupation of Paris by the Allies on 31 March 1814 spelled the end of Napoleon's reign. Charles-Maurice de Talleyrand (1754–1838), Napoleon's former Foreign Minister, had been working behind the scenes against his master for some years. On 1 April, he formed a provisional government and manoeuvred to bring back the Bourbon monarchy. The next day, 2 April, he persuaded the Imperial Senate to depose Napoleon. The Senate, which had always been a rubber-stamp institution during the empire, now attempted to secure its future by an empty show of independence. In the following proclamation, the decision to depose Napoleon is explained to the people of Paris. He is reproached, somewhat hypocritically under the circumstances, with violating the Constitution.

From the provisional government to the French people

Frenchmen
At the end of our civil discord [that is, the Revolution], you chose for a leader a man who appeared on the world scene with a character of grandeur. You placed all your hopes in him; those hopes were deceived. On the ruins of anarchy he built despotism.

He should have at least, out of gratitude, become French with you. He has never been [French]. He never stopped carrying out, without objective and without motive, unjust wars, like an adventurer who wants to be famous. Within a few years, he devoured your riches and your people.

Every family is in mourning; all of France groans: he is deaf to our plight. Perhaps he yet dreams of gigantic projects, even when incredible defeats punish with such brilliance the pride and the abuse of victory.

He did not reign either in the national interest or in the interest of his own despotism. He has destroyed all that he wanted to create, and recreated all that he wanted to destroy. He believed only in force, force overwhelms him today, a just payment for a senseless ambition!

Finally, that tyranny without precedent has ceased to exist: the Allied powers have just entered the capital of France.

Napoleon governed us like a barbarous king; Alexander and his magnanimous allies speak only the language of honour, justice and humanity. They have come to reconcile with Europe a brave and unfortunate people.

Frenchmen, the Senate has declared *Napoleon deposed from the throne*; the *patrie* is no longer with him. Only another order can save France. We have known the excesses of popular abuse. Let us re-establish the true monarchy by limiting, through wise laws, the various powers which compose it.

So that within the protection of the paternal throne, an exhausted agriculture may flourish again; so that commerce weighed down with shackles may regain its liberty; so that youth may no longer be the harvest of arms, before having the strength to carry them; so that the order of things may no longer be interrupted, and the old may hope to die before their children! Frenchmen, let us rally; past calamities are about the finish and peace is going to bring the upheavals of Europe to an end. The august Allies have given their word. France will rest from its long disturbances, and, more enlightened by the double trials of anarchy and despotism, it will find happiness in the return of a titular government.

Source: *Archives parlementaires de 1787 à 1860*, Deuxième série (Paris, 1868), vol. 12, pp. 11–12.

Abdication of Napoleon at Fontainebleau, 11 April 1814

A week after he was formally deposed by the Senate, faced with a political coup in Paris and the unwillingness of his generals to fight on, Napoleon reluctantly decided to abdicate in favour of his son, the 3-year old king of Rome, a provision that was rejected by the Allies. On 6 April, Napoleon abdicated unconditionally. The next evening, he attempted to commit suicide by poisoning himself. By the Treaty of Fontainebleau, worked out between the tsar and Talleyrand, Napoleon (against Talleyrand's protests) was given the island of Elba with pensions for both him and his family.

The Allied powers, having declared that the Emperor Napoleon was the only obstacle to the re-establishment of peace in Europe, the Emperor Napoleon, faithful to his oath, declares that he renounces, for himself and his heirs, the thrones of France and Italy, and that there is no personal sacrifice, even that of his life, that he would not be ready to make in the interest of France.

Done at the Palace of Fontainebleau, 11 April 1814

TREATY BETWEEN THE ALLIED POWERS AND THE EMPEROR NAPOLEON

Article 1. His Majesty the Emperor Napoleon renounces for himself, his successors and descendants, as well as for all the members of his family, all right of sovereignty and dominion, both to the French Empire and the Kingdom of Italy as well as to every other country.

Article 2. Their Majesties the Emperor Napoleon and the Empress Marie-Louise shall retain their titles and ranks, to be enjoyed during their lives. The mother, brothers, sisters, nephews and nieces of the emperor shall also retain, wherever they may reside, the title of princes of his family.

Article 3. The island of Elba, which the Emperor Napoleon has chosen as his place of his residence, shall form during his life a separate principality, which he shall possess in full sovereignty and ownership. There shall be given besides in full property to the Emperor Napoleon an annual revenue of 2,000,000 francs, carried over as pension upon the ledger of France, of which the sum of 1,000,000 shall revert to the empress.

Source: Buchez and Roux, *Histoire parlementaire de la Révolution française*, vol. 39, pp. 512–14.

23

THE HUNDRED DAYS

Louis XVIII's entry into Paris, 3 May 1814

Louis entered the capital he had left twenty-five years earlier on 3 May 1814. Although few could remember the royal family, the city was nevertheless bathed in white flags and cockades to welcome the man they hoped would be the guarantor of peace and the restorer of liberty. In the carriage at the king's side sat the morose Duchess of Angoulême, Marie-Thérèse, daughter of Louis XVI and Marie-Antoinette, who had been imprisoned in the Temple during the Revolution and who had never forgotten or forgiven the people of Paris for the treatment handed out to her family. She did not make a good impression. Even the Countess of Boigne, an ardent royalist, was disappointed in the day's proceedings.

We went to see the king's entry from a house in the rue Saint-Denis. There was a large crowd. Most windows were decorated with white garlands, slogans, white lilies and white flags.

The foreigners had the good grace . . . to consign their troops to the barracks. The town was given over to the National Guard. . . . Everybody noticed the absence of foreign uniforms. General Sacken, the Russian governor of Paris, was the only person to appear in the town. He was liked well enough, and people felt that he was keeping a look-out for the maintenance of order given to his own troops.

The procession was escorted by the old Imperial Guard. Others will tell of the tactlessness committed against them both before and after this moment; all I will say is that they were imposing but icy. They advanced in great strides, silent and gloomy, full of past memories. They stopped with one look the enthusiasm towards those who were arriving. Cries of 'Long live the king!' fell silent when they marched past; now and then cries of 'Long live the guard, the old guard!' were heard, but they were no better received and they seemed to greet them with derision. As they marched past, the silence increased; soon only the monotone noise of their quick steps could be heard, pounding on one's heart. Consternation prevailed and the contagious sadness of these old warriors gave the ceremony the appearance of the emperor's funeral much more than the accession of the king.

It was time for that to end. The group of princes appeared. Their passage had been badly prepared; nevertheless they were received warmly enough but without the enthusiasm that had accompanied [the entry of] Monsieur [on 12 April].

Were people already worn out? Were they already dissatisfied with the brief administration of the lieutenant general, or was it the guard's aspect which had brought about this chill? I do not know, but it was noticeable.

Monsieur was on horseback, surrounded by marshals, general officers of the Empire, the King's Household and the House of the Line. The king was in a carriage, completely open, Madame sitting beside him; in front were Prince Condé and his son, the duke of Bourbon. . . .

I have to admit that, for me, the morning was distressing from every point of view and the occupants of the carriage had not met the hopes I had placed in them. I was told that Madame, on arriving at Notre Dame, collapsed onto her prayer stool in such a gracious, noble and touching manner, there was both so much resignation and acknowledgement in that action, that tears of tenderness flowed from everyone's eyes. I was also told that on arriving at the Tuileries, she was as cold, as awkward, as surly as she had been beautiful in church.

At that time, Madame, Duchess of Angoulême, was the only person in the royal family who was remembered in France.

The younger generation knew nothing about our princes. I recall that one of my cousins asked me at that time if the Duke of Angoulême was the son of Louis XVIII and how many children he had. And yet everyone knew that Louis XVI, the queen and Madame Elisabeth had died on the scaffold. For everyone, Madame was the orphan of the Temple and on her head was united all the interest acquired by so many terrible disasters. The blood spilt had baptised her daughter of the country.

So much was owing to her! But any expressions of regret had to be received with benevolence. Madame was not able to make the distinction; she imposed by her haughtiness and only accepted testimonies with curtness. Madame, full of virtue, generosity, a French princess in her heart, had found the way to make herself appear as though she was mean, cruel and hostile towards her country. The French believed themselves disliked by her and in turn finished by disliking her. She did not deserve it and, certainly, one was not disposed to do so. It was the result of a disastrous misunderstanding and of a false pride. With a small dose of feeling added to her noble nature, Madame could have been the idol of the country and the palladium of her race.

Source: *Mémoires de la comtesse de Boigne, née Osmond*, 2 vols (Paris, 1986), vol. 1, pp. 256–8.

Napoleon returns from Elba, 1 March 1815

Napoleon was on the island of Elba less than a year when he decided to return to France in an attempt to regain power. The decision was in part motivated by Louis XVIII's refusal to comply with the treaty stipulations by which Napoleon was to receive an allowance of 2 million francs per year. He landed in the south of France on 1 March 1815. His proclamation to the French people was a transparent attempt to justify what was a desperate gamble. It is interesting to note that, whether sincere or not, he blames others for his initial defeat. It is obvious that he had not learnt from the first abdication.

Napoleon, by the grace of God and the Constitution of the State, emperor of the French, etc., etc., etc.

TO THE FRENCH PEOPLE

Frenchmen, the defection of the Duke of Castiglione [Marshal Augereau] delivered Lyons defenceless to our enemies. The army, of which I had confided to him the command, was, by the number of its battalions, the bravery and the patriotism of the troops which composed it, capable of defeating the Austrian army which opposed it, and of arriving at the rear of the left wing of the enemy threatening Paris.

The victories of Champaubert, Montmirail, Chateau Thierry, Vauchamp, Mormans, Montereau, Caronne, Rheims, Arcis-sur-Aube and Saint Dizier, the insurrection of the brave peasants of Lorraine, Champagne, Alsace, Franche-Comté and Burgundy and the position that I had taken in the rear of the enemy army separating it from its supply depots, its reserve parks, its convoys and all its equipment, had placed it in a desperate situation. Frenchmen were never on the point of being more powerful, and the élite of the enemy army was left without resources. It would have found its grave in those vast regions that it had so pitilessly plundered, when the treason of the Duke of Ragusa [Marshal Marmont] surrendered the capital and disorganised the army. The unexpected behaviour of these two generals, who betrayed at the same time their *patrie*, their prince and their benefactor, changed the outcome of the war. The disastrous situation of the enemy was such that, at the end of the incident which took place before Paris, he was without ammunition through the separation from his reserve parks.

In these great and new circumstances, my heart was torn apart, but my spirit remained resolute. I consulted only the interest of the *patrie*; I exiled myself on a rock in the middle of the sea. My life was and still had to be useful to you, I did not allow the great number of citizens who wished to accompany me to share my fate; I thought their presence useful in France and I only took with me a handful of brave fellows necessary as my guard.

Raised to the throne by your choice, all that has been done without you is illegitimate. For twenty-five years, France has had new interests, new institutions, a new glory, which could only be guaranteed by a national government and by a dynasty born in these new circumstances. A prince who would reign over you, who would sit on my throne by the force of the same armies which ravaged our territory, would seek in vain to bolster himself by principles of feudal rights; he could only assure the honour and the rights of a small number of individuals, enemies of the people who, for twenty-five years, have condemned them in all our national assemblies. Your peace at home and your respect abroad would be forever lost.

Frenchmen, in my exile I heard your complaints and wishes; you were claiming that government of your choice, which alone is legitimate. You were blaming me for my long sleep, you were reproaching me for sacrificing to my rest the great interests of the State.

I crossed the seas amid all sorts of dangers; I arrived among you to regain my rights, which are yours. Everything that these individuals have done, written or said since the taking of Paris, I will always ignore; it will have no influence on the memory that I retain of the important services that they have rendered, because there are events of such a nature that they are beyond human comprehension.

Frenchmen, there is no nation, however small it might be, which has not had the right to remove itself and may not be withdrawn from this dishonour of obeying a prince imposed by a temporarily victorious enemy. . . .

It is likewise to you alone and to the brave soldiers of the army that I give and will always give every duty.

Signed: Napoleon
At Gulf Juan, 1 March 1815

Source: Buchez and Roux, *Histoire parlementaire de la Révolution française*, vol. 40, pp. 46–8.

━━━▷◦◦◦◁━━━

The 'Acte Additionnel' to the new Constitution, 22 April 1815

When Napoleon returned from Paris to re-establish the Empire, he commissioned the writer, Benjamin Constant, to frame a new Constitution, called the Additional Act to the Constitutions of the Empire, that was meant to demonstrate a new, liberal Napoleon, and which was submitted to a referendum. The document thus contained a declaration of the rights of man, guaranteeing equality before the law, eligibility of office, freedom of religion, and liberty of the press. The executive power was nevertheless confided in the person of the emperor. One can surmise that Napoleon would have found it difficult to maintain the liberal nature of his new régime had he continued in office after Waterloo. Note Napoleon's defence of his past conquests: his objective was to create a European federation.

ADDITIONAL ACT TO THE CONSTITUTIONS OF THE EMPIRE

Napoleon, by the grace of God and the Constitutions, Emperor of the French, to all present and to come, greetings.

Since we were called fifteen years ago by the will of France to the government of the State we have sought at different times to improve the constitutional forms, according to the needs and desires of the nation and by profiting from the lessons of experience. The Constitutions of the Empire have thus been formed by a series of acts that have received the acceptance of the people. Our purpose then was to organise a great European federative system, which we had adopted as in conformity with the spirit of the age, and favourable to the progress of civilisation. In order to bring it to completion and to give to it the scope and the stability of which it was susceptible, we had postponed the establishment of several domestic institutions, more especially designed to protect the liberty of the citizens. From this moment on, Our aim is to increase the prosperity of France by strengthening public liberty. Hence the necessity of several important modifications to the Constitutions, Senatus Consulta, and other acts which govern the Empire. For these reasons, wanting, on the one hand, to retain from the past whatever is good and salutary, and on the other, to make the Constitutions of the Empire entirely conform to the national wishes and needs, as well as to the state of peace which we desire to maintain with Europe, we have resolved to propose to the people a series of provisions tending to modify and improve these constitutional acts, to support the rights of citizens with all their guarantees, to give to the representative system its full extent, to invest the intermediary corps with worthwhile importance and power; in a word, to combine the highest point of political liberty and individual security with the strength and centralisation necessary to make the independence of the French people and the dignity of Our crown respected by foreigners. Consequently, the following articles, forming a supplementary act to the Constitutions of the Empire, shall be submitted for the free and solemn acceptance of all citizens, throughout the whole extent of France.

TITLE 1 GENERAL PROVISIONS

Article 2. The legislative power is exercised by the emperor and by two chambers.

Article 3. The first chamber, named Chamber of Peers, is hereditary.

Article 4. The emperor appoints its members, who are irrevocable, they and their male descendants, from eldest to eldest in direct line. The number of peers is unlimited.

Article 7. The second chamber, named Chamber of Representatives, is elected by the people.

Article 8. The members of this chamber are in number 629. They must be at least 25 years of age.

Article 13. The Chamber of Representatives is entirely renewed by right every five years.

Article 14. No member of either chamber can be arrested, except if caught in the act, or prosecuted for a criminal or correctional matter during the sessions, by virtue of a resolution of the chamber of which he is a part.

Article 21. The emperor can prorogue, adjourn and dissolve the Chamber of Representatives. The proclamation which pronounces the dissolution convokes the electoral colleges for a new election, and indicates the meeting of representatives within six months at the latest.

Article 23. The government can propose laws; the chambers can propose amendments; if these amendments are not adopted by the government, the chambers are required to vote upon the law as it has been proposed.

Article 24. The chambers have the right to invite the government to propose a law upon a defined subject, and to draw up what appears to them suitable to insert in the law. This request may be made by each of the two chambers.

TITLE 3 OF THE LAW OF TAXATION

Article 55. No direct or indirect tax in money or in kind can be collected, no loan can be made, no entry of credits upon the ledgers of the public debt can be made, no domain can be alienated or exchanged, no levy of men for the army can be ordered, no portion of the territory can be exchanged, except in virtue of a law.

Article 56. No proposal for taxation, loan or the levy of men, can be made except by the Chamber of Representatives.

TITLE 6 RIGHTS OF CITIZENS

Article 59. Frenchmen are equal before the law, whether for contribution to public taxes and charges, or for admission to civil and military employments.

Article 61. No-one can be prosecuted, arrested, detained or exiled except in the cases provided for by law and according to the prescribed forms.

Article 62. Liberty of worship is guaranteed to all.

Article 63. All property possessed or acquired by virtue of the laws, and all state-credits, are inviolable.

Article 64. Every citizen has the right to print and publish his thoughts in signed form, without any prior censorship, subject to legal responsibility, after publication, by jury trial, even when there may be occasion for the application of only a correctional penalty.

Article 66. No place or any part of the territory can be declared in a state of siege, except in the case of invasion on the part of a foreign force, or of civil disturbances.

Article 67. The French people declare that, in the delegation which it has made and which it makes of its powers, it has not intended and does not intend to give the right to propose the re-establishment of the Bourbons or any prince of that family upon the throne, even in the case of the extinction of the imperial dynasty, or the right to re-establish either the old feudal nobility, or feudal and seigneurial rights, or the tithe, or any privileged and dominant religion, or the power to bring any attack upon the irrevocability of the sale of the national domains; it especially forbids to the government, the chambers and the citizens any proposition of this kind.

Done at Paris, 22 April 1815

Source: Buchez and Roux, *Histoire parlementaire de la Révolution française*, vol. 40, pp. 129–34.

The plebiscite of 1815

Once again the new Constitution was put before the French people, but this time there was a poor turnout. Only about 1 million voted in favour, while about 4,200 expressed their opposition to it. Most of the unfavourable comments were directed at Article 3 introducing hereditary peerage.

Hostile responses

From the Landes

Constant in my principles, faithful to my legitimate sovereign, I do not want either Bonaparte, or his dynasty, nor his constitutions.

Source: Archives nationales, F1cIII Landes 3.

From Plumelec

No—having already desired the abolition of hereditary nobility, which is re-established in the peerage.

Source: Archives nationales, BII 915.

A 'yes, but . . .' from the Eure

The critical situation . . . demanding that all good citizens rally to the government, I accept the Additional Act even if it appears to me to be defective . . . if it were permitted to vote on sections of the Act, I would reject the unfortunate article on hereditary peerage, as well as the implicit preservation of entailed property, because equality before the law with the hereditary titles and privileges is to maintain two opposing and absolutely incompatible principles . . . I reject two other articles also, the one which accords the right of the emperor to adjourn or dissolve the chamber, and the jury for press crimes. Finally, I do not at all like the Anglomaniacal denominations of the Chamber of Peers and the Chamber of Commons which represent a disastrous absence of national spirit.

Source: Archives nationales, BII 880.

Napoleon's second abdication, 22 June 1815

The defeat at Waterloo (18 June) made it impossible for Napoleon to remain in power. In what has to be one of the greatest understatements of all times—'Circumstances seem to me to have changed'—Napoleon relinquished the throne in favour of his 4-year-old son and asked the Senate to proclaim him Napoleon II. The Senate refused, and awaited the return of Louis XVIII.

DECLARATION TO THE FRENCH PEOPLE

Frenchmen, in beginning of the war to maintain national independence, I counted on the reunion of all efforts, of all wills, and on the cooperation of all the national authorities. I was justified in hoping for success, and I defied all the declarations of the powers against me.

Circumstances seem to me to have changed. I offer myself as a sacrifice to the hatred of the enemies of France. May they be sincere in their declarations and in only wishing for my person! My political life is at an end, and I proclaim my son, under the title Napoleon II, emperor of the French.

The present ministers will temporarily form the Government Council. The interest that I have in my son binds me to invite the chambers to organise without delay the regency by [passing] a law.

Unite for the public safety, and to remain an independent nation.

At the Elysée Palace, 22 June 1815

Signed: Napoleon

Source: Buchez and Roux, *Histoire parlementaire de la Révolution Française*, vol. 40, p. 228.

24

FRENCH MEN AND WOMEN REFLECT

On the French Revolution

Baron Trouvé on southern peasants

Charles-Joseph Trouvé was a highly intelligent and politically adaptable man from an artisan family to whom the Revolution offered opportunities which would have been unthinkable under the *Ancien Régime*. In 1794, when just 26 years old Trouvé had become editor of the *Moniteur*, and ambassador to Naples three years later. He was stridently anti-Jacobin, but no less hostile to *Ancien Régime* élites and the Church. As Baron Trouvé, he was prefect of the department of the Aude from 1803 to 1816. He recognised the improvement in the peasants' standard of living, but claimed that unchecked land clearances had wreaked environmental damage.

The suppression of feudal dues and the tithe, the high price of foodstuffs, the division of the large estates, the sale in small lots of nationalised lands, the ending of indebtedness by [the inflation in the value of] paper currency, gave a great impulse to the industry of the peasantry. . . .

In this region, people have always complained about the fury of land seizures and clearances. Decrees and laws were made to repress it. The storms of the Revolution having released this brake, now powerless against anarchy, seizures multiplied, clearances became an almost general calamity; and a region formerly covered with pastures and flocks suddenly found itself threatened with losing the raw material for its manufactures, the principal source of its wealth. Through the wish to expand the cultivation of grain crops, the hills and mountains have been given up to destruction; bushes and trees have been uprooted; and the fields on the hillsides, formerly so fertile and useful, were no longer held together by the tree-roots and were washed into the streams which they have blocked and forced to overflow onto the river-flats, and to cover them with the gravel and stones with which their beds were obstructed. . . .

Although the Revolution had an impact on the diet of the people of the countryside, this impact was even more marked on clothing. They seem to have more interest in clothing their bodies than in feeding themselves. In the old days, rough woollen cloth, or homespun linen, was their finest apparel. They disdain that today; cotton and velveteen cloth are the fabrics they desire, and the large landholder is often confused with his sharecroppers because of the simplicity of his clothing.

Source: Charles-Joseph Trouvé, *États de Languedoc et département de l'Aude*, 2 vols (Paris, 1818), vol. 1, pp. 452–3, 530–1, 563.

The Marquise de La Tour du Pin on her family

The Marquise de La Tour du Pin was born in 1770 as Henrietta-Lucy Dillon, the descendant of English and Irish Jacobites who had been exiled to France after the defeat of James II in 1691. Her husband was an army officer from an ancient and wealthy family. Her liberal father-in-law was Minister for War in 1789–90, but his support for Louis XVI during his trial led to his execution. Lucy and her husband emigrated to Boston in 1793, returning in 1796. Lucy de La Tour du Pin wrote the first part of her memoirs in 1820 and the second in 1843.

. . . the happenings of the night of 4 August when, on the motion of the Vicomte de Noailles, feudal rights were abolished, should have convinced even the most incredulous that the National Assembly was unlikely to stop at this first measure of dispossession. This decree ruined my father-in-law and our family fortunes never recovered from the effect of that night's session. It was a veritable orgy of iniquities. The value of the property at La Roche-Chalais lay entirely in feudal dues, income from invested money and leases or from the mills. There was also a toll river-crossing. The total income from all these sources was 30,000 francs per year and the only charge on that sum was the salary of the agent who, on an appointed day, received payments in grain or the money equivalent of the grain at the current market price. . . .

We also lost the toll crossing at Cubzac on the Dordogne, which was worth 12,000 francs, and the income from Le Bouilh, Ambleville, Tesson and Cénévrières, a fine property in the Quercy which my father-in-law was forced to sell the following year. And that was how we were ruined by the stroke of a pen. Since then, we have been forced to contrive a living, sometimes by sale of some of the few possessions remaining to us, sometimes by taking salaried posts . . .

And so it is that, inch by inch, over a long period of years, we have gradually slid to the bottom of an abyss from which we shall not emerge in our generation. . . .

In December [1796], when I had recovered [from giving birth], my husband went to visit Tesson, Ambleville and La Roche Chalais where all that remained to us of the 30,000 franc income from the property was a few old, tumble-down towers. I remained alone in the great house at Le Bouilh with Marguérite, two maidservants and old Biquet, who got drunk every evening. The farm workers were some distance away. The unfinished part of the ground floor was secured only by a few dilapidated planks and it was the time when gangs of brigands known as *chauffeurs* (thieves who tortured their victims with fire) were spreading terror throughout the south of France. Every day fresh horrors were told of them. Only two leagues away from Le Bouilh they had burned the feet of a certain M. Chicous, a Bordeaux shopkeeper, to force him to tell them where he kept his money. Many years later, I saw this unfortunate man, still on crutches. I am ashamed to admit it, but these gangs filled me with a paralysing terror. I often spent half the night sitting on my bed, listening to the barking watchdogs, thinking that at any moment the brigands would break through the flimsy planks covering the ground floor windows. How I longed for my farm, my good Negroes and the peace of those months. My days were no happier than my nights. It was midwinter, and all my thoughts were with my husband, travelling about the countryside on a poor horse, over the terrible roads of the southern provinces, which in those days were especially bad.

Our financial position was another constant worry. . . . I will not go into details of our ruin; in any case, I never knew them very exactly. I only know that when I married, my father-in-law was understood to have an income of eighty thousand francs. Since the Revolution, our losses have amounted to at least fifty-eight thousand francs a year.

Source: Felice Harcourt (ed. and trans.), *Escape from the Terror: the Journal of Madame de La Tour du Pin* (London, 1979), pp. 93–4, 243–4.

Marie-Victoire Monnard on making ends meet

Marie-Victoire Monnard was just 12 years old when the Revolution began. She was the daughter of a *laboureur* or farmer from Creil, 60 km north of Paris. In 1790 she was sent to Paris as an apprentice to Madame Amé, a linen merchant. Here she describes how the inflation of the revolutionary years gave her the chance to establish herself as a draper. Marie-Victoire died aged 92 in 1869.

At that time the conversation was only about the Revolution, which was not very interesting for a young person of thirteen years. . . . Mme Amé believed that she had seen signs in me of intelligence and curiosity; she chose me from among her young charges to go to listen to everything that was being said in the National Assembly, at the Jacobin Club, and to the denunciations being made at the churches in the evenings. . . . The first important mission with which I was charged was to go and see Louis XVI and his family on their return from Varennes. . . .

A general decree that the National Convention passed among others which were disastrous was that which finally ended the tithe on grains. My father had a contract from the monks for the tithe for the canton of Creil and this law left him without work.

During all these troubles, the three years for which I had been placed with Mme Amé had passed. I was searching for a position for myself, so as to no longer be a burden on my parents. A widow . . . let me know of one. This lady was an excellent woman, even though a Jacobin; she told me that she had recently remarried, to General Vachot, and that their marriage had been 'republican'. Wanting to know of this new way of marrying, I asked her. She told me that, wearing a tricolour cockade and a red cap, she had sworn on the altar of the homeland to take the republican Vachot for her spouse and that mutually, in the name of liberty, they had promised fidelity to each other unto death and that this bond was more solid and natural than the old way of marrying. I recounted these details to Mme Amé who forbade to see this immoral woman again. It seems that the basis of her republican marriage was not so solid, because the symbols of freedom, like the tricolour cockade, the red cap and the patriotic oaths did not stop citizen Vachot from leaving his republican wife three months later, without needing recourse to a divorce, which was then recognised by the law. . . .

The *assignats*, the paper currency of the time, were losing value and gave to whoever wanted the chance to open a shop with little merchandise. A few samples were enough to buy and sell. That gave me the idea of setting up on my own. I told my father, explaining the advantages I had in mind; he wasn't opposed, but did not give me any money to get started. . . . But, to begin a small business, one has to have either some goods or the money to buy them; having neither the one nor the other I cut my sheets into towels because they were too coarse for anything else; I sold them, as well as a nankeen dress with wide stripes that I still had, plus a pillow. I earned in total about 40 francs and used them to buy ten lengths of calico, which I immediately sold, making 8 francs' profit. I was so happy with this beginning to my business that I would not have given up my position for that of the greatest ruler in the world. The continued decline in the value of the *assignats* facilitated the sale of all kinds of merchandise; they only had to be put up for sale and they were sold.

Source: Marie-Victoire Monnard, *Souvenirs d'une femme du peuple, 1777–1802* (Creil, 1989), pp. 62–5, 86–7, 95–6.

On Napoleon and the Empire

Mme de Staël on Napoleon's political doctrine

Here Mme de Staël reflects on the reasons why Napoleon was unable to found a lasting and stable dynasty. Like many historians today, she found that the answer lay with Napoelon's character.

The two main reasons for Napoleon's power in France were his military glory especially, and the art of re-establishing order without attacking the interested passions which the Revolution had given birth to. But not everything consisted in these two problems.

People pretend that in the middle of a Council of State Napoleon used to show universal wisdom in the discussions [which took place]. I would cast some doubt on the mind of an all-powerful man . . . Nevertheless, one is not master of Europe for fifteen years without having a penetrating view of men and the world. . . . His successes were stunning; his defeats were even more stunning. What he did with energy for the nation is admirable; the state of torpor in which he left the country can barely be conceived. The number of intelligent men he used is extraordinary, but the characters which he degraded harmed liberty more than all the faculties of intelligence could serve liberty. To him alone can one apply the wonderful image of despotism in [Montesquieu's] *Spirit of the Laws*: he cut the tree by its roots in order to get its fruit, and he has perhaps even parched the land.

Finally, Bonaparte, absolute master over 80 million men, meeting no opposition from anyone, was unable to found either an institution in the State or a stable power for himself. What then was the destructive principle which followed in his triumphant footsteps? What is it? The [answer lies in a] disdain for men, and consequently for all laws, for all study, for all establishments, for all elections, the basis of which is respect for the human race. Bonaparte got drunk on the bad wine of Machiavellism; in many respects he resembled those Italian tyrants of the fourteenth and fifteenth centuries and, as he had read very little, in his mind education did not combat his natural disposition. . . .

[Bonaparte] only listened to momentary considerations, and only examined things from the perspective of their immediate use . . . He was not bloodthirsty, but he was indifferent to the life of men. He only considered the life of a man as a means of attaining his objective, or as an obstacle that had to be pushed off the road. He was not even as angry as he often appeared to be: he wanted to frighten with words, in order to spare himself the necessity of acting. Everything in the man was a means to an end or an objective; there was nothing unintentional about him, [he was] neither good nor evil.

Source: Germaine de Staël, *Considérations sur la Révolution française* (Paris, 1983), pp. 421–3.

Alfred de Vigny recalls his childhood

Alfred de Vigny (1797–1863) was a romantic French poet who joined the army in 1814. His memoirs, an extract of which is cited below, reflect the impact Napoleonic propaganda had on him as a young boy, fed as he was on a diet of Bulletins and battle accounts. The nostalgia for the past associated with Napoleon felt by men like de Vigny helped consolidate the Napoleonic legend after his death in 1821.

Towards the end of the Empire, I was a distracted schoolboy. The war was alive in the *lycée* [grammar school], the beating of the drum drowned out the voices of the teachers, and the mysterious voices in books spoke only in a cold and pedantic language. Logarithms and tropes were in our eyes nothing more than steps on the path to the Legion of Honour, the most beautiful star in the heavens for children.

No meditation could for long enchain minds constantly deafened by the sound of cannon and the ringing of bells for 'Te deums'! When one of our comrades, who had left the college a few months before, reappeared in a hussar's uniform with his arm in a sling, our books made us blush and we threw them at our teachers' heads. The teachers themselves constantly read the Bulletins of the Grande Armée to us, and our cries of 'Vive l'empereur!' interrupted Tacitus and Plato. Our tutors looked like heralds in arms, our study rooms like barracks, our recreation like manoeuvres, and our exams like reviews.

Source: Alfred de Vigny, *Servitude et grandeur militaires* (Paris, 1965), pp. 13–14.

George Sand on Napoleonic propaganda

George Sand (Aurore Dupin, 1804–76), playwright and romantic novelist, was the daughter of Maurice Dupin de Francueil, an aide-de-camp in Napoleon's army, and Sophie Delaborde, who was a camp follower. When her father died, the aristocratic grandmother, who disliked her working-class daughter-in-law, raised Aurore until she was 13, before sending her off to a boarding school. In this extract of her memoirs, Sand recalls how her grandmother used to spread bad rumours about Napoleon. The Bulletins had the opposite effect to what was desired and tended, according to Sand, to undermine people's faith in the regime.

My grandmother had no enthusiasm for the emperor. My father did not have much either . . . And yet, during the last years of his life, he became attached to him. He often said to my mother: 'I have a lot to complain about, not because he did not automatically place me among the first ranks. He had other things to think about, and he was never short of people who were more successful, more capable, and bolder than I. I complain because he liked courtesans and because it is not dignified of a man of his stature. And yet, in spite of the wrongs he did the Revolution and himself, I love him. There is in him something, I don't know what, apart from his genius, which forces me to be moved when my look encounters his. He does not scare me at all, and that is why I think that he is worth more than the airs which he gives himself.'

My grandmother did not share this secret sympathy which had won over my father, and who, combined with the loyalty of her spirit, the warmth of her patriotism, would certainly have prevented him, not from I would say betraying the emperor, but from rallying to the Bourbons after the fact . . .

And yet my grandmother feared the emperor more than she loved him. In her eyes, he was an ambitious man without peace of mind, a killer of men, a despot by character more than by necessity. Complaints, criticisms, calumnies, false or real revelations did not fill the columns of newspapers. The press was not only muzzled, but degraded. It was not only obliged to keep quiet, it was careful to humiliate itself and to heap admiration on power. This absence of polemic gave conversations and individual preoccupations a character of partiality and extraordinary gossip. Official praise did more harm to Napoleon than twenty hostile newspapers would have done. People were tired of the extravagant, bombastic eulogies, of the servility of bureaucrats, and the arrogant mysteriousness of courtesans. They got their revenge by disparaging the idol in the impunity of intimate conversations, while recalcitrant salons became dens of denunciation, of the subject of ante-chambers, of small culumnies and small anecdotes which was to give life back to the press later under the Restoration. . . .

Source: George Sand, *Histoire de ma vie*, in *Oeuvres autobiographiques*, 2 vols (Paris, 1970), vol. 1, pp. 692–3.

INDEX